COORDINATORS

COORDINATORS

a new focus
in parish religious education

by

JOSEPH C. NEIMAN

SMC

st. mary's college press
christian brothers publications
winona, minnesota 55987

Cover Design: Joanna Barinotti-Braun

To

John P. LaGoe

A priest and prophet

CONTENTS

LIST OF CHARTS

INTRODUCTION

Professional Coordinators (Directors) are the new frontier in parish religious education. These dedicated, visionary, and skilled men and women are forging ahead into new possibilities, and, as a result, they are presently meeting endless difficulties.

The high frustrations which they feel are an acute expression of the present state of religious education as we move into the decade of the 1970's. Most everyone working in the field feels that what he is doing is good, but not great; that it is a holding measure until some major change in the religious education of youth and adults occurs. This high frustration level might be viewed as the evolutionary temperature rising toward the point when a new leap of creativity will occur. I for one think it is.

In the summer of 1968, I started *Project Coordinator* in an effort to gain some national perspective on a diocesan project which the Religious Education Office had begun under the wise leadership of Monsignor Victor P. Gallagher. Project Coordinator is a national research project on the role of parish coordinators in which hundreds of participants from around the United States and Canada took part in varying degrees. Two things have become very clear to me since the project began; namely, the great potential which the phenomenon of parish professionals offers and the desperate need for

1

wise leadership in bridging the gap between what is and what might be in religious education.

The response to Project Coordinator was much greater than could have been anticipated. There were many more parish coordinators (directors) working than anyone had imagined. Yet each one was working more or less alone in his area and felt a great need for communication and sharing with others, and the flood of mail to Grand Rapids was overwhelming.

The flow of mail brought with it cries for help, notes of hope and success, and a general impression that a quantitative change far exceeding the changes wrought by the Eichstaett-Bangkok Congresses was underfoot. Whether that massive change, that quantitative leap into a new and creative form of parish religious education will occur, is dependent upon many variables. One variable is the introduction of significant information about coordinators and their potential into the national, regional, diocesan, and parish discussions about this new focus. This book was written with that intention in mind.

The other variable which will allow the significant change to occur or will retard it is the wise leadership mentioned above. Monsignor Gallagher has said throughout the post-Vatican developments: "Priests like me are so badly malformed that we will probably never get over it. But I believe God is alive and the Spirit is at work in the world and in the Church, and we just have to risk going ahead even though we cannot completely understand many things that are being proposed by the new religious educators."

This wise leadership has not been a passive and uncritical one. Those of us who are proposing new ventures have the responsibility to present a convincing case to those who make the decisions, but the decision-makers also need a risk-spirituality in responding.

I wish to thank the many hundreds of parish coordinators who have participated in Project Coordinator thus far in either the surveys, research reports, and/or the many workshops and personal discussions. I have gained much from you, and I hope this book provides some basic information for you, so we can move quickly into new problems and get on with the metanoia which must come in the educational mission of the Church. If you care to react to this book, please do so. The dialogue about this new potential must continue at all levels.

I wish also to thank particularly Monsignor Victor Gallagher for his wise leadership and deep friendship throughout my years of work in the Grand Rapids Diocese. His approach in hiring me might be an example for parish Boards. He asked Bishop Allen Babcock in 1964 if he could proceed to hire a layman. The Bishop asked what this man would do. Monsignor replied, "I do not know for sure, but I am sure we need to take this step, and if he hasn't done something significant within a year, I will personally fire him."

Thanks are also due to Mrs. Lenora Triggs for her exceptional secretarial skills, to Mr. Patrick Usas for his manifold duties in handling the materials related to Project Coordinator, to Sister Rita Panciera, RSM, and Sister Mary Frances Prior, SC, for assistance with the manuscript, and to Dr. Beryl Orris for his many insights into the nature and scope of religious education.

Joseph C. Neiman, Director
Project Coordinator
Divine Word International
Centre of Religious Education
London, Ontario, Canada

Summer 1970

Chapter One

WHY PARISH COORDINATORS?

Throughout the United States and parts of Canada, a new focus is appearing in parish religious education — the professional. Parishes or groups of parishes are hiring a professional person to work exclusively in youth and adult religious education. This person is called a Religious Education Coordinator (REC) or a Director of Religious Education (DRE), depending upon the area of the country in which he is hired. This trend appears to have begun about 1967, and should reach major proportions by 1975 (As of 1970 there are at least 1,500 persons employed in this capacity).

No one reason accounts for this development, rather many variables in combination are producing a general climate which leads to such a decision. Before discussing the details about parish coordinators, it is important to examine the situation out of which this new focus is developing.

First, the climate which is generating this new development is also placing expectations and limitations upon it. If coordinators are to be successful, they will have to meet some of these expectations or at least grapple with them before moving on to achieving goals which they deem important to realize. Part of the great frustration which coordinators are experiencing lies in this unconscious confrontation of differing expectations.

Secondly, the present situation of Christian education within the Church presents a significant opportunity for radical (meaning *root*) change. Coordinators and those concerned with the educational mission of the Church in the '70's can either improve the present approaches, striving for excellence, or they can evolve radically new and more effective approaches. In either case, an understanding of the present crisis climate in Christian education in the Church and of the way in which this accounts for the growth of parish coordinators is necessary.

GROWING CONCERN FOR RELIGIOUS EDUCATION

One of the more indirect causes for the development of parish coordinators lies in the growing importance of religious education within the parishes. Since the Eichstaett and Bangkok International Congresses on Missionary Catechetics in the early 1960's, great emphasis has been placed upon the teaching of religion. The advances in theology, liturgy, Scripture, and the behavioral sciences were introduced into catechetics largely through the impetus of these Congresses and the events and persons surrounding them (Fathers Hofinger, Nebreda, and VanCaster played important roles in these Congresses and in spreading the discussions throughout the North American continent). One need only look at the rapid increase in published materials about religious education since 1960 to see this growth. "It is beyond question that a great concern with religious education has been generated within a very short time," Brother Gabriel Moran wrote in 1966 (1).

This early concern led to professionalization of personnel, especially on the diocesan level, and to a greater awareness of the need of improvement in the content and scope of school and parish religious education programs. A few large parishes — generally those without schools — strove to hire a professional religious educator to extend their program and to train the teachers. Schools worked to train religion teachers, to introduce new curriculums, and to secure a professional as department head, wherever possible. A few diocesan offices, college programs, and centers of various kinds sprang up to prepare people for the changes launched by these two International Congresses.

The Second Vatican Council in the mid-60's gave further impetus to this thrust and especially highlighted the need for adult religious education. The changes in the liturgy, the increased participation in parish decision-making, and the move into ecumenical and community involvements demanded adult education for leadership and understanding. Parishes that could afford it hired professional educators to assist with improving youth programs and to launch adult education. More generally, however, parishes relied on diocesan offices for assistance in providing "effective" youth programs and for educating adults through renewal programs.

By the end of the '60's, the head of steam generated by the Congresses and the Council was exhausted, leaving behind confusion and polarization in parish religious education. The response to the urban crisis — the introduction of the social gospel in youth and adult programs — further frustrated volunteer teachers in parish programs and confused the rest of the parishioners. Thus, by the end of the decade, dissatisfaction with parish religious education was widespread, and beleagured pastors and parish leaders began to look seriously for new alternatives for program improvement. Hiring a parish professional became one of these alternatives.

Perhaps the sociological and economic problems which were coming to the surface in Catholic education by the end of the '60's were more directly responsible for the broad climate which has led to the hiring of coordinators of parish religious education. The influence of these factors on the education situation is seen mainly in their importance in the decline of the Catholic school.

SOCIOLOGICAL CHANGES AFFECTING CATHOLIC EDUCATION

It is beyond question that the overwhelming majority of Catholic youth receive their education in the public elementary and secondary schools of our land. At the college level, the number of Catholic young people who attend Catholic colleges is exceedingly small in proportion to the total number of Catholics attending college.

This is a sociological fact. Opinion begins when speaking of the desirability of this fact and/or the quality of education which is received in schools or parish religious education programs.

The Greeley-Rossi Study showed that the majority (81%) of Catholic young people attend public schools for all or part of their formal education (see Chart 1:1). Hence, they depend upon the parish CCD program for all or part of their formal religious education. The same study indicates that these parish programs do not reach half of the youth. "Parents of 44 per cent of the Catholic children not in Catholic grammar schools and 24 per cent of the high school group reported their children to have had some religious instruction" (2).

The Notre Dame Study (see Chart 1:2) indicated that in the 1962-63 school year, 54% of the Catholic youth of school age attended public elementary and secondary schools, and 46% attended Catholic Schools (3). In that year, Catholic schools had an enrollment of some 5.3 million. By 1967, the school enrollment had passed through a crest of 5.6 million (in 1964) and declined to an enrollment of some 5.2 million nationally (4).

Bishop Joseph Bernardin of the United States Catholic Conference told the National Catholic Education Association audience: "In two years, the number of children in Catholic elementary schools has dropped by almost 500,000. Even when allowance is made for consolidations and the elimination of sub-standard conditions, the fact still remains that our Catholic school system is shrinking. In all likelihood, the situation will probably worsen rather than improve in the foreseeable future" (5).

CHART 1:1

THE EDUCATION OF CATHOLIC YOUTH
(Greeley-Rossi Study)

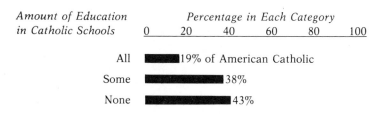

Amount of Education in Catholic Schools	*Percentage in Each Category* 0 20 40 60 80 100
All	19% of American Catholic
Some	38%
None	43%

Andrew M. Greeley and Peter H. Rossi, *The Education of Catholic Americans* (Chicago: Aldine Publishing Co., 1966), p. 25.

CHART 1:2

THE EDUCATION OF CATHOLIC YOUTH
IN CATHOLIC SCHOOLS AND PUBLIC SCHOOLS
(National Enrollment Facts — 1962-63 School Year)

Based on Reginald A. Neuwein, ed., "Enrollment of Catholic Schools," *Catholic Schools in Action, A Report of the Notre Dame Study of Catholic Elementary and Secondary Schools in the United States* (Notre Dame, Indiana: University of Notre Dame Press, 1966). p. 27-37.

Total Number of Catholic Youth of School Age

11.4 million

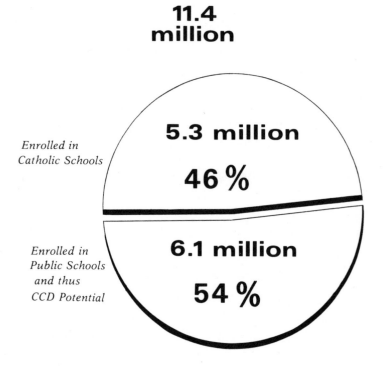

Enrolled in Catholic Schools

5.3 million

46%

Enrolled in Public Schools and thus CCD Potential

6.1 million

54%

A census taken in the Grand Rapids Diocese (Michigan) by Census Management in 1968, indicated that of the total Catholic population of the Diocese, 49.5% were 21 years of age or older. The other 50.5% were under 21 years of age. The majority of those in school (61.9%) attended public schools (see Chart 1:3) (6).

CHART 1:3

THE EDUCATION OF CATHOLIC YOUTH
(Grand Rapids Census)

Category	Percentage in Each Category
	0 20 40 60 80 100
Total Number of Youth in School	████████████████████ 77,793
Number in Catholic School	████████ 38.1% (28,994)
Number in Public School	████████████ 61.9% (47,008)

Census Management, Inc., "Summary Report, Diocese of Grand Rapids, Census Survey—1967 (Grand Rapids, Mich.) unpublished manuscript.

Thus, sociological evidence clearly shows that the majority of Catholic youth attend public elementary and secondary schools and depend upon parish programs for their formal religious education. What records there are in diocesan and parish CCD offices also show that these parish programs are failing to reach a large percentage of these youth.

Educational leaders, diocesan and parish Boards of education, pastors, and religious communities have begun to collect and examine these and similar sociological facts in order to face hard priority decisions. Bishop Bernardin notes further in the same speech to the NCEA:

"Still, if we are honest we must admit that, in an individual case, the continuation of a school could mean using a disproportionate share of our talent and resources, with the result that the religious education programs for those who are not in Catholic schools — both children and adults — would be impaired. In such a case, then, the decision may have to be made to deploy our resources in a radically different way" (7).

After serious study of their educational problems and mission, St. Mary of the Lake Parish in suburban Minneapolis phased their school and CCD program into a Family Learning Center and total educational program. Their Board of Education hired a carefully selected team of religious educators and worked closely with them(8).

Many parishes and dioceses, after studying these sociological facts, hire a parish coordinator or a diocesan regional team to extend the scope and deepen the quality of parish youth and adult programs, largely because they came to the realization that religious education is the most essential part of the Church's educational mission (9) and that the majority of the youth and adults of the parish were not being given quality opportunities for religious education (10).

Thus the renewed emphasis upon religious education stemming from the Congresses and the Council and a study of the sociological facts about the education of Catholic youth and adults provide some of the general influences leading to the employment of parish (and area) religious education coordinators. The economic factors, however, are equally important.

ECONOMIC FACTORS AFFECTING CATHOLIC EDU-CATION

Economics is always important in the decision-making process about priorities for education. This is equally true in the Catholic Church. The popular theory that the Church (especially the diocese), like the government, has "unlimited" funds to spend upon programs is simply a myth. Especially since the introduction of lay representative Boards of Education at the parish and diocesan levels, the economic factors affecting educational decisions are being studied closely.

The Notre Dame Study on Catholic Education, in projecting what the enrollments would be in the 1968-69 school year based upon the variables used in the 1962-63 count, predicted an increase in expenditures of $721,610,000 dollars for space alone(11). Neither the increased enrollment nor the projected income was attained.

In the Archdiocese of New York, the reported operating costs per pupil in 1958 were $55.00. They increased to $156.00 by 1968, and are projected to reach $379.00 per pupil by 1972(12). It simply costs more to educate a child today in all academic areas including religion, This increased cost is hitting Catholic schools very hard. Father Virgil Blum, strong advocate of governmental assistance to non-public schools stated: "We have a financial crisis in non-public school education. These schools cannot exist more than four or five years at the most, under present conditions"(13).

The late Monsignor O'Neil C. D'Amour, an outspoken advocate of Catholic schools at any cost, said that "there can be no doubt that unless something is done and done soon, there will be no Catholic schools. The crisis is a financial one" (14). He indicated that the present modes of solving the crisis—increased tuitions and restricting enrollments—would further the decline of the schools.

This decrease in the amount of funds available for Catholic education is not limited to schools alone. CCD programs in parishes and in dioceses have always suffered from a lack of funding (15). There is much dispute as to what constitutes the actual amount spent on parish CCD programs versus the stated amount, but the fact remains that parish CCD education is poorly funded, and the recent cutbacks in diocesan programs indicate that these programs will suffer a financial pinch also (16).

The financial bind which is affecting all of the educational attempts of the Catholic Church seems to arise from a number of factors, not the least of which is the prevailing polarization within the Catholic community itself.

The Catholic community is in disagreement over the developments within theology and the methods in liturgy and education. This controversy ranges from bishops to the man-in-the-pew.

A reevaluation of the effectiveness of Catholic education is taking place. Liberal lay groups claim that schools consume too much of the human and material resources of the Church. The much discussed but poorly interpreted book by Mary Perkins Ryan, *Are Parochial Schools the Answer?* (Holt, Rinehart, & Winston, New York, 1964), is a good example of this position, as are statements by the National Association of Laymen. Conservative groups are disturbed by the changes in the content of the religious education programs; they desire a return to orthodoxy and a renewed emphasis on schools.

Taken together this polarization of the left and the right, which is representative of a larger disunity in society itself, accounts for a "credibility gap" regarding Catholic schools and parish religious education.

The man-in-the-pew is using his voting power in the Sunday collections to voice his lack of interest, disapproval, or confusion. Hence, there is not sufficient money to fund present and planned educational objectives. Hard priorities have to be set by parishes, schools, and diocesan offices. Catholic educators have responded in a variety of ways, not the least of which is Educaid, the drive for governmental assistance for the secular purposes of parochial shools. Another method is the development of parish or regional centers employing religious education personnel.

An additional economic (and sociological) factor which may change the priorities concerning the Church's educational mission is the increased teacher cost stemming from the growing number of non-religious personnel being employed by the Church and the rise of salaries of both lay and religious personnel to just rates. "Rising costs and a dwindling number of religious personnel— just to mention what are undoubtedly the most serious difficulties—have forced us to do things which we would have completely rejected just four or five years ago" (17).

With the renewal launched by the Second Vatican Council, many men and women have sought other life styles and vocations outside the religious communities. In addition, the communities have expanded into new work such as human relations, social services, and the like, to respond to the needs of the times. Furthermore, the democratization of the religious communities (under the principle of subsidiarity) has allowed the individual members much more choice regarding the areas in which they will work. Many have chosen not to work in schools but rather in parish religious education or other apostolates.

Thus the number of lay personnel in Catholic schools has increased greatly. The NCEA notes that approximately 44% of all teachers in grade schools and 41% of all teachers in high schools are lay (non-religious) personnel(18). This means salaries include a greater part of the educational budget. Salaries of religious have also increased as communities realize that sisters and brothers cannot be treated as interchangeable parts at a fixed rate and that poverty is in the way in which the money is spent and not in the amount received. Furthermore, communities need more money to pay for needed specialization and to care for the growing number of retiring religious.

The buildings themselves are another economic factor affecting priority decisions. Many Catholic schools are advanced in age and ill-suited for the multimedia, flexible learning styles required by education today. The cost of renovation is prohibitive of change. The population shift from older inner-city parishes to suburban sites also accounts for the decline of funds available for renovation or even increased operating costs.

The present efforts to secure private and governmental funding for Catholic schools may ease the economic burden to some degree *if* successful, and this in turn may free some Church funds for religious education. However, these efforts are not without opposition and are long-range in most parts of the country. The financial crisis facing parishes is immediate, making school closings "inevitable" as Cardinal Cushing put it(19).

Thus, through representative Boards of Education at the parish and diocesan levels(20), many Catholics are finding it "cheaper" to fund two sisters or one lay religious education coordinator for all of the youth of the parish (and perhaps the adults) rather than several sisters and lay teachers for a minority of the youth in a school. Whether or not it will be "cheaper" than schools in the long run in terms of effectiveness and growth of the Church only history will show.

"Catholic people have more money available for schooling than ever before in their history," Monsignor D'Amour argued(21), but the fact remains it is not forthcoming nor is governmental assistance being secured rapidly. This economic situation facing the Church in the educational mission is one of the chief factors behind the decline of the Catholic school and the rise of parish religious education coordinators(22).

CHANGING CONCEPTIONS OF THE EDUCATIONAL MISSION

The decline of the Catholic school and the growing concern for extending parish religious education to all the youth of a parish and to adults are perhaps the chief immediate causes for the growth of the parish coordinators. The more lasting pressure for this new focus of a professional religious educator at the parish level will come from the changing conceptions about the educational mission of the Church itself. With a rapidity that unsettles publishers and program planners, religious education is evolving out of the Eichstaett-Bangkok and early Vatican II eras into new goals, content, and processes.

The Eichstaett-Bangkok Congresses introduced the *kerygma*(23) as a new content arrangement to replace the catechism and introduced (or greatly advanced) the Munich Method with audio-visual aids of a limited nature as the new instructional style for the teaching-learning situation. These changes neces-

sitated teacher education for both volunteers and professionals, a relatively easy task for diocesan offices
and other groups to provide in the early and mid-1960's.
Concern for professionalism was voiced throughout
the catechetical milieu, but this concern was infrequently translated into action except at the diocesan
and regional levels—or in some cases where a parish
(generally without a school) hired professionals for
large-scale CCD programs or for catechetical centers.

By the late 1960's and with the advent of the '70's,
the content of religious education itself is to be found
increasingly *within* the media of films, music, print,
and life experiences. These are no longer supplemental
to the basic *kerygmatic* message and are not, therefore,
easily dropped "if there is not sufficient time." Flexibility in curriculum and instructional styles have also
advanced rapidly. The "theme" curriculum for adolescents and the "CCD Sundays" are examples of new flexibility.

The increased sophistication in the teaching-learning situation and in the total parish programming for
youth and adults necessitates a professional near at
hand to lead all the volunteers in making decisions
to plan and implement "multi-sensory" or "life-centered" or "multi-media" curriculums.

There is no doubt that what is presently being
done in religious education for adolescents is vastly
inadequate. The design of new materials is flexible
and media-oriented, placing them nearer in appeal to
youth but more out of reach for the teachers in terms of
usefulness. The introduction of parent-pastor-teacher-
child materials in elementary programs has made the coordination problems more complex. Consequently,
parishes are beginning to feel acute frustration not only
from their inability to "reach" all the youth but also from
their inability to start *any* effective program for youth.

Coupled with this is the growing conviction that faith is adult in character and that unless adult religious education is taken seriously, the efforts of the youth programs can never be effective. The Greeley-Rossi Study indicates that "there does not yet seem to be any substitute for the predispositions created by the family milieu—at least short of the college level"(24).

Adult religious education is new to parishes, and committees approach it with a school model in mind (including lectures, classes, seminars). Thus, success is minimal.

The easy answer to this general frustration with youth and adult religious education appears to be to hire a professional religious educator trained in catechetics (or *religious studies, theology, religious education, multi-discipline courses*—depending upon which fad is popular that year) to make sense out of the chaos, as it were. This feeling of hopelessness, frustration, and complexity, as well as a desire on the part of some people for new goals and new programs accounts for much of the general climate leading to the hiring of parish coordinators. It is no wonder friction arises when they do not seem to deliver immediate and startling results.

SUMMARY

No precise reason can be given for the development of the parish coordinator across the North American continent. Many variables contribute to the general climate out of which a given parish makes the decision to launch such a new focus in parish religious education. Even the broad cultural "American way" of solving new problems or old problems which are out of hand—set up an office and hire a professional—permeates the thinking of the pastor and parish leaders who sit down to answer what can be done in X Parish to solve the educational problems.

Within the current crisis situation facing the educational mission of the Church, the following variables can be identified as part of this general climate:

1) The majority of Catholic youth attend public schools and are not being reached with quality opportunities for formal religious education.

2) There is a declining amount of financial resources available to the Church for education; the current polarization within the Church, the rising costs of living and operating, the more specialized needs in education for human and material resources, the increase of *non-religious* personnel at a higher salary rate—these are part of this general financial bind. The current drive for *Educaid* and private funding of Catholic schools may ease the situation for *schools*, but it will not solve the financial problems confronting the total educational work of the Church.

3) There are a declining number of *religious*, men and women, available for achieving the educational objectives of the Church. This specialized personnel makes possible certain types of educational work (e.g., in urban or rural poverty areas, parish missions).

4) The aging, outdated facilities and the shift of population groups further complicate the educational picture.

5) The changing conceptions of the objectives of the Church's educational mission—the importance of adult religious education, educational service to man's special needs, and the nature of the parish itself—are also factors.

6) The increased sophistication demanded in the teaching-learning situation by the introduction of specialized media make religious education and general education more complex and costly.

A local parish generally faces one or a combination of these variables and is forced to think through (formally or informally) the educational mission of the Church and make priority decisions. Typically the decision is to close the school and/or to hire a professional coordinator (an individual or a team) to handle the educational work. *Other options are possible* and ought to be taken into consideration before a final decision is made. There is no *generic* or *objective* or *essential* reason flowing from the nature of the Church which would compel a faith community (parish) to hire a professionally prepared person to lead in its educational mission. This is not to say that it is not a good idea to hire such a person or that the role of a coordinator cannot be seen as integral to a Christian community. Rather it is a warning that a faith community ought to know *why* they are hiring a professional and what he will do for and with them.

NOTES FOR CHAPTER 1

1) Gabriel Moran, FSC, "Catechetics for the Real World," *America* 115, no. 3, (July 16, 1966), pp. 57-59.

2) Andrew M. Greeley and Peter H. Rossi, *The Education of Catholic Americans* (Chicago: Aldine Publishing, 1966), p. 285.

3) Reginald A. Neuwien, ed., *Catholic Schools in Action* (Notre Dame, Indiana: University of Notre Dame Press, 1966), pp. 27-37.

4) Neil G. McCluskey, *Catholic Education Faces Its Future* (New York: Doubleday, 1968), p. 45.

5) Joseph L. Bernardin, "Catholic Education Serving a Troubled Society," *NCEA Bulletin* (August, 1969), p. 7.

6) Census Management, Inc., "Summary Report, Diocese of Grand Rapids, Census Survey — 1967 (Grand Rapids, Mich.), unpublished manuscript.

7) Bernardin, "Catholic Education Serving," p. 8.

8) Michael Farren, "Family Learning Center: A New Approach to Religious Education," *The Living Light* 6, no. 3, (Fall, 1969), p. 62. Detailed description and rationale is given here by one of the team members.

9) Cf. Walter M. Abbott, ed., *Vatican Council II, Declaration on Christian Education, The Documents of Vatican II* (New York: Guild Press, 1966). Bishop Bernardin in his speech to the NCEA quoted here stated: "We must give priority to the religious education of all Catholics" (Bernardin, "Catholic Schools Serving," p. 8).

10) Studies made on the future of Catholic education in parishes before about 1965-66 tend to re-arrange priorities by phasing into a catechetical center or a released/shared time program. The study of St. Joseph's Parish in St. Joseph, Michigan, is a good example: "How Long Can the Door Stay Open," (1965), report of a committee of the Home and School Association.

11) Neuwien, ed., *Catholic Schools in Action*, p. 36.

12) UPI New Release, "Catholic Schools Caught in Bind," *Grand Rapids Press* (August 30, 1969).

13) "Father Blum Says Money Crisis Could Kill Parochial Schools," *Catholic Messenger* (Diocese of Davenport, Mich., February 27, 1969).

14) Rt. Rev. Msgr. O'Neil C. D'Amour, "Catholic Schools Must Survive," *NCEA Bulletin* (November, 1968), p. 5.

15) Census Management, Inc., "National CCD Survey" (1968), an unpublished research report for the National Conference of Diocesan Directors.

16) "Dilemma: How Do You Pay for Professionals?" National Catholic Reporter July 16, 1969.

17) Bernardin, "Catholic Education Serving," p. 7.

18) Catholic Education 1969 — An Overview, (Washington, D.C.: National Catholic Education Association, 1969).

19) USCC News Release, "State Aid Chief Hope for Schools," The Western Michigan Catholic (February 20, 1970).

20) The NCEA notes that there were some 4,000 parish boards in 1968, with a forty percent increase expected in 1969 (Catholic Education 1969).

21) D'Amour, "Catholic Schools Must Survive."

22) USCC News Release, "Religious Formation Programs Gain Status," The Western Michigan Catholic (April 11, 1969).

23) Sister Miriam, OLVM, "A New Terminology for Catechetics," Catholic School Journal (May, 1966), p. 30: "This, then, is the idea of the kerygmatic teaching: A God-centered synthesis of the essential truths as revealed by God Himself in Holy Scripture and as lived and realized in daily life through the liturgy."

24) Greeley and Rossi, Education of Catholic Americans, p. 197.

Chapter Two

SECURING A COORDINATOR

Parishes planning to hire a professional person to handle their religious education work ought to be particularly concerned about the process which leads to that decision. Those parishes which have already hired a coordinator may profit from re-examining the basis on which the decision was made; certain elements need to go into the decision in order for the program with a coordinator to succeed. If they have not, some remedial steps can be taken. Project Coordinator data would indicate that initial mistakes made in this area later become major problems.

The very first area to examine is precisely who decides (or decided) that the parish needs a religious education coordinator. If the pastor makes an arbitrary decision, however well intended, chances are poor that success will be achieved. To proceed to hire a coordinator without consulting the teachers and others who are involved in the religious education program is to indicate to them that their efforts are not appreciated and clearly demonstrates a lack of communication and openness, qualities essential to the new focus.

PREPARATION OF THE PARISH

All those who will be directly involved with the work of a parish coordinator ought to be in on the discussions that lead to the conclusion to hire such a person. This obviously does not mean that *all* are involved to the same degree, but that they are involved or represented to an appropriate extent, perhaps determined by the closeness of contact which they will have with this project.

Those involved should include the pastor, the associate pastors, the school principal, the teachers in the religious education program, heads of educational organizations or committees, the Board of Education, and/or the Parish Council. The parish at large should be informed and consulted as the process is initiated and proceeds. *The broader the base of support for the decision, the better the chances of success both educationally and financially.*

Perhaps as much as a year of preparation should be done before an organized search is begun to secure a particular coordinator (lay or religious). During this year the parish as a whole—but especially the people dealing directly with the educational mission of the parish—should probe the questions: What should we as a parish do in Christian education? What are the strengths and weaknesses of our present efforts? What are our particular educational needs? (This may lead to the deeper questions about the nature of the Church and its relationship to society and man. It ought to be noted that these are questions that cannot be "answered" but can be "resolved" in the sense that some on-going understandings can be articulated which provide the basis for working decisions.)

At first it would seem that involving the parish in this type of questioning is doing precisely what the coordinator ought to be hired to do, but it is not. Rather, this is a process which leads many to become aware; first, aware that Christian education is an essential part of the Church's total mission and, second, aware that the educational needs of this parish which are great now and which will expand in the future can be met partially by hiring a professional religious educator.

Frequently a parish which would at first think it could not hire such a coordinator and finance that kind of a program will discover in this questioning process that the vitality of the faith of the whole parish is to a large degree dependent upon the quality of Christian education. Collections—that voting sign of the non-involved laity—drop off when people begin to feel that faith as expressed in the life of this parish is not too important. In all areas of life, people "pay" in psychic or tangible ways for what they need, want, and believe in. Religious education helps people to become more aware of themselves and their lives in relationship with faith and hence can strengthen the total faith life of a given parish—including a renewed commitment demonstrated by increased collections and involvement.

Board of Education The parish Board of Education, or a similar committee representative of the parish and responsible for the educational mission, should head this process of preparation in conjunction with the pastor.

This preparation process can take many forms. Presenting the educational problems (the variables discussed in Chapter 1) to the total parish for consideration through public meetings, parish bulletins, personal letters, homilies, or whatever vehicle can show the need for a thorough re-examination of what is presently being done by the faith community in its educational mission.

Next an in-depth discussion of what ought to be done and why would be in order. Speakers, discussion groups, panels, ad hoc committees, neighborhood-action sessions, or any suitable vehicle can be used to probe the questions described above.

Besides involving many in examining the problems to which the coordinator and an expanded program may provide a partial solution, the Board and the pastor will also be defining more precisely with the parish its educational needs; from this the job definition for the coordinator will arise. When a parish knows to a large degree what it wants to do and why, a professional can assist in achieving it. Or the professional can point out to the parish what is wrong or incomplete or inaccurate in what it is seeking to do and why.

At this point, an "outside agent" may be of assistance in helping the Board and the pastor. The Diocesan Office may be able to provide this kind of assistance. The outside agent with the Board brings to formal articulation in a report the discussions about the educational mission of that parish. He also assists the Board in drafting a long-range "ideal" plan for meeting these stated educational needs. This plan is again presented to the total parish for discussion. It may include such broad steps as closing the school or hiring a coordinator.

In some parishes, presenting this long-range plan to the whole parish can be done by presenting it to the Parish Council which then reacts to the plan from the perspective of all the various efforts of the parish.

In dioceses where a strong Diocesan Board of Education is operative, this plan would also have to be presented to that body for discussion and/or approval. Showing how the envisioned parish plan would handle diocesan goals and policies already established would need to be demonstrated in the plan or the reason for the variance clearly explained.

It cannot be stressed enough that it is *not* the work of the coordinator to draft this long-range plan. The professional puts the flesh on this skeleton by showing the parish how they can best reach these goals and what will be necessary to do so. Given the present state of confusion in the Church about the educational mission, the coordinator *may* be hired to assist the parish in determining what it will seek to do in the coming year or two. If this be the case, the preparation process is still necessary so that the large body of the parish knows that this is precisely what the professional will do and so that they sense the need for it to begin with.

In undertaking this preparation process, the parish may decide that it can best meet its educational needs by an option other than hiring a professional coordinator. Total parish support for the school and an expanded program built around it could be achieved. If a school is present in the parish, there are already educational resources (human and material) available. The problem may be with the relationship of these resources to the educational needs and goals of that parish. A re-arrangement of the resources (introduction of teacher-aides, shared time, new instructional styles) may provide for the total religious education desired there.

CONTRACT-ROLE DESCRIPTION — FIRST DRAFT:

From the long-range plan the Board of Education can begin to identify the kinds of responsibilities which it will ask a professional person to fulfill. A contract with supplements is useful as a tool for the articulation of this expectation. Preparing the first draft of the supplements accompanying this contract from the job content information (long-range plan) not only helps the Board to know what to say to the prospective coordinator, but also helps the teachers and others who will be closely connected with the coordinator to know what help they can expect from this person. A certain measure of cooperation is already started when the catechists see that someone can help them with certain of their needs.

Although many executives in business, industry, and in education work with a verbal agreement alone, the predominant trend within education is toward a written contract for teachers and administrative personnel. For reasons which should become clear in this discussion, contracts will be necessary for coordinators of parish religious education, at least for the present.

Parish Boards need not have scruples concerning the use of contracts in religious affairs. Our theological and Scriptural background will tell us that a contract (covenant) is a formalized agreement between two parties regarding the nature of their relationship and the responsibilities and benefits accruing to each party of the contract. The very core of Judaeo-Christian religions is the covenanted relationship between God and his people. Contracts for coordinators ought to be viewed in this light rather than as mere business affairs to be avoided by dedicated religious people.

Religious communities have made contracts in the past with bishops and pastors committing personnel to apostolates. Contracts are not new in the Church even in this business sense. Catholic school personnel also utilize the formal agreement and will do so more in the future.

Parishes cannot realistically expect qualified persons to move any distance to accept the responsibilities of a parish coordinator merely on the verbal say of one individual—be it pastor or Board member—or without the assurance that the parish will employ the coordinator for at least a year.

A contract, however, will not solve all the problems

of working relationships; for in fact the contract in the case of coordinators carries little legal weight, compared with other business contracts. Its chief benefit is not in the security afforded the coordinator or the parish, but rather in the process of formalizing the relationship and clarifying what is expected of one another.

A contract can be written many ways. The model presented here (see Chart 2:1) is offered for discussion and adaptation. Each parish will have to prepare its own or use a diocesan model. Basically, a contract does four things:
1) it states who the parties are,
2) what their relationship is to one another and what responsibilities are required of that relationship,
3) what benefits accrue,
4) and how to terminate or extend the agreement and (perhaps) how to handle grievances.

Who Agrees The contract for coordinators ought to be an agreement between the faith community and the individual coordinator. This would even apply with *religious* personnel today. The parish is represented by the pastor and the Board of Education (or Parish Council) con-jointly. The pastor is essential for the legality of the contract in the present status of Church legal relations. The Board is essential as it should be representative of the people of the parish and will be the group with whom the coordinator will work (See Chapter 5). The Board also provides continuity when pastoral changes are made. These parties then sign the agreement or contract.

In some places, the Diocesan Office also becomes a party to the agreement. There does not seem to be any real reason (perhaps a psychological one) for this, unless the Diocesan Office also agrees in the contract to offer certain services to the parish and/or the coordinator.

CHART 2:1

CONTRACT
RELIGIOUS EDUCATION COORDINATOR

This agreement is between the Pastor and the People of _____ (hereinafter termed the BOARD) and _____ as Coordinator of Religious Education (hereinafter termed COORDINATOR).

The BOARD agrees to hire the above party as COORDINATOR of Religious Education for _____ Parish to fulfill the responsibilities described in *Supplement A* accompanying this Contract. For the fulfillment of these responsibilities, the BOARD agrees to pay the COORDINATOR a salary of _____, payable in ____ equal install-ments over a ____ month period, beginning _____ and ending _____. This salary shall increase by an annual increment of _____and shall be subject to the usual payroll deductions required by law and other authorized deductions. The BOARD also agrees to provide the personal benefits and professional support described in *Supplement B* accom-panying this Contract.

The COORDINATOR agrees to fulfill the responsibilities assigned (*Supplement A*) for the development of Religious Education in _____ Parish for the duration of this Contract.

This Contract is for a ____ year period, subject to annual review. Either party may terminate this Agreement in the event of a willful and material violation of the terms of the Agreement, which violation shall be judged by the Diocesan Office of Religious Education. In the event of a termination, the responsibilities of each party cease.

SIGNED: _____ COORDINATOR
           _____ Pastor
           _____ President, Board of Education

           DATE: _____

(Copies of Contract and Supplements to Coordinator, Board of Edu-cation, Pastor and Diocesan Office of Religious Education.)

The Relationship The relationship of the coordinator to the parish is generally conceived of as the role of the coordinator. This role or job description or definition of assigned responsibilities becomes Supplement A to the basic contract (It is discussed in detail in Chapter 3). Supplement A describes in detail the responsibilities which the coordinator will fulfill for the parish and to whom and in what way the coordinator will relate both to the parish and to groups outside the parish.

Benefits Accruing Supplement B to the contract explains the benefits accruing to the coordinator for the fulfillment of the assigned reponsibilities (Supplement A). These include both personal and professional support. As with Supplement A, the details of Supplement B need to be worked out to fit each particular parish. It is appropriate, however, that some general reasoning about the items to be included is mentioned here.

Salary There is a great deal of variation across the country in the salaries paid to coordinators. This is due to many factors besides the obvious variations expected from one economic area to another.

The majority of coordinators are religious women. The next largest group would be single women, many of whom are former religious. Men make up the smallest ratio of the total number of coordinators — a growing and vocal group, however. This factor causes the salaries to vary. Men and women who have worked in professional "secular" capacities in the course of their work career expect and receive higher salaries. Religious and former religious are seen and see themselves differently and the salary they accept is one manifestation of this.

In speaking of the salary for religious, the variance must also be seen against the difference between actual salary paid (money) and the real salary provided in housing, transportation, and the like. The real salary for many religious includes the following components:

1) Base salary for religious in diocese: This will soon change as religious communities begin to ask for salaries commensurate with the competence of the individuals and as religious are hired on an individual basis rather than through the community.

2) Housing: Frequently a convent is provided for religious working as coordinators. This is often desirable for communal life style and is frequently possible where schools are or were present. Housing is part of the real salary and details about it should be stated in Supplement B when applicable to religious.

3) Transportation: In the case of religious, a parish car is frequently provided or a fleet car is utilized by the religious as a member of a larger community. If a car is provided, details are described in Supplement B under salary or in the more general category for transportation.

4) Benefits: Often members of religious communities have their own medical and retirement plans which the individuals pay out of the salary which they receive. This ought to be taken into consideration and an additional amount put into the salary, if this is the arrangement. Otherwise, the parish benefit plan can be followed and described in separate sections.

In some dioceses, communities of religious women also receive a "housekeeper's fee" for hiring out the cooking, cleaning, and similar domestic service. This should be taken care of out of the base salary and not be a separate item in a contract with religious. This is a matter of personal budget and not a part of the educational budget being described here. The base salary, however, should be sufficient that personal budgets can provide such assistance. Many diocesan norms in this regard are inadequate.

Salary Schedule Salaries should be based upon (1) the responsibilities assigned, (2) the education, and (3) the experience of the coordinator being hired. Since the salaries of coordinators vary so greatly, it would be inappropriate to present a national average as a sample salary schedule. Some guidelines can be given, however, to assist parishes (and dioceses) in setting a proper salary for coordinators, proper for the area, the responsibilities assigned, the education, and experience of the coordinator.

The National Catholic Education Association has suggested that Catholic school salaries ought to be approximately 80 to 90 percent of comparable public school salaries. This can be one guideline for parishes.

Generally, coordinators are given responsibilities similar to those in public schools working with instructional services over against those actually teaching. If the role of the coordinator is largely administrative (see Supplement A for that parish), then the job of the assistant superintendent for curriculum and instruction may be comparable. If the role is that of resource person or consultant, then the supervisory jobs at the local public school district would be similar.

Nationally, classroom teachers holding a Bachelor's Degree and teaching in a moderately sized school district received between $5,500 and $8,000 in 1967-68. Inflation would increase this at least 10% a year. With a Master's Degree, classroom teachers of these districts received from $6,000 to $9,000. Those teachers above the Master's level received a maximum of $10,500 (1).

Assistant superintendents in moderately sized school districts, in 1967-68, received an average of $18,294 for their services. Master teachers — teachers with an advanced degree and administrative or supervisory responsibilities — received an average of $10,772. Coordinators of programs — largely an administrative type of work in new projects—received $12,454 for their work(2).

These national statistics can serve as a very broad guideline for the salary schedule. They show that a parish can expect to pay a coordinator with a Master's Degree approximately $8,000 to $15,000, depending upon the personal and experience qualifications of the individual and the responsibilities assigned.

Medical and Retirement Benefits Supplement B ought to include a definition of the coordinator's medical and retirement benefits. Parishes around the country are beginning to participate in provincial or diocesan plans and the coordinator's participation should be stated.

Vacations and Sick Leave These personal benefits should be described in Supplement B. The suggestions presented in Chart 2:2 are a possibility in this regard. Religious women will soon move in this direction—year-round employment—especially when the parishes begin to provide for continuing education. The school year model with its "automatic" vacations is not a good model for a coordinator, as frequently the coordinator's work will intensify at the holidays (depending, of course, on the responsibilities of the REC). Furthermore, much of the summer will be used for continuing education and preparations if we are to take religious education seriously.

Professional Support In addition to the salary, medical, vacation, and similar items which can be considered the personal benefits accruing to the coordinator for fulfillment of the responsibilities assigned, Supplement B ought to state what professional support will be provided for the coordinator. This would include at least transportation arrangements, office and secretarial assistance, and continuing education.

Transportation The coordinator should be reimbursed for travel involved in executing the responsibilities of religious education at a rate of ten cents per mile, if he provides his own car. If a car is provided, then the transportation section of the Supplement would describe the other transportation provisions such as travel to conferences, diocesan workshops and institutes, national affairs, and the like. How much will be assumed by the parish and what will be assumed by the coordinator? This question needs to be answered.

CHART 2:2

SUPPLEMENT B
PERSONAL AND PROFESSIONAL BENEFITS

PERSONAL BENEFITS:

Salary:
Example: The Board of Education will provide the salary as indicated in the Contract. The salary shall be paid by the Secretary-Treasurer of the Board from the Educational Budget on the 15th and the 30th of each month.

Medical Insurance:
Example: The COORDINATOR shall be enrolled in the Blue Cross-Blue Shield Group Medical Plan through the _____ Catholic Conference at parish expense. Additional enrollees of the COORDINATOR'S family shall be at the COORDINATOR'S expense.

Retirement:
Example: The COORDINATOR shall be enrolled in the comprehensive retirement program through the _____ Catholic Conference at parish expense.

Vacation:
Example: The COORDINATOR shall be given vacation in the following manner:

One year employment . . . . 2 weeks
Three years employment. . . . . 3 weeks
Five years employment. . . . . 4 weeks

In addition, the COORDINATOR shall also receive with pay the usual Holy Days and Holidays.

Sick Leave:

Example: The COORDINATOR shall be entitled to 12 sick days per year. These sick days are accumulated at the rate of 1 day per month.

PROFESSIONAL SUPPORT:

Office:

Example: The COORDINATOR shall be provided with an office and working space necessary for the fulfillment of the responsibilities assigned. Secretarial assistance shall also be provided.

Transportation:

Example: The COORDINATOR shall be reimbursed for travel involved in the fulfillment of the assigned responsibilities at a rate of 10¢ per mile. The amount of transportation shall be estimated and included with the total program and budget projection each year. Additional travel to regional, diocesan, and national conferences shall be subject to Board approval, as they arise.

Continuing Education:

Example: The COORDINATOR is encouraged to attend Diocesan Education Programs and other conferences and conventions designed to continue his professional development. These shall be anticipated in advance and shall require Board approval. Once approved, the Board will pay expenses incurred for such education.

During the summers, the COORDINATOR shall enroll in _____ to continue work toward a Master's Degree in _____ The Board shall provide for these expenses provided the COORDINATOR will be returning to the parish for work in the year to follow the summer program.

Office The parish, generally, would be expected to provide an office and basic office equipment for the coordinator. How much secretarial assistance and additional items will be provided should also be listed here in Supplement B. At this time in history, with parish religious education still largely a second best operation to Catholic schools in many places and with many coordinators being forced to work under adverse conditions, a parish would be wise to spell out in more detail than would usually be assumed, these office provisions, so prospective coordinators (as well as the parish) will know what to expect.

Education If the parish will send the coordinator (with a 3-year contract, it would seem likely) for continued studies, an explanation of this should appear in Supplement B. Sometimes, a coordinator does not initially have all the requirements in education which the parish would desire. Then a plan for fulfilling these requirements can be worked out and stated here. Frequently, the participation of the coordinator in diocesan education programs (workshops, institutes, regular meetings, etc.) are viewed as continuing education and the parish stipulates in Supplement B that the coordinator is expected to go to these and that the parish will pay for the cost involved.

It might be expedient in preparing Supplement B for presentation to prospective coordinators (in cases where the parish is just moving to this area) to state the professional support (program budget) which the parish expects to give to the religious education program the coordinator will implement (or design). The clearer these items are in Supplements A and B, the better the chances of communication with prospective coordinators.

FINDING A COORDINATOR

Once the parish has gone through this preparation process and the Board of Education has worked out the first draft of the contract and the Supplements, an organized search can be begun to find a person to covenant with that parish to assist in achieving excellence in their youth and adult religious education.

The contract and supplements provide a mirror of the parish for prospective coordinators who will be contacted. This "mirror" of the situation is especially important in recruiting personnel from a distance. The interest in hiring a professional person for parish religious education is growing rapidly across the country. The competition is great and the supply from colleges and universities limited. Hence, coordinators (lay and religious) will search out those situations which present the best possible climate for achievement. The parish which demonstrates that it is taking religious education and the role of the coordinator seriously will have the best chance of securing competent personnel.

Money is not the key factor here. Offering a good salary, benefits, and a working budget are certainly important and are part of demonstrating the serious commitment which the parish is making to religious education. It is this latter factor, however, which will most appeal to the dedicated men and women (lay and religious) who are moving into this field at the present time. No educator works for the Church because of wages—although social justice demands that they be appropriate. Religious educators are idealists and are more apt to work with people who take ideals of Christianity and religious education seriously. If a parish has gone through the above described preparation process, clearly reflected in the contract and supplements and in the interview process to be described below, its chances are much better than those of a parish which just offers a high salary.

Even in contacting a religious community for personnel in poor urban or rural situations, the more the parish can demonstrate the seriousness of its commitment in both solving money problems and in providing a broad base of support for the program, the more apt it is to obtain personnel.

Search Committee A committee of the Board of Education (or other group representative of the parish and responsible for the educational program) should become a Search Committee with the pastor. Again, the presence of both the pastor and the Board is essential at this time. The presence of representatives of the parish in the search and interview process demonstrates to the prospective coordinator that the parish is involved, is interested, and will assist with the religious education program. The pastor's word for this usually will not replace the actual involvement of representatives as pastors frequently overestimate the cooperation of the laity in the parish. The presence of the pastor is essential, for he is the chief spiritual leader of the people of that faith community and unless he is behind the hiring of a coordinator and demonstrates this by his presence, the coordinator will (or should) suspect that the offer may be the idea of only a few people in the parish concerned about religious education. Searching together for a coordinator indicates working together and this, like the seriousness of the commitment described above, appeals to potential coordinators or religious communities.

Diocesan Office The Diocesan Office can usually assist in the search by contacting colleges and universities and religious communities for personnel. Some Diocesan

Offices also help by screening the prospective coordinators and making recommendations to parishes. A few even have sufficient personnel to assist with the interview process or at least provide ideas and information that can help the parish Search Committee with this.

Personal contacts through letters, advertisements in national catechetical magazines that show imagination and a personal touch, contacts through the Religious Education Exchange (REX) program of the National Religious Education Center (CCD) in Washington, D.C. (1312 Massachusetts Ave., N.W.), letters to colleges and universities, visits to religious communities, and similar means are possible ways in which the parish Search Committee (or the diocese) can contact potential coordinators.

The Interview Once the initial contact has been made and the coordinator has responded with some interest and information (see Chart 2:3 for a sample professional profile form), the Search Committee narrows down the choices and presents the list to the Board of Education. The Search Committee ought to have worked out in advance the criteria for the coordinator (qualifications desired in that parish) for the Board and get these approved. The "problem" of hiring a former sister and/or priest should be resolved before the interview. The Board (perhaps in conjunctions with the Diocesan Office and/or neighboring parishes) then arranges with the prospective coordinator for an interview. With few exceptions, the interview is essential and is paid for by the parish.

The pastor, president of the Board of Education, and the chairman of the Search Committee (with a member of the Diocesan Office, when possible) meet with the prospective coordinators. The discussion can focus on the expectations of the parish as reflected in Supplements A and B. These should be given to the coordinator in advance of the interview and the Coordinator's reactions to the expectations of the parish become part of the interview. Discussion of the individual's vision of religious education, educational background and experiences, and similar items can be part of the interview. A tour of the parish plant should be conducted after the interview by some member of the Board and/or the educational staff of the parish. The actual decision to hire should *not* be made during the interview.

   After the interview, the Board and the pastor can go over the data gained (someone should take notes during the interviews) and work toward a final choice. Such questions as the following are raised and resolved:

1) Does this coordinator have the educational background best suited to fulfill the responsibilities to be assigned? Can it be adequately augmented by continuing education?

2) Has the coordinator had experience which would relate to the responsibilities to be assigned? (Many will not have had experience, hence, the parish needs to consider: Does this coordinator demonstrate in his educational experience the type of working style that leads us to conclude he can gain the necessary experience on the job?) How much support will be necessary for this person, given the work experience background?

3) Is our understanding of the responsibilities to be assigned realistic in light of the expectations and reactions of this coordinator? The parish should be listening to what the coordinator says about the parish's expectations (Supplements A and B).

4) Are the coordinator's personal qualities (age, sex, personal traits, etc.) best suited for the working relationships which will be needed in this parish?

CHART 2:3

PROFESSIONAL PROFILE

NAME: _____   Permanent Mailing Address:
ADDRESS: _____   _____
CITY: _____   _____
STATE: _____ ZIP: _____   _____

PERSONAL DATA:
Date of Birth: _____ Social Security: _____
(Religious Community: _____) Married ___ Single ___

EDUCATION:

Degrees:	Year:	Place:	Major:
_____	_____	_____	_____
_____	_____	_____	_____
_____	_____	_____	_____

Other:

EXPERIENCE:

Year:	Place:	Nature of Experience or Job:
_____	_____	_____
_____	_____	_____

Why are you interested in Parish Religious Education?

What do you think ought to be the chief work of a Parish Religious Education Coordinator?

REFERENCES:
(On the reverse side, please list three persons for personal and three persons for professional references and their mailing addresses.)

At this time, during the evaluation of the interviews, it might also be advisable to re-open the question of whether or not a coordinator is really needed in this parish and whether or not the expectations of the parish are realistic in light of the reactions received in the interviews. If it is still deemed vital to the long-range plan for the educational mission of that parish, and, if one of the prospective coordinators appears to be suited to the responsibilities, then a contract can be prepared and the final form of Supplements A and B worked out between the Search Committee and the coordinator who will be hired. When the pastor and the Board and the coordinator have reached agreement on the contract and the Supplements, the contract can be signed and copies sent to the Diocesan Office.

If there is some question about hiring a particular person which is difficult to resolve, then the discussions and possibly the search ought to be continued. *For no reason should a person be hired "on a temporary basis."* One does not make a temporary or partial act of faith nor should a parish make a partial covenant with a person. The very bond of a "total" commitment for a period of time provides the strength which can make success in achieving the educational mission possible. Mistakes flowing from a partial commitment are very costly in psychological terms for both the coordinator and the parish. It is not simply a matter of removing one coordinator and hiring another if the first choice, in a partial commitment, proves to be a mistake. Confusion and division of the parish will follow as people will take sides, as it were. Unless the parish (pastor and Board) are reasonably confident that the parish needs a coordinator and wants this particular person, then it is better to proceed with the present educational program and volunteer help alone.

This is not an argument for tenure for coordinators.

Tenure is not necessary in a community of people who have common goals, a lasting commitment to one another, and who are animated by the "gospel spirit of freedom and charity." In a case where the full commitment is given to a coordinator and then problems arise, there is still the commitment to work out the problems, even if breaking the contract is the ultimate answer. Resolving the problem right through to the end, that is, to the point where all concerned see the wisdom in the resolution step and accept it, is necessary if the parish seeks to be a real Christian community, and practical if the parish wants a successful educational program. Working out such problems is adult education in Christian community living at its fullest. Bypassing them breaks the communal bond which negates faith community existence.

LAUNCHING THE PROGRAM WITH A COORDINATOR:

Once a final choice has been made, the Board can begin to "launch" the program. If the preparation process described above has been followed, then there will be great parish awareness and a celebration event can be the proper thing to launch the program. The coordinator might be introduced at the liturgy, a coffee reception could follow after each of the Sunday Masses. Any type of event such as this which will alert the whole parish to the arrival of the new member of the parish educational team is appropriate.

If a parish has already hired a coordinator without the preparation, perhaps a parish event at the beginning of a new year could be a remedial step during which the purpose of the educational program and the responsibilities of the professional could be presented.

"Getting to Know You" For the coordinator, the initial steps center around getting to know the persons with whom he will be working and translating the assigned responsibilities into reality.

Establishing the office, if it has not already been done in advance, and becoming familiar with the parish resources and the past educational programs will be the first order of business before any of the assigned responsibilities can be assumed.

After this initial period (the length varying from parish to parish), the coordinator can begin to put the flesh on the skeleton long-range plan which the Board has developed and specifically that which relates to the immediate year ahead by drafting a Program and Budget Projection for the coming year (See Chapters 5 and 6 for details about this work).

In parishes where the questioning process about the nature of parish, about the educational mission, and about the very goals of religious education itself have been taken quite seriously, the parish may have hired the coordinator to assist them further with the questioning, that is, to work out goals for the next decade. In such a case, the expectations would be quite different. The coordinator would be expected to spend the majority of his time in this search process and a smaller amount in helping with the present program during that year.

Given the present educational climate within the Church and the present changes within the North American and world cultures, hiring a professional to help the people of a parish think through in an organized way who they are as Christian people bound together in a faith community and what kinds of responses they ought to make to the larger communities of which they are a part and to the Lord might be the most appropriate challenge to embrace. Certainly the present youth and adult programs will limp along for another year during which time the coordinator and the Board (in conjunction with the larger parish represented, perhaps, through the Parish Council) could work out an approach to the educational mission of that parish which would be more than a "band-aid" approach. Frequently today the very root assumptions about the parish and its educational work are the source of the problems and not the educational programming or skills. A professional person with educational skills and a mature faith could assist the parish to re-examine these root assumptions and develop more lasting approaches for the '70's.

In either case, the parish needs to know why it is securing the professional services of a person called a coordinator of religious education and in general what it expects of him. Then, together, they can work to achieve excellence in their educational mission. A coordinator is no educational messiah and the parish needs to learn this through the preparation process before they hire someone and grow "disappointed" in what he or she accomplishes.

NOTES FOR CHAPTER 2

1) "Economic Status of the Teaching Profession, 1967-68," *Research Report:* 1968-R4 (Washington, D.C.: National Education Association, Research Division), Table 12, p. 19.
2) *Ibid.,* Table 13, pp. 20-21.

Chapter Three

DEFINING THE ROLE

Religious educators are particularly sensitive to
the subject of role or job descriptions. This concern is
a reaction, to a certain degree, to the heavy emphasis
in seminaries and novitiates on the "model" priest or
sister and the related stress upon the "model" catechist
and layman.

This syndrome, which has many side effects in other
areas that will be discussed later, accounts for part of
this sensitivity but by no means all of it. An additional
source for this concern is to be found in the vastly differing conceptions in approaches to religious education
between religious educators and those whom they would
serve.

Pastors, board members, and those generally raised
in the "old" catechetics, wish a teacher and, therefore, a
coordinator to *accomplish* certain things deemed essential to religious education in a parish. Religious educators
versed in "new" catechetics — to use superficial labels
for the purpose of discussion — are raised in an atmosphere
of personalism and community and want to be "real" to

youth and adults, to be "where it's at" in the world, and to build "community" in the parish rather than accomplish something. Simple program accomplishment and achievement are viewed as institutional "hang-ups" derived from American pragmatism and structured views of the Church in the world.

This is a philosophical difference not accounted for by the "model" syndrome mentioned above and yet it is related to it; for it is an expression of the striving for a "perfect" mode of existence and relationship although different visions of what that "perfection" is exist. Similarly each group tends to demand its vision rather than accept diversity and work with it.

Faith and Christianity are rather profoundly simple. Christian people, according to most recent major theologians, would seem to have two main areas of endeavor differentiating them from any group of people: namely, celebrating and nourishing their faith in the Spirit of Jesus (now-already eschatology) and serving man and his world by sharing this faith and by ministering to his needs (yet-to-be-realized eschatology) in light of the Spirit of Jesus.

The educational mission of the faith community is a part of this total pastoral mission and contributes to it. The educational mission in its broadest terms is concerned with "teaching" the reflections on the present and past (especially Apostolic) faith community to those who have come to believe in the Lord, with challenging those who have not heard the word, and with bringing the Gospel to bear upon the present and future human needs and the ideas (culture) of the age, from an educational perspective.

Although faith is simple, given the human condition and the Church as an organization, formal education and parish work present complex problems to be overcome. The Church (and the parish) as a group of people working together in an organized way faces certain problems which can be identified and resolved on the level of applied knowledge from theoretical disciplines — education, psychology, management, and so forth. One of these problems is the role or relationship of the professional educator to the parish and their educational mission.

Project Coordinator data indicates that one of the most pressing problems in this new focus of the professional in parish religious education is precisely the lack of a formalized understanding of the responsibilities and relationships involved in this new phenomenon.

The need for a formalizing of these organizational relationships and responsibilities should not be too surprising. Again, the history of Judeao-Christian religions shows us that the covenanted relationship between God and his people has always had formalized expressions; e.g., Ten Commandments, Beatitudes, *Constitution on the Church.*

SUPPLEMENT A: COVENANTED RELATIONSHIP AND RESPONSIBILITIES

The preparation process described in Chapter 2 in which the parish, through the pastor and Board of Education, thinks out its educational mission in general and why in specific it wishes to hire a professional is much more important than the actual first draft statement of Supplement A, which is prepared for the recruiting and interviewing. This process can also be seen as one through which the faith community comes to a clearer understanding of its identity — a necessary step before one enters into any or a number of covenanted relationships.

In the first stages of this preparation process, the

Board has gathered together the *job content* information by identifying the educational needs and general goals of the parish. Out of this long-range plan, the first draft of Supplement A — the parish's first vision of what ought to be the responsibilities and relationships of the co-ordinator and the parish — is prepared. This first draft is used for the recruiting and the interviewing.

After the interviews, during which the prospective coordinators have reacted to the parish's vision of the relationship and responsibilities with their own, the parish should review and revise its side of the contract especially with the person most likely to be chosen in mind. Then, the final chosen coordinator and the Board work out the second draft of Supplement A together.

This process of working out a detailed and semi-final version of Supplement A brings the differing philosophical and theological assumptions about the Church and education to the surface where they can be separated to a certain extent from attitudes and emotions and dealt with. In actuality, the pastor and the Board members may have a different conception of the educational mission of a parish than the coordinator, but the reality of the situation is that both visions are part of the Church and Church history clearly demonstrates that there are many models of what parish, priest, and educator can be and do.

These differing assumptions (or beliefs) cannot be totally resolved nor should a tight consensus be sought. Rather, the diversity should be recognized; for it is apt to be representative of the total parish community and should become a "creative tension" out of which genuine progress toward the attainment of the educational mission is achieved. Faith itself always provides both a "continuity" with the past and present experiences as well as a "discontinuity"; the evidence of things seen and the essence of things hoped for.

When the Board and pastor and coordinator have agreed to the second draft of Supplement A, a full commitment can be made and the covenanted relationship (contract) signed. This Supplement should be reviewed at the end of the first year (or sooner) and changes made as the relationship matures.

Purpose of Supplement A There are actually five reasons why Supplement A or an equivalent vehicle of definition is essential to the covenanted relationship:

1) It determines the reason for the position. It is crucial that the parish and the person being hired have clearly in mind why a professional is being hired for parish religious education.

2) It assigns the responsibilities. All who will be involved with the professional want to know and have a right to know what he will do and what his responsibilities are.

3) It designates his "limits of authority." This could be included in the assignment of responsibilities but given the present "syndrome" of authority in the Church, it is an important item in and of itself.

4) It establishes the basic relationships with other personnel and groups. To whom does the coordinator answer? How does he relate to the pastor or the school principal professionally?

5) It can state the qualifications which are being sought in the person to be hired. This is important especially in the first draft and should be revised later with the coordinator in the final draft in the event of looking for a replacement.

The sample form for Supplement A given here (Chart 3:1) can be used as a grid or outline which the Board of Education and the pastor expand and arrange according to the local situation. The actual Supplement A will probably fill a couple of pages when the skeleton is completely fleshed out.

CHART 3:1

CONTRACT SUPPLEMENT A
RESPONSIBILITIES OF COORDINATOR

GENERAL PURPOSE:
Here the reason why the coordinator is being hired; i.e., the total area of responsibility is stated.

SPECIFIC RESPONSIBILITIES:
The major tasks to be accomplished; e.g., development of curriculum for youth and adults, are stated. It is important that the specific duties, e.g., meeting with the teachers monthly, are *not* stated. These are a matter for the coordinator's professional discretion.

EVALUATION:
The means by which the parish will evaluate the achievement of the above responsibilities is stated here; e.g., the coordinator shall present a yearly evaluation of the total program to the Board.

RESPONSIBLE TO:
It is imperative that it be clearly stated to whom the coordinator is responsible for the execution of the above responsibilities; e.g., the Board of Education.

RELATIONSHIPS WITHIN THE PARISH:
The relationship with other professionals and groups over whom the coordinator has no authority should be stated. These would include: (1) the pastor, (2) the associate pastors, (3) the school principal, (4) the Home and School Association, (5) the Liturgy Commission of the parish, and similar persons and groups.

RELATIONSHIPS OUTSIDE THE PARISH:
The relationships which the coordinator is expected to have outside the parish are stated here. These might include (1) Diocesan Office, (2) other parishes, (3) ecumenical groups, (4) civic groups, and the like.

QUALIFICATIONS OF THE COORDINATOR:
Here the parish states expected personal and professional qualifications which it will look for in the coordinator.

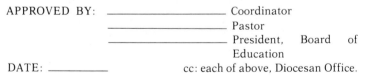

APPROVED BY: _____ Coordinator
              _____ Pastor
              _____ President, Board of
                                Education
DATE: _____   cc: each of above, Diocesan Office.

SUPPLEMENT A: GENERAL PURPOSE OF COORDINATOR

The very first area to be determined is the purpose for hiring a professional, or stated in another way, what the role of the coordinator is. The total scope of the responsibility and relationship should be stated in general terms.

"Director"(DRE)versus"Coordinator"(REC) Across the country, there is a vast difference in the role descriptions for the professional in parish religious education. The fact that professionals are hired on an area basis by the parishes or the diocese also further confuses the problem faced by a parish; namely, determining the responsibilities and relationships to be covenanted.

In some parts of the country — the distinction seems to run according to areas and dioceses — the professional in parish religious education is termed the "director of religious education" (DRE) whereas in others he is called "religious education coordinator" (REC) or something similar. The reasons for the differing titles are both obvious and subtle.

The most obvious reason for the difference is to be found in the responsibilities assigned. In some parishes, the professional is to organize, implement, and evaluate the total youth and adult program in a strict administrative fashion. Other parishes ask the professional to advise them about curriculum, to teach teachers and adults, and similar consultative services. This is an obvious difference in role conception.

The subtle reason for the title difference centers around a definition of authority and arises out of a very distinct educational history in the American Catholic Church.

The overwhelming emphasis of the Catholic Church

in America in education has been on the parochial school. Father Neil McCluskey's books on Catholic education document the times, places, and issues or reasons why this strong emphasis arose (1). As a result, the Confraternity of Christian Doctrine (CCD) as a canonical organization was given the responsibility for the religious education of the "youth *not* attending Catholic schools" (note the negative definition of this responsibility) and of adults—this latter, however, never really succeeded except in a few isolated areas.

In a typical parish with a parochial grade school, the majority of the human and material resources went (and still go) into that school leaving the CCD program with volunteer teachers, poor facilities, and substandard educational materials. In the 1950's and the '60's, "liberal" Catholic parents, who *chose* to put their children in the public schools, and teachers in CCD programs who had been growing in their knowledge and awareness of the educational mission of the parish, began to demand an equal amount of attention for the educational needs of the youth in public schools. Pastors and defenders of the schools reacted rather adversely dismissing the CCD as "ineffective" and dealing with "marginal Catholics" anyway in places where there was a school to which the youth could be sent.

Hence, out of this context of conflict, parishes which have begun to seek a professional for the religious education program often demand that he have "authority."

The title of "director" is chosen and a job description in which his authority is clearly stated is prepared and forced upon the pastor and/or the Board of Education. The duplication of educational structures—School Board versus Confraternity Board—is a clear example of this fight for authority. (Boards of Education in parishes originally arose as *school* boards and were concerned only in a token fashion with the problems of the non-school education programs. Unfortunately, this is still largely the case. See Chapter 5 for details.)

Peabody's distinction between formal authority and functional authority might clarify part of this problem here (2). Parents have the *formal authority* for the religious education of their children. Church law and state law both recognize this. This authority is shared to a certain degree with the larger community of which they are a part—parish or state—in the sense that the corporate community has the right and the responsibility to see to it that parents exercise their authority.

Schools, teachers, catechists, and coordinators have a *functional authority* given to them by both the parents and the larger community. The professional coordinator or director has no *formal* or legal authority for parish religious education. His is a *functional authority*, that is, he is given certain responsibilities and resources which will make it possible for him *to help* the parents and the pastor (and adults in general) in achieving *their* goals in education. His authority is one of competence but always geared to the *service of others* who need and request it. Vested with the *authority of competence*, the parish professional needs to build a climate of confidence in which those who have the authority and the responsibility can achieve their goals—however they are defined.

Thus, the parish professional is a leader of the educational team whose only authority is his knowledge about religious education and his skill in the leadership process. Since he may also be "temporary" in a given parish—especially with religious working as coordinators—and because of the very nature of parish itself as a *communal* effort, the title of "coordinator" is more suited than that of "director" which is more the pastor's role with the Board of Education.

It is important for the immediate future that the

actual description of the parish professional's role become more settled and yet stay fluid. In each parish and perhaps in dioceses, a particular style ought to be closely identified, studied, and reported. Eventually, out of the various experiments and out of organized research on the part of coordinators themselves, a much clearer understanding of this new focus will arise(3).

Coordinator as Generalist As far as his relationship goes with other professionals and non-professionals outside of the area of religious education, the coordinator is a *specialist*. He specializes in religious education. Within the educational framework, however, the coordinator has to be a *generalist*. He carries many responsibilities or wears many hats. This makes it difficult to describe his responsibilities and relationships closely. This is difficult for other reasons also.

First of all, what the coordinator does accomplish is usually not visible. The personal inspiration given to teacher or parent, the right word at the right time in solving an educational problem, the support given in and for the program in a thousand little ways—these are difficult to demonstrate in words or symbols.

Second, each person whom the coordinator serves expects something different from him. Hence, there are as many job descriptions as there are people affected by the parish religious education program.

Third, as was mentioned above, the coordinator shares his responsibilities with others: Board, pastor, teachers, parents, and so forth.

Fourth, the coordinator works in many places. While the coordinator should have an office, his work will carry him into many different situations which further confuse the role expectations.

Lastly, the development of the coordinator in parish religious education is a new focus and until it becomes more clearly defined, each person will project his own image onto what the coordinator should be and judge the present person by that image.

These areas of confusion about the very role of the parish coordinator again highlight the need for the process of working out Supplement A and further show that the coordinator is truly a *generalist* in the parish religious education program.

When it comes to translating this into the general purpose of the coordinator in a parish, it might become a statement such as: *"The Coordinator is responsible for organizing, implementing, and evaluating the total religious education program for youth and adults."* This would place the coordinator in the position of being the professional who leads the Board in fulfilling its responsibilities. (See Chapter 5 for a thorough discussion of parish Boards of Education and the parish educational mission).

Parishes which still wish to perpetuate the separate boards and educational personnel for school education and parish education would define the general scope differently. They might put the school principal in the position of being the executive of the parish Board and place the coordinator as the "assistant" in charge of religious education. However, since the chief educational responsibility of the parish is religious education, it would seem that the coordinator should shoulder that total responsibility with the Board and coordinate the work of other groups (school, Cursillo, Pre-Cana, and the like) into a total parish thrust.

Placing the coordinator in the position of an executive responsible for the total parish religious educational program would seem to make him an administrator. In a sense, it does. However, the definition which Peter Drucker gives to an "executive" is what is intended here. Drucker says: "Every knowledge worker in modern organization is an "executive" if, by virtue of his position or knowledge, he is responsible for a contribution that materially affects the capacity of the organization to perform and to obtain results"(4).

However else the coordinator is viewed, he is expected to help the parish achieve something — even if that something is defined as "a communal sense of relatedness to one another in the Spirit of Jesus." To do this he must bring the theoretical knowledge which he has obtained in the theologic or God-oriented disciplines and the anthropic or man-oriented disciplines to bear upon the actions needed to fulfill that expectation. This makes him an "executive" for "executive" means "to effect" and this is precisely what the coordinator is asked to do.

SUPPLEMENT A: SPECIFIC RESPONSIBILITIES

Translating this general purpose or responsibility of the coordinator into more specific terms will also vary from parish to parish. It is important, however, to understand what type of things should be considered for inclusion and what should be excluded.

In this part of Supplement A, the Board should be careful *not* to list specific duties. Rather it should designate major tasks or areas of responsibility which concretize the general responsibility to that parish. Specific duties are professional decisions about the way in which the responsibilities are met.

For example, a specific duty might be stated: "The coordinator shall visit the homes of those parents who do not send their children to the youth program." Another might be: "The coordinator shall order the textbooks and audio-visuals for the religious education program and the school and shall organize a religious education library in the parish." These are *too specific* and are matters of professional decision. Each of these could be carried out by a volunteer member of the parish without the expense of a professional educator. The professional may create the climate of support and expertise whereby these duties are taken care of, but the means should be his decision.

REC as Leader of Teaching-Learning Team One of the major tasks of the Coordinator who shares the total responsibility with the Board of Education is to pull together all those persons who are working directly with the teaching-learning situation into a dynamic team. This is one major task the REC cannot avoid. All groups and all helpers and all teachers who work directly with the youth and adult religious education program of the parish would come under the leadership responsibility of the coordinator. Those who are only indirectly related are included in the "Relationship Within the Parish" section of Supplement A. Those over whom the coordinator will have "authority" are listed here as sub-points under this major task. This major task might be listed under the *Specific Responsibilities* section as: *"The coordinator shall organize, recruit, and coordinate all who are directly involved in the youth and adult religious education programs."* Under this, as sub-points, would be listed all the groups of persons who would be involved in that parish: e.g., helpers, teachers (youth and adult), action committees, and the like.

Serving as leader of the teaching-learning team is an essential part of the professional's work. Much of the actual work can be delegated, that is, the coordinator can extend himself with the assistance of individuals and groups, but this responsibility is rightfully his.

REC as Supervisor of Teachers In addition to the more administrative task of organizing the present groups and individuals who are working with the religious education program into a team and recruiting others as needs become manifest, the coordinator also has the responsibility as leader of the teaching-learning team for teacher education (see Chapter 7, "Assisting Teachers," for an in-depth discussion of this responsibility). This is so much a part of his work that it should be listed as a separate item in Supplement A with the emphasis upon the improvement of *instruction;* that is, the teaching-learning process. It might be stated: *"The coordinator shall work with the teachers in improving the teaching quality at all levels."*

It is prudent not to suggest by a more direct statement that the present teachers do not know what they are doing and need "in-service education" or "in-depth training." Creating a dependency upon another in attitude or fact for one's teaching style predisposes the teachers to look for something from the coordinator which he can never give no matter how qualified; namely, confidence in themselves. Confidence is the essential ingredient for creative and innovative teaching. Even volunteers can have confidence in their ability to lead others in probing faith, for faith is not professional.

REC as Curriculum Specialist Another area in which the coordinator needs to lend a great deal of specialized service is the area of curriculum—helping the parish (Board, teachers, etc.) translate their aspirations and good intentions into action.

The vision of what might be and how the Gospel can be seen in the culture of the day and the lives of the *seekers* or learners is the essence of curriculum work here. Selecting the right resource materials for the learning experiences takes a professional sense and skill much akin to that of a doctor selecting the right medicines for the illness diagnosed. The media (print, audio, video, and tactile) available for religious education for youth and adults have been greatly improved in both quality and flexibility in the last few years and a greater movement in this direction is planned by publishers. The coordinator must help (1) begin the process of analyzing the parish educational needs, (2) set goals that are appropriate to those needs and to the authentic teachings of the Church, (3) design a curriculum (selection of media materials and instructional style) appropriate to achieving those goals, and (4) implement and evaluate that curriculum.

It is in this area that the coordinator orders the texts, gathers a library, makes available audio-visuals, and similar duties. The responsibility for curriculum is rightfully the coordinator's and should be so stated; the specific duties necessary to implement that responsibility are the coordinator's decision. This major task might be stated in Supplement A as follows: *"The coordinator shall design and implement a curriculum suitable to the religious education needs and goals of the youth and adults of the parish, subject to the approval of the Board of Education."* The approval of the Board of Education and the actual designing of the curriculum will be discussed in subsequent chapters (see Chapter 5, "Working with the Board," and especially Chapter 6, "Preparing a Program and Budget").

The coordinator will gain "authority" largely to the extent that he is able to demonstrate competence in this area of translating a vision into a reality.

REC as Innovator An area which is generally spoken about but seldom acted upon is research or innovation. The Board should definitely ask the coordinator to organize his work to such an extent that some time is available for research either by the coordinator himself or under his direction.

The era in which we live is an era of change. Change

may be good or bad, depending upon its direction and impact upon people. Growth, that is, change related to the past, integrated into the total person (or organization), and motivated by a vision for the future, is desirable change. Research, especially into alternatives for action and decision in the future, is essential to growth. Marshall McLuhan notes that "any medium has the power of imposing its own assumptions on the unwary"(5). This is true of the basic geographical organization of the parish; of the media of education — schools, CCD classes, lectures; and of many other aspects of parish life. Parishes and religious education have not always been in their present forms and these forms are not holy in themselves. Research in religious education can assist a parish in sorting out the viable forms and media from those which are merely a "flash in the pan." In this era in which there are so many problems, research is not a luxury but *an essential aspect* of a coordinator's work. This ought to be recognized and so stated in Supplement A as one of the coordinator's major tasks: *"The coordinator shall organize, direct, and/or coordinate research concerning all aspects of the youth and adult religious education programs as deemed necessary for achieving quality."*

As with all of the above major tasks, the coordinator ought to involve as many other persons as possible and necessary in research, that is, in examining what is happening and why and what might be possible. An innovative atmosphere is essential for all involved in the religious education program, if the creativity needed for the *root* changes in programming are ever to occur.

REC as Board of Education Executive This is another major task of the coordinator as a knowledge worker-executive as described by Drucker. It is cited in the

Supplement A sample given here under the section on "Responsible to" and discussed in specific in Chapter 5.

SUPPLEMENT A: EVALUATION

Research into the basic goals and processes of parish religious education is essential in this era of change. Equally as essential is evaluation of the "new" as well as the "tried and true," lest the former be mere "sounding brass" without substance and the latter become the "tired and trivial."

It was emphasized strongly above that the parish needs to know why it hired a professional person to lead the educational work and should state this reason as the *General Purpose* in Supplement A. This General Purpose is expressed in specific terms in the *Specific Responsibilities*. It is appropriate that an evaluation of the coordinator's fulfillment of these responsibilities be done regularly, but at least annually and as a formal process.

In recent years, religious educators have become rather touchy about evaluation respective to religious education. They are confusing marking (grades and other symbols) with genuine evaluation. Evaluation is as proper to religious education as the examination of conscience and the regular retreat are to growth in prayer and a Christian life style. Evaluation is essential as "feed-back and feed-forward," that is, it assists all involved in the educational mission of the parish to see what validity their assumptions and goals have, what progress they are making towards them, and what kinds of decisions are yet to be made and evaluated.

The Board of Education, representing the parish, has the responsibility to evaluate the effectiveness of the decision to hire the coordinator. The coordinator has the right to know on what basis the Board will make this evaluation and that the Board will do so in a formal and objective fashion rather than on personal emotions and opinions.

Perhaps the best form of evaluation will be in the continued reporting of the coordinator to the Board on the progress being made in the fulfillment of the major tasks assigned. This is part of the coordinator's regular mode of operation with the Board (see Chapter 5). An annual evaluation of the total program by the coordinator (see Chapter 6) also provides the Board with a picture of the wisdom of their decision.

Over and above these operational forms of feedback which the coordinator provides the Board and which the Board requests, the Board should undertake a formal evaluation of the covenanted relationship embraced. The original Search Committee of the Board which worked with the coordinator could serve as the ad hoc committee for this purpose. At any rate, some small group of Board members with the pastor should initiate the process of gathering independent (independent of the coordinator's reportings) information from the parish at large and especially from those involved in the parish educational work concerning the extent to which the coordinator has fulfilled the assigned responsibilities.

If the coordinator has not fulfilled them, it is important to determine if the lack is due to personal and professional failure on the part of the coordinator or to other reasons. These problems might include: the failure of the Board to assume its leadership role, the lack of needed resources and assistance for the coordinator, a special parish crisis which consumed most of the time of the coordinator, and other such items.

Whether success or failure emerge from the evaluation, it is important to know why. If the coordinator has been the leading reason for the success, then this might provide the basis for an increase in salary and other benefits. If failure emerges, a change of approach will need to be worked out. In Supplement A, under Evaluation, the Board may express its intent as follows: *"The coordinator shall submit regular reports and an annual report to the Board of Education concerning the progress of the parish religious education program for which he is responsible. The Board will evaluate these and gather additional information to evaluate the effectiveness of the coordinator in fulfilling the assigned responsibilities."*

Although the contract (covenanted relationship) may be reviewed annually, it is appropriate to state the length of the contract for a 3 to 5 year period. The coordinator could not possibly achieve all of the stated responsibilities in one year, but should at least have made noticeable progress toward them. The coordinator also needs the security of the long-range perspective in order to plan and to work successfully. Only for a serious breach should the contract be terminated.

When there is controversy about the qualitative aspects of the achievement of the coordinator (e.g., the "rightness" of certain programs introduced in terms of the authentic teachings of the Church or some other standard), the Diocesan Office could be called in as an advisor and judge for the situation.

SUPPLEMENT A: RELATIONSHIPS

The formalized relationships between the coordinator and the other professionals (and groups) within the parish and between the coordinator and groups related to the parish from the outside should also be a part of Supplement A. Many of these kinds of relationships are assumed in other organizations because they have existed over a period of time. The relationship between the principal of a school and the teachers is frequently assumed and not clearly stated. The coordinator role is too new and too threatening for this area to be left to implicit assumptions.

REC and the Board of Education: Throughout this book, it is assumed that the primary relationship of the coordinator as a professional in the educational work of the parish is with the Board of Education which represents the people of the parish and carries the parish's responsibility for its educational mission. The way in which this relationship between the Board and the coordinator is carried out is discussed later (Chapter 5). It should be stated in Supplement A, however, as a separate section due to the problems arising in this area, that the coordinator is responsible to the Board of Education before any other relationships are described. An example of such a statement is as follows: *"The coordinator is responsible to the Board of Education of X Parish for the execution of the above responsibilities. The coordinator shall submit to the Board for approval an annual Program and Budget for the parish religious education program. Once approved, it shall be the coordinator's responsibility to implement the Program."*

As will be seen, the pastor (and/or the Parish Council) has the veto power over the decisions of the Board and should not be involved in carrying the responsibility for the coordinator's work.

REC and the Pastor: Coordinators frequently want "to run the parish" or at least not have to depend upon the decisions of the pastor for what they do. It is necessary that the coordinator know clearly what is expected of him and thence have the freedom to implement his responsibilities without needless interventions. *However*, it is the pastor who has the authority for one aspect of religious education within that faith community. As the formal representative of the larger faith community (diocese) and of the bishop, it is his responsibility to see that the parish meet its educational responsibilities in an authentic manner, that is, in a way which is in keeping with the magisterium of the Church.

The coordinator assists the pastor with this responsibility (see Chapter 4) and the parish through the Board with their responsibility, by virtue of his competence.

Because of the "authority syndrome" described in part above, it is essential that the relationship between the pastor and the coordinator be clearly stated, both for them as individuals and for the members of the parish who have expectations concerning them. This should be stated in Supplement A: *"The coordinator shall be mindful that the pastor is the main religious leader of the people of the parish and, therefore, the coordinator shall keep the pastor regularly informed (in depth) concerning the development of religious education within the parish. The advice of the pastor shall also be taken into consideration in planning and implementing the religious education program."*

Pastors and coordinators both should note that this recommendation does not say that the coordinator shall implement the advice of the pastor, but rather, that the coordinator shall take that advice into consideration in his professional work.

REC and the Associate Pastor(s): The formal relationship of the coordinator to the other priests within the parish should also be clearly stated. If the priest is to be the chief advisor on religious education within that parish for the coordinator, then this should be so stated. It may even be necessary to determine and state what the major tasks of the associate pastor relative to religious education shall be as compared with those of the coordinator (*Specific Responsibilities*) in order to minimize confusion, ineffectiveness, and possible conflict. The pastor would also wish to know what the Associate Pastor will be doing relative to parish religious education, in order to make effective pastoral plans.

REC and the School Principal: Second only to the need for clarifying the relationship of the priests and the coordinator is the need for a clarification of the relationship of the professional educators to one another in fulfillment of the educational mission. In parishes with a parochial school, this applies chiefly to the relationship between the coordinator and the school principal. In places with a team of professionals, this relationship between the professionals over and above what is stated for each as *Specific Responsibilities* would deal with their relationship to the team leader.

A basic decision has to be made by the parish (through the Board and/or Parish Council) whether the school principal shall become the executive agent of the Board of Education or whether this responsibility shall be with the coordinator to be hired. This decision must take into consideration the relationship of the school to the total educational mission of the parish (present and possible future relationship); the capabilities of the present principal (and those experienced in this role) to plan for non-school education; and the priorities which the parish wishes to set for its educational work in the coming decade.

It is recommended here that the coordinator become the executive agent of the Board and that the Board have the total responsibility for the educational work of the parish. Obviously, the coordinator and the principal of the school would need (and want) to work together closely, utilizing their strengths and resources toward the achievement of the parish's educational goals. But the school, by its very nature, will demand constant and single purpose attention. The principal must respond to this need, but unless he is especially skilled and astute, he is apt to neglect setting aside the time and energy necessary to generate programs to meet the non-school needs of the parish—needs which are growing in size and complexity.

Whatever decision the Board makes about this relationship between the two professionals must be stated clearly in Supplement A. The process of making this decision might also result in a clarification of the responsibilities assigned to the principal—a step which may benefit those in the school.

REC and the Parochial School Teachers: There would be such a category only if the parish has decided (a) to place the principal as the executive agent of the Board and place the coordinator in a semi-autonomous position, responsible for non-school religious education, or (b) to allow the existing separate structures of school versus CCD to remain, thus appointing the coordinator the executive agent of the CCD Board and the principal as the executive agent of School Board.

In the event that the relationship of the coordinator to the professional teachers within the parochial school in the parish has not been stated in the *Specific Responsibilities* section of Supplement A, it should be stated here.

Relationships Outside the Parish: The relationships which the coordinator will be expected to have (or to avoid) outside the parish within the community and/or

the diocese should become part of the covenanted relationship also. The more that these items are clarified,
the better the chances of effective working relationships. When individuals and groups have become aware
of how the coordinator will relate to them, they have
also become aware of what that person can do for them
and are partially disposed to cooperate.

This section might include relationships between
the coordinator and the public school personnel, the
coordinator and the professionals (or leaders) in ecumenical groups, the coordinator and the regional and/or
diocesan personnel, the coordinator and a supervisor
or consultant of the religious community, and so forth.
In general, this section will define the relationship between the coordinator and any individual or group whose
decisions will bear upon the responsibilities assigned
to the coordinator.

No specific examples can be given since each parish
has differing relationships possible. However, it is appropriate to emphasize the necessity of making these
expected relationships formal in Supplement A, given the
present climate within the Church, the "authority syndrome" battle, and the many problems which have already arisen in this new phenomenon of hiring a parish
professional which could have been avoided if these
expectations had been examined beforehand.

QUALIFICATIONS OF A COORDINATOR

The qualifications which a person needs for a job
depend upon the assigned responsibilities. Each parish
will, therefore, look for a coordinator with slightly differing qualifications, depending upon what that parish
has determined he will do (Supplement A).

Currently, parishes seem to look for an expert who

has education and experience in everything from pediatrics to geriatrics—all with a theological bent. (Job descriptions gathered in Project Coordinator show a variety of responsibilities assigned to persons working as parish coordinators or directors of religious education.) Colleges and universities are graduating people who could be classified as generalists in theology. They typically have a background in fundamental and moral theology with some work in ecumenical theology; Scripture; liturgy (both theoretical and experiential); catechetics; perhaps some media experiences and a bit of theory; and general courses covering psychology, sociology, anthropology, and other items. These graduates have worked with others of similar convictions and background in their theoretical studies and experienced many "happenings" together. When each goes forth to a "reality" situation of a parish, he finds few people who appreciate and understand what he has learned and experienced. He has vision and they have problems. He has experienced a bit of "community" and they have experienced disunity and understand "community" in very limited terms. He is interested in solving problems which they are not aware of, or give little priority to, e.g., adult education for community and for social concern. It is no wonder conflicts and frustrations arise.

Besides this dilemma in which the coordinator is not prepared for what the parish would like him to assume, there is a common worship of the M.A. Degree which permeates both the religious educator and the parishes. "A coordinator must have an M.A. Degree in theology or an allied conglomerate." This assumption must be challenged. A coordinator should be prepared to assume the responsibilities which the parish gives him in the covenanted relationship. What this means in terms of degrees and course work will have to be thought through in much more depth in the next few years. Some general discussion of the qualifications which a parish might expect a coordinator to have is appropriate here, however.

Theologic Disciplines Parishes can and should expect that coordinators will have competence in the God-oriented (theologic) disciplines: theology, Scripture, liturgy, and the hybrid areas of religious psychology, religious sociology, and the like.

The coordinator is given the responsibility of assisting the pastor and the people in deepening their awareness (adult and child) of life in relationship to the Lord; that is, in growing in their knowledge, understanding, and application of revelation to their lives. Thus, the coordinator must have a very firm grasp of revelation both theoretically and experientially. This latter would cover the usually stated qualification of a strong personal faith. Without a doubt the coordinator must be a man of the Spirit.

To put it another way, the coordinator must have a strong vision of faith that is translated into a Christian life style before he can assume the leadership responsibilities of helping others to organize for growth in faith for themselves or their children. Faith simply has to make a difference in the coordinator's life. And he must know why with both experiential and theoretical reasons.

Brother Gabriel Moran has consistently stressed that religious educators need a greater understanding and awareness of theology. This is essential for the coordinators. They must know how to "theologize" as well as know the conclusions of theologians. They must know the Scriptures as the poetry of their lives. Liturgy in its total spectrum from contemplative Latin solemn high Mass to extemporaneous (or pentecostal) prayer must be a part of their experience and their ability to lead. Prayer, fasting, alms-giving, and other charity forms need to be readily available to the coordinator in his daily life style. In brief, a coordinator's life must be animated by the Spirit of Jesus. This does not mean that he "baptizes" or "smears Christ" on everything. It simply means that life in its totality is seen (directly at times, but always indirectly) in the Spirit of Jesus because of the individual's faith, and that professionally he is able to explain why with all the theologic disciplines ready at his command. In the interview process, the coordinator should be able to give "testimony" to his faith; that is, he should be able to relate theoretical theology to practical terms. Parishes should look for and expect this in a coordinator. Do not, therefore, be "snowed" by high sounding theology. If it can't be translated, it will not be helpful to the parish.

Anthropic Disciplines This fancy term refers to all of the areas of knowledge that study man, his extensions or creations, his relationships, and his times. In actuality, this means that the coordinator should have some education and experience with sociology, anthropology, and in particular psychology. In-depth knowledge of the growth and development pattern of youth and adults is essential for the educational responsibilities assigned to a coordinator. Coursework in the psychology of learning generally probes this area. Individual reading could also achieve the same results.

Over and above course work at a college or university in this general area, the parish should look for a person who is aware of the times. Familiarity with contemporary films, music, political events and issues, world affairs, ecumenical and community problems, and the like should *show*. This is not an argument for the coordinator ideally to have knowledge about *all* things. That ideal is for each Christian and never attained in any one person. *However,* the Board in interviewing a prospective coordinator should look for and expect a life style which demonstrates that this person *lives in the present.*

Education or Religious Education If a coordinator is being asked to work with the teachers in the improvement of instruction; to organize, design and implement a curriculum for youth and adults; and to lead the total teaching-learning group; then, the parish should expect the individual to have education and experience in what could be termed "education" or "religious education."

Teacher education is a specialized task as is curriculum design. A good many coordinators graduating from the present programs offered by colleges and universities do not have such formal education. Many have gained it through individualized study or experience. Many have not. If a parish expects a coordinator to assume these specialized tasks of teacher education, curriculum design, and instructional leadership, these kinds of skills and understanding should be sought after in the search and interview process. Knowledge of and experiences with the dynamics of individual and group behavior is necessary for leadership responsibilities. An understanding of the process of curriculum building over and above an in-depth understanding of theology is needed for developing goals, assessing textual materials, for selecting media, and for implementing the program with continuity and balance, and with a scope large enough to involve all the seekers of a faith community.

Executive and Research Life Style Over and above this more formalized educational and experiential background, the coordinator should have executive ability, described by Peter Drucker as "the ability to bring knowledge to bear upon the capacity of the organization to perform and to obtain results"(6). This means the individual must be able to make decisions, to assume responsibility, and to lead others (in particular the Board of Education of the parish) in making the right decisions and in assuming responsibility for them.

A coordinator will be expected to lead the Board of Education in understanding its responsibility and in executing it. This calls for executive or administrative ability. In practice it will mean the ability to plan and execute meetings, develop reports and policies and goals for adoption, organize and maintain records, plan budgets, and similar activities.

It is also important that the Board look for a person who has the blend between this creative administration talent and scholarship. Research ability (or the ability to stimulate research by the identification of problems and resources) is essential in this era. A coordinator needs to know not only how to get a job done, but why that job ought to be done.

Summary It may appear that no person is educated or experienced in all of these areas of competence. Generally, this is true. There are some people with these talents available and parishes can look for them. Most coordinators applying, however, will have strengths in one or more of these areas. The Board will either have to revise its expectations and the assigned responsibilities (Supplement A) or find ways of building on the strengths of this particular person and augmenting his weaknesses from other sources. Members of the parish, for example, may have certain of the needed skills and understandings and could supply these on a voluntary part-time basis to assist the coordinator. Another possibility for some parishes is a team of professional educators each with different talents.

The total process of preparing for and implementing a parish religious education program with a coordinator might be analyzed as follows:

First The Board of Education with the pastor engage the parish in an examination of its educational mission, seeking to develop some long-range goals and a skeleton of a plan to implement them (e.g. close/expand the school, hire a coordinator, re-arrange the parish structure).

Second Out of this long-range plan — if appropriate — the Board (or an ad hoc committee) prepares the *first draft* of the Contract and Supplements A and B, which will be used in securing a professional person to work as coordinator.

Third This *plan* and *first draft* are presented to the parish at large (Parish Council) and the diocesan Board of Education (where applicable) for discussion, revision, and/or approval.

Fourth The Board (with the assistance of the Diocesan Office) searches for prospective candidates to serve as coordinator sending them a *professional profile* form (see Chart 2:3) to secure a personal and professional description together with either the *long-range plan* and the *first draft Contract* and *Supplements A* and *B* or, (and more appropriate) a synopsis of why this parish is looking for a coordinator and what in general will be expected of him.

Fifth From the responses, a selection of likely prospects is determined and interviews arranged. The prospective coordinators should receive the *long-range plan* and the *first draft supplements* to have a clear picture of the parish's *initial* expectations.

Sixth After the interviews, the parish (pastor and Board) re-examines its expectations in light of the reactions of the coordinators interviewed and the talents of the persons available.

Seventh Then, if the parish has a definite person in mind and wishes to proceed, a *second draft* of the contract and supplements is prepared by both the Board and the coordinator working out a consensus on the general purpose, on the assigned responsibilities, and on the expected relationships.

Eighth The coordinator is introduced to the parish and those working in the educational mission with "a parish event" or something appropriate.

Ninth After the first six months or a year, the Supplements are revised by the Board and the coordinator, according to their evaluation of the situation.

These steps do not take into consideration other things which the parish will have to do when it begins to secure a coordinator; namely, thinking through the possibilities (and perhaps acting on some) of an office for the coordinator, budget, professional assistance possible, living situation (for religious particularly), and similar items. Other different kinds of decisions might also be necessary if the parish is to secure the services of *religious* as coordinators. A team approach in which one sister serves as the coordinator and another as an assistant (or internship, perhaps) might be needed. In such a case, matching persons of varied talents would be desirable.

In summary, it cannot be emphasized enough that the parish (the broad base of people involved in the decision) must know clearly why it is hiring a professional and what it expects that person to do *with* them. Thinking through its own educational mission and the part which a professional can play in that work and formalizing this into a role description (Supplement A) can greatly benefit the total faith community. The "thinking through" process itself is of great merit. The clarification of expectations reduces the major source of conflict and failure in this new phenomenon in parish religious education and provides a base for creative accomplishment so desperately needed in this crisis era in education in the Church. The very nature of a coordinator's role is to work with change and produce growth. Hence, it is essential that the responsibilities and relationships be as stabilized as possible, lest the creative tension inherent in change be turned toward the coordinator rather than toward the growth step.

NOTES FOR CHAPTER 3

1) Neil G. McCluskey, *Catholic Education Faces Its Future,* especially Chapters 1 and 2. See also Neil G. McCluskey, *Catholic Viewpoint on Education* (Garden City, N.Y.: Hanover House, 1959), a more detailed analysis of the history of Catholic schools in America.

2) Robert L. Peabody, *Organizational Authority* (New York: Atherton Press, 1964), p. 117ff.

3) The currently existing research in management and education can be of great assistance here. The research on "supervisors" in the Association for Supervision and Curriculum Development of the National Education Association is particularly helpful. See William H. Lucio, ed., *Supervision: Perspectives and Propositions* (Washington, D.C.: ASCD, 1967).

4) Peter F. Drucker, *The Effective Executive* (New York: Harper and Row, 1966), p. 5. This is a *must* book for coordinators since their professional education is generally lacking the "skill" aspect of applying theoretical knowledge to action.

5) Marshall McLuhan, *Understanding Media* (New York: Signet, 1964), p. 30.

6) Drucker, *Effective Executive,* p. 5.

Chapter Four

WORKING WITH THE PASTOR

The work of the coordinator cannot be discussed adequately without relating it to the role of the pastor in parish religious education. This will be done first theoretically and then experientially.

Some people express the concern that the coordinator role is developing because the pastor is not suitably prepared to assume his rightful responsibilities for Christian education in the parish. Others would explain this new phenomenon as a pragmatic extension of the pastor, deemed necessary due to the size of the parish and the scope of the educational mission today. In either case, the coordinator role is viewed as a practical compromise from what ought to be ideal in a Christian community. These are misconceptions, for the work of the coordinator can be seen as a proper role, distinct from that of the pastor, within the "ideal" Christian community.

THE CHRISTIAN COMMUNITY IDEAL

"At all times, among every people, God has given welcome to whosoever fears Him and does what is right (cf. Acts 10:35). It has pleased God, however, to make men holy and save them not merely as individuals, without any mutual bonds, but by making them into a single people, a people which acknowledges Him in truth and serves Him in holiness." This is the way in which the Bishops of the world expressed the nature of the People of God or the Christian community in the *Dogmatic Constitution on the Church* (#9).

God is present to all men at all times. When a man has "heard the word" and come to believe in the Lord, he finds that the very root principle of Christianity is belief in a Triune God and that Christianity is in essence a communal religion. It is the community of men whose lives are animated by the Spirit of Jesus and who celebrate that faith in liturgy (1 Pet 2:5), who preach the word to all men and grow in its understanding themselves (Acts 2:17), and who minister to the needs of one another and to the needs of their fellow men (Jn 13:35). This community of believers, as a whole the Church, is called to be holy by faithfulness to the Lord in the fulfillment of this three-fold mission: *preaching* the word (education), *priesthood* (liturgy), and *charity* (social action). This mission has both present (now-already eschatology) and future (yet-to-be-realized eschatology) aspects(1).

The Bishop stands in the center of this community both expressing the centering of the community in their mission, and ministering to the Church in order that they may be able to fulfill their mission — the mission Jesus gave to his apostles *and* disciples, that is, to the whole community. As a successor of the Apostles, who gave personal witness to what Jesus said and did, the

Bishop has a role of primacy vis-a-vis the community, but, like them, he is always and foremost to be faithful in all things to the Lord who is the *primary* person or center (cornerstone) of the faith community (Col 1:16).

The Second Vatican Council has clearly taught that the Bishop is not simply an administrative unit or extension of the Pope. He and the community around him are proportionately the whole Church. His is a rightful place within the Church because he is ordained bishop. The fullness of Church rests in him. He preaches, teaches, consecrates, guides—all *functional* activity of the Church in Christian mission rests with each Bishop by virtue of his ordination, that is, his call by the Lord, by the community, and by the college of Bishops to become an apostle(2). The Bishop, in turn, shares his mission of service with his priests who stand in his place in the local Churches(3).

The pastor as "presbyter" (elder of the community) is both called forth by the Christian community to lead them in their mission and sent by the Bishop to stand in his place as priest of the local Church. His chief responsibility, like that of the Bishop, is to minister to the community in the fulfillment of its mission. Having been sent by the Bishop, he has primary authority to preach, celebrate, and minister (Acts 20:17-35).

Educational Mission The very purpose of the Christian community is to be like Christ and thus to manifest the Spirit and to serve man (Lk 22:27). Chief among the ways in which this is fulfilled is the proclaiming of the Word (Acts 6:4), or, broadly conceived, the educational mission. This mission of proclaiming the Word, like other aspects of the Church's mission, is the responsibility of the whole community (1 Cor 2:12). Hans Kung explains that "every believer can and must, having been taught by God, teach others; can and must, having received the word of God, be its herald in some form or other"(4).

Thus, within the ideal Christian community, the responsibility to preach the Gospel is of central importance to all members—each according to the gifts of the Spirit which have been given to him and/or according to his appointed role within the community (People of God). Hans Kung states it: "Every Christian is called to be a preacher of the word, in the widest sense, even though, in view of the variety of the gifts of the Spirit, not everyone can, by any means, do everything"(5).

Furthermore, it is the Spirit who teaches each and every man what is truly of God. Thus, the Bishop (and pastor) does not "save" his flock by the sedulous care which he gives to the word. "But you have not lost the anointing he gave you, and you do not need anyone to teach you, the anointing he gave teaches you everything (1 Jn 2:27). Rather, the role of the apostle who stands at the center of the community is to affirm that the preaching and teaching is of the Spirit as well as to give testimony himself to the saving words and deeds of Jesus as he has come to understand them in prayerful openness to the same Spirit(6).

Since there are a variety of gifts of the Spirit within the whole community, the responsibility of the whole community and the Bishop to preach the word is made possible. "There are a variety of gifts, but always the same Spirit; there are all sorts of services to be done, but always to the same Lord; working in all sorts of ways in different people, it is the same God who is working in all of them" (1 Cor 12:4-6). The role of the apostle (Bishop) to preach may be the role of primacy within the community but it is not the only role in conjunction with the preaching of the word over and above the general responsibility shared by all believers. The New Testament mentions several ministries related to the Gospel.

"And to some, his gift was that they should be apostles, to some, prophets; to some, evangelists; to some, pastors and teachers; so that the saints together make a unity in the work of service, building up the body of Christ" (Eph 4:11-12).

The New Testament Prophet The existence throughout the Old and New Testament accounts of a distinct group known as prophets cannot be overlooked in this discussion. The conceptions about the role of the prophet in the Old Testament most frequently view him as an ecstatic seer, one who foretells the future events or who calls forth punishment upon the community for its failures to remain faithful to Yahweh. The accuracy of this characterization as complete, is open to question, as McKenzie notes(7), but this view of the prophet is clearly present there.

In the New Testament, prophets were different. They played an important and more functional role within the Christian community. The list of ministries related to preaching the Word frequently mentions two other groups besides the apostles and in order after the apostolic ministry: "second, prophets; third, teachers" (1 Cor 12:28). The community "has the apostles and prophets for its foundations" (Eph 2:20). The prophet in the early Christian community, therefore, was called by the Spirit to speak in God's name (1 Cor 12:1) about the Scripture (1 Pet 1:10-12) and about the mystery of God at work in the world through Christ (cf. 1 Cor 13:2; Eph 3:5; Rom 16:25ff). Unlike those who spoke in tongues, the prophets of the early Church were to speak in an intelligible fashion for the building up of the whole community (1 Cor 14).

These prophets in the early Church were called by the Spirit, as was the apostle, and share in a special way the gifts regarding the Word which all believers receive in the anointing (baptism). However, unlike the apostle, their gift is to be ju̇dged by the community "to see if they come from God" (1 Jn 4:2), and if they are contributing to building up the body of Christ (1 Cor 14). Thus, the prophet is subject to the authority of the apostle who stands vis-a-vis the community on his own authority for preaching the Gospel; and to the community who are to discern the widsom of the prophecy (1 Cor. 14:16)(8).

Many Roles in the Educational Mission By defining the educational mission broadly within the Christian community as that pertaining to preaching the Word, it can be seen that there are many roles, therefore, pertaining to such a ministry. Religious education coordinators are not necessarily a new expression of the prophet role in the ideal Christian community—although a good case might be made for this. Their responsibilities and education, however, do place them in a position in reference to the Gospel much like that of the prophet and also like that of the teachers mentioned in the early Church accounts (cf. Acts 13:1; 1 Cor 12:28).

The main point in this consideration of the roles in the ideal Christian community relative to preaching is that the pastor, as a representative of the Bishop (apostle) and as presbyter or elder of the community, is *not the only* person responsible for preaching the Word. Pastors exist for and within a Christian community. Their responsibility for preaching is primary but not limited to them. All of the community shares in the gifts of the Spirit and in the responsibility to preach the Word. In addition to this general sharing, individuals within the community have special charisms for prophecy and teaching and have a definite leadership role or ministry for building up the community. Hence, the coordinator role is not merely a pragmatic compromise, but can be seen as a focus proper to the educational mission of the parish, a focus not unlike that of the prophet in the early Church.

THE CHRISTIAN COMMUNITY REALITY — 1970's

Since the Church always exists within a given historical context and with men who fail, this ideal Christian community is always in the process of becoming. The reality of Christian community is to be found in the parishes and people present in the 1970's, and both are in need of continual reformation.

In the real parish situations of the 1970's, the relationship of the apostle and prophets and presbyters to the believing community is buried beneath customs, mentalities, and rituals which have grown up in the Church in America throughout the decades. Both pastor and people do have an unclear understanding of the parish as the local Church and of the many gifts and roles which the whole believing people (the parish) share as a result of the Spirit.

For the past several decades, the local Church has relied upon the pastor as the chief preacher and teacher. The religious in the parish school were also credible in the teaching mission to a certain limited extent. This over-dominance of the pastor within the parish community was not limited to the areas of preaching and teaching, but often extended to the total mission of the parish. Lay men and women shared in all the duties of the parish or the parish mission in a very secondary way.

Within the last decade, lay men and women gradually began to enter into the educational mission of the parish, first as lay teachers in parochial schools and/or as catechists in the parish schools of religion and, eventually, as participants in the decision-making process regarding the parish's educational mission in committees and Boards of Education. A few lay persons were also recognized as competent speakers for religious education programs, Cursillo, and retreats. Even then, however, these types of sessions were always under the direct guidance of a priest.

Thus, because the history of the Christian community (Catholic parishes) in the last few decades has been dominated by the pastor as the chief preacher and teacher, the entrance of a professional into the area of religious education, religious or lay, has not been without problems for pastor, coordinator, and people alike. At this present time in history, the working relationship of the coordinator with the pastor and the people is high charged emotionally, for reasons which are both personal and professional.

Personal Problems Both the coordinator and the pastor bring into this new focus of parish religious education personal anxieties which are not germane to the coordinator role itself, but which do cause over-reactions to the real problems that are involved. These personal anxieties are found with both the pastor and the coordinator, especially religious.

Priests and sisters, in recent years, have been forced to make a radical change in life style in both their working and living conditions. Young priests come into the parish (or diocese) with new ideas and a new style of life which threatens the pastor who was raised in another tradition. Often conflicts within the rectory living situation wear the pastor's patience thin so that when he becomes involved in a working relationship with the coordinator, his emotional reactions are frequently not based upon the actual situation, but stem from his living conditions. The same applies to assistant pastors who work with coordinators and have a poor living arrangement in the rectory.

The radical change for the coordinator who is a sister coming from a large community style of life into a small community of perhaps two sisters, produces living problems which also are carried into the pastor-coordinator working relationship by the coordinator.

In addition to the significant adjustments demanded of both pastor and sister coordinator in their living conditions in the 1970's, the working relationship between pastor and coordinator also touches on another problem which plagues both, namely, heterosexual relationships.

The pastor, typically, has been raised in a context in which his contacts with women have been largely pastoral or family relationships. Accepting a sister as a coequal in the teaching mission of the Church is difficult enough because it is a challenge to his status as the chief teacher; but, secondly, it opens up the problem of working in an intensive way with a woman. This problem of heterosexual relationships in a working situation can be seen in other professions where women have only recently entered into the work. Within the parish, however, it is much more intense due to the long history of celibacy on the part of the priest and the implicit second place status given to women within the Church. Hence the pastor, as a man, has a difficult time establishing a harmonious working relationship with a woman coordinator, religious or lay. His problem becomes greater with young women coordinators and sisters in contemporary garb, for both their youth and their femininity pose unconscious obstacles for the pastor.

Heterosexual relationships are also problematic for religious who, only recently, have begun to establish intensive working relationships with men, either as educators or as pastors. Novitiates and spiritual formation in religious communities have an implicit negativism toward men built into them. This is equally true, of course, with seminaries and their view of women. In either case, this problem of the heterosexual relationship between a pastor as a man and a coordinator as a woman is often unconscious, yet quite serious.

In addition to this personal problem of heterosexual relationships, both priest and sister in the last decade have been forced to change their working style in drastic ways. Formerly, both priests and sisters worked alone within the framework of the parish church on the teaching apostolate without much involvement in the public community or with a large number of people. A high degree of involvement in the "secular" world and with many people is demanded today in the teaching apostolate of the Church. This new involvement produces anxiety which contributes to the emotionally charged situation in which the pastor and coordinator must work.

Concomitant with this high degree of secular involvement and the anxiety which it brings, there is a general threat today to the very existence of religious life and the nature of priesthood. The waves of confusion which sweep our society and the Church do not affect the priest and sister solely as academic issues. The pastor and the sister-coordinator each have invested much of themselves in a life style deeply integrated into Church and this life style is now open to serious questioning. The defections from religious communities and from priesthood and the many debates, pro and con, on the nature of priesthood and religious life cannot help but produce anxieties which are brought into the working situation.

These personal problems exist over and above those which all people face and bring into a working context. They are problems that are part of the "syndrome" which plagues priests and religious (and a certain number of lay people) working in all areas within the Church today. Such problems *are not inherent* in the working relationship between the pastor and a coordinator as such, but they are real and definitely contribute to the highly emotional atmosphere in which ordinary professional problems must be faced.

Professional Problems There are some very definite professional problems which *are inherent* in the working relationship between pastor and coordinator that must be faced if this new focus in parish religious education is to survive and become effective. Project Coordinator data frequently indicates that the working relationship between pastor and coordinator is volatile. An identification of some of the problems inherent in this professional relationship may help to improve the situation.

1) General Parish Polarization: The confusion within the Church not only poses a personal threat to the pastor and to the coordinator, but it also affects the whole parish and puts a special strain upon the educational mission. The launching of Sputnik in 1957, and the effect which this had upon education in the United States is a good example of this general principle. The high degree of confusion and polarization within the Church today places a heavy demand upon education for solutions. Various factions arise with partial answers which they seek to legislate into religious education as the chief means for overcoming the confusion and polarization and "saving the church." Each comes with certain demands for change in parish education programs. The demand for the return to the catechism is a conservative example of this; the demand for a

social gospel in all religious education programs is a more liberal example of the same principle.

This phenomenon is not all bad. Parish religious education exists for the service of the people of the parish. Educators have frequently complained about apathy on the part of people. The appearance of pressure groups can be seen, therefore, as a good sign, for people who are pressuring are interested in what is taking place. The extent of the pressure today, however, definitely has an emotional impact upon pastor and coordinator. Both the pastor and the coordinator are approached by such groups. Frequently the pastor is approached by the more conservative groups and the coordinator by the more liberal groups. Each in his dedication feels intense professional concern to meet the needs of the groups pressuring. This can lead to a struggle between the pastor and coordinator, whereby each seeks to convince the other of the "rightness" of the direction he or she wishes to take to meet the needs of those groups to whom he or she is listening.

2) Apathy and Misconceptions: The vast majority of the people of the parish, however, are not organized into pressure groups. They are simply apathetic about what happens in any phase of parish work.

In all areas of life today people are faced with change. The rate of change often produces a type of shock in which people simply withdraw. Unable to meet all of the changes demanded and unable to relate the changes which are made to their past and to their basic sense of what life means, people must protect themselves: They let go of some of their concerns and involvements and, hence, become apathetic toward and withdrawn from many areas of their lives. Many of these people have looked to their Church for a stabilizing effect. The over-emphasis in Catholicism upon the

unchangeableness of Church and theology further reinforced this tendency toward permanence. Suddenly —
when seen in terms of the local parish — the whole of
the Church is in a state of upheaval. The last bulwark
against change, so to speak, has itself begun to change.
It is no wonder people have become apathetic in this
area of their lives also.

One of the changes which confronts the average
parish is the development of new roles within the parish
mission. The layman has grown accustomed to seeing
the pastor as the dominant force in whatever happens
in the parish. With the introduction of new roles into
the liturgy and the decision-making process of the parish,
an initial threat to these expectations of the pastor and
of parish life was provided. The expectations towards
sisters have also been thoroughly shaken. The parish
had become accustomed to seeing the sisters working
in the parochial schools, solely with children, with
little other involvement. With the close of the school,
and perhaps the addition of a sister coordinator to the
parish, sisters have become more involved with adult
education; they visit homes and are seen in the community and, in general, live and work in a way which is for-
eign to the conception the parish has had of them.

This apathy and these misconceptions are real
elements which must be dealt with in the educational
mission of the parish. Frequently they are part of the
reason for the lack of success of educational programs.
They are the ghost, so to speak, which the coordinator
and the pastor must face in seeking to accomplish their
objectives. Just as the pastor and coordinator are anxious
to meet the needs of the pressure groups, similarly
they are anxious about the lack of response from the
majority of the members of the parish and this anxiety
is present in the working relationship and influences
many decisions.

3) Confusion Regarding Goals of Religious Education: In addition to the problem of polarization and general apathy, the working context between the pastor and the coordinator is plagued by a general confusion about the goals of religious education. Pastor, coordinator, catechist, and parents have each been raised with definite views about what the Church ought to do in educational work and today these views are frequently conflicting. Caught between pressure groups, surrounded by apathy, and confused about what ought to happen, it is no wonder the pastor and coordinator find their working relationship emotionally tense.

4) Lack of Immediate Feed-back: Once a goal is agreed upon and a program begun, another problem comes into play; namely, the lack of immediate feed-back which enables one to see the results of the educational endeavor.

Coordinators by and large have come out of a teaching background in parochial schools. In that context, one could see the immediate effects of a good lesson. This immediate feed-back provided evaluation — the evaluation of the goals and the program — and encouragement that the efforts put into it were worth it. Even the pastor could look at the day to day operations of the parochial school and see some visible evidence of the attainment of the parish's educational mission.

General parish religious education does not have this immediate feed-back. Neither pastor nor coordinator can see "the results" of their efforts when the youth and the adult contacts are on a weekly or less frequent basis. This lack of feed-back produces a sense of frustration that perhaps the programs are not good enough and spurs both pastor and coordinator to be highly critical of the effectiveness of what they are doing and, eventually, of each other.

As it has been shown, the working relationship between the coordinator and the pastor is highly charged with emotion for both personal and professional reasons. The personal anxieties of each produces a sensitivity and a frustration which frequently causes an over-reaction to the professional problems which are inherent in the working relationship and to those general problems which impinge upon it at this time in history. The professional problems are new since the focus of a professional in parish religious education itself is new. Because they are new, they are vague and ill-defined. The net result is a volatile climate in which pastor and coordinator are expected to work. It is no wonder immense problems are arising in this particular area.

Steps to Minimize Anxiety There are a number of steps which can be taken to minimize these anxieties. Each parish will have to solve this problem in its own unique way, but one or more of the following should definitely help.

1) Solve Personal Problems Elsewhere: Both the pastor and the coordinator need to identify the personal problems which cause each a great deal of frustration and anxiety. These will have to be solved outside the working relationship itself. Both a pastor and a sister-coordinator, for example, will have to cope with the threat to their life styles as priest and religious within their own peer groups. A priest or sister who finds heterosexual working relationships difficult should attack the problem with a counselor or in some other way. The problem ought to be solved, but this cannot be accomplished in the working relationship itself. It is understandable when one compares these personal problems to the problems which a lay person, working as a coordinator, may have with his marriage or family. He should be, and is, ex-

pected to solve these problems outside the working context.

2) Preparation Process and Expectations: The preparation process described in Chapter 2 can do much to change the expectations of the pastor and the people of the parish toward the role of a coordinator. Involving a large part of the parish in this preparation process can help to reduce the apathy of many and temper the special interest pressures of others.

3) Supplement A and Role Definition: The process of arriving at the Contract and Supplement A described in Chapter 3 can clarify the expected working relationship between the pastor and the coordinator. The general framework of the working relationship must be clearly defined so that the pastor knows what to expect of the coordinator and the coordinator knows what to expect of the pastor. This will do much to put both at ease and lessen many of the potential tensions. Allowing the working relationship simply to evolve without clear definition is very costly and seldom works.

4) "Take Each Other Into Account": Earl S. Johnson, in writing about the relationship between supervisors in public education and principals, explains that "the most important feature of human association is that the members of it, the participants, take each other into account"(9). This type of human relationship whereby two people are aware of one another and take one another seriously, as people and as professionals, should be inherent in any working relationship. It is especially important in a working relationship within the Christian community, which is attempting to show, by its very belief, the importance of human beings. For either person to deny this importance in the work-

ing relationship between pastor and coordinator is in effect to deny the very belief which the educational program is seeking to foster in other people.

Both pastor and coordinator can strengthen their unity and working relationship by praying together, celebrating together, and suffering together. Each share the same general aim for the parish and this can be formalized into prayer to enrich one another in pursuing their joint apostolate; each can share in the accomplishments which the parish makes. Occasions should be sought out to celebrate formally. Similarly, the pastor and coordinator can sustain one another in facing the frustrations and in meeting the failures which the program will encounter.

It is imperative that the pastor attempt to see the problems which the coordinator faces and the coordinator attempt to see the problems which the pastor faces. In this way, they can both take one another into account on a very human level.

On a more professional basis, the coordinator needs to realize that the pastor has had theological education and much pastoral experience which can be brought to bear upon the educational efforts of the parish. On the other hand, the pastor needs to take the coordinator into account for the same reason. The coordinator is educated formally in religious education and has much to offer to the pastor in assisting him and the people of the parish in the accomplishment of their goals. The pastor needs to learn to work with the coordinator as a coequal in the teaching and preaching mission of the Church. This in no way lessens his priesthood. Rather, it intensifies it.

5) Focus on Strengths Rather Than Weaknesses: "The effective executive makes strengths productive"(10). Both pastor and coordinator have strengths as well as

weaknesses. Focusing on the strengths and accepting the weaknesses can further improve the working relationship. The pastor, for example, in his style of management may find written reports of much more help than dialogue appointments. Coordinators should respect this characteristic of the pastor and utilize it for the benefit of the total program. The pastor, in turn, should find the strengths which the coordinator can offer to the total work of the parish and capitalize on these rather than lament his or her weaknesses and mistakes. Strong people always have strong weaknesses. St. Peter is a good case in point. His faith was strong, but so indeed were his denials (cf. Matt 66:18 and Mark 16:22).

6) Formalize Communications: Regular times and means of communication should be established between the pastor and the coordinator in their working relationship. When and how such communication occurs should obviously be based on the preferences of the individuals involved and should take their personal life styles into account. Whatever the method, effective two-way communication must be established on a regular basis.

The coordinator should bear in mind that the pastor should never hear about something of importance regarding the educational mission of the parish second-hand. As will be explained later, the professional day to day decisions of the coordinator are not subject to veto on the part of the pastor, except in extraordinary circumstances. However, the effects of these decisions should not reach the pastor second-hand. When meetings are going to be held, for example, the pastor should know about the meeting and its agenda before it occurs and hear about the results afterwards.

The pastor, on the other hand, should keep the coordinator informed about comments from parishoners, about decisions being made by the diocesan structure or by the parishes in the area, and other events and items which would bear upon the work of the coordinator in the educational mission of that parish.

Some parishes find weekly meetings between pastor, coordinator, and those working in the educational mission absolutely essential. Others have found simple written reports suffice with bi-weekly cr monthly meetings as the need arises. Whatever the particular style in a given parish, this type of communication must be effected and maintained with sedulous care right from the beginning of the coordinator's work in that parish. Once trust is broken between the coordinator and the pastor, it is exceedingly difficult to re-establish.

7) Be Led By Vision: A Methodist bishop in Michigan once remarked that we should live our life led by our visions and not pushed by our problems. In management, this would mean that personnel focus on the attainment of the goals and find a unity with one another by identification with those goals.

Both the pastor and the coordinator have the same end in mind; namely, the attainment of the mission of the Church in that parish. In the educational area, both want what is best for the youth and adults. Thus, there is an immediate unity in motivations. This unity in motivations should be further augmented by consensus in a general vision or general purpose in religious education which the pastor and coordinators seek to accomplish in that parish. The pastor and coordinator need not agree on all aspects of that vision—nor should they—but there should be a general agreement on the basic direction and basic priorities and an acceptance of the plurality of the vision itself. As one person put it, if there is not a difference of opinion between two people working on the same general task, one is not needed. It is important that this vision be articulated, perhaps in the program goals for the parish (cf. Chapter 6) or in some other way. It is not enough to let this vision be worked out on a weekly basis in confronting problems. When the pastor and the coordinator can share a general vision of religious education, accepting one another's differences, each can trust the other to solve problems appropriate to his work without apprehension.

8) Discuss Conflicts With Peers: Although personal problems must be solved outside the working relationship, professional problems need not. In the process of regular communication described above, the pastor and the coordinator ought to bring up, as agenda items, areas of conflict which are plaguing the working relationship. Some of these problems can be solved simply by an open discussion. Others will need a more elaborate discussion among peers — in this case, pastors and coordinators in similar situations.

The coordinators working in a diocese or same area should meet together and, in this peer situation, discuss common problems and gain insights. The same applies to pastors. It is also beneficial to have the pastors and the coordinators meet together as one large group and discuss common problems which they all face, such as communications, working with the Board of Education, and differing visions of religious education. Discussion of problems in this context makes them problems to be solved rather than battles to be won.

PASTORAL ASPECT OF EDUCATIONAL MISSION:

As indicated above, the responsibility for proclaiming the Word is the responsibility of the whole Christian community and of the pastor, who is always to be seen in relationship to a Christian community. The pastor, however, as a representative of the bishop (apostle), does have a primary responsibility in reference to preaching the Word. The educational mission of the whole community and the primary responsibility of the pastor in reference to it might be summarized as follows:

People:
1) *Hear the word of God and preach it in actions and words* (cf. Acts 4:31; Rom 10:14-17; 1 Cor 1:24; 1 Pet 2:9; 3:15 and Constitution on the Church, par. 17).
2) *Teach their children* ("Parents, moreover, have the right to determine, in accordance with their own religious beliefs, the kind of religious education that their children are to receive." *Declaration on Religious Liberty,* par. 5).
3) *Work for quality education for all men* ("All men of every race, condition, and age, since they enjoy the dignity of a human being, have an inalienable right to an education. . . . *Declaration on Christian Education.*

Pastor:
1) *Preach the Gospel* (Mark 1:35-38; 1 Cor 1:17; Rom 11:13; 2 Cor 3:6; 4:1; 6:3).
2) *Discern the authenticity of the teaching and preaching of the word in the local Church* (Acts 20:28-35; 1 Tim 5:17; 1 Pet 5:1-4; 1 Tim 3:2-5). This means to relate it to the Gospel and to the teachings of the Apostles (Church) with the aid of the Spirit.
3) *See that opportunity for catechetical education is provided for all ages* (Constitution on Pastoral Office of Bishops, par. 14).

To summarize it another way, "the principal duty of both lay men and lay women is to witness to Christ by their lives and words, in the family, within their social circle, and in their working environment"(11). The pastor as representative of the bishop shares in *his* duties. "Among the principal duties of bishops, the preaching of the Gospel occupies an eminent place. For bishops are preachers of the faith, who lead new disciples to Christ, and they are authentic teachers, that is, teachers endowed with the authority of Christ, who preach to the people committed to them the faith to be believed and put into practice, and by the light of the Holy Spirit they illustrate that faith, bringing forth from the treasury of revelation new things and old, making it bear fruit, and vigilantly warding off any errors that threaten their flock"(12).

Preaching It is inappropriate to attempt to translate this pastoral responsibility into minute specifics. We have lived through a cultural era in which a man tried to conform himself to a closely defined role and we have seen the loss of individuality and personal charism which resulted. Thus, we know that it is better for each man to fulfill this pastoral responsibility in the way in which he is best suited. It is appropriate, however, to attempt to discuss this general responsibility in more specific terms which flow from the nature of the call to ordination and the responsibility of a pastorate.

The priest as a representative of the bishop who gives testimony to the saving Words and deeds of Jesus cannot avoid the responsibility to preach the Word, that is, to give testimony. He need not be a good preacher, but preach he must. He must preach, first of all, to the believing community with whom he works and prays. This is most frequently done at the Sunday liturgy during which he assumes his responsibility of leadership for that community. He also gives testimony at more formal sessions; namely, educational conferences, meetings of various organizations, school assemblies, etc. It is at these more formal sessions, in reference to proclaiming the Word, where the pastor's responsibility and that of the coordinator are apt to clash. The pastor is frequently called upon to theologize and philosophize about everything in the parish, including the educational program, at meetings such as this. He should be very careful at these times to give witness to the expertise or the authority of the coordinator in that area of competence rather than speak of it specifically himself. If the pastor and coordinator can have a consensus on the basic direction of religious education in the parish as described above, the pastor, when called upon to give testimony at various formal meetings, can speak about this general consensus rather than speak of specific program ideas and possibilities.

The pastor also preaches the Word in a variety of informal ways throughout his work with the believing community. In visits to the sick, in marriage counseling, in many other contacts with the members of the parish the pastor is continually relating the Gospel to the situation and in that way proclaiming the Word. Preaching is intimately tied up with sacraments and other ministries in which the pastor works.

In addition to his responsibility to preach to the believing community, the pastor, as priest and representative of the believing community, should proclaim the Word before the whole community of man, that is, the civic community of which he and the parish are a part. Giving testimony to what Jesus said and did at various civic meetings and ecumenical meetings is the prime responsibility of the pastor when an official representative is requested. This responsibility might be shared with the President of the Parish Council in some specific sessions or with the coordinator at others, but it is chiefly the pastor's responsibility to give testimony to the civic community.

This testimony to the civic community would also include convert work. The pastor's responsibility toward converts is primary. The coordinator may assist the pastor in the educational program for persons becoming members of the parish, but the pastor cannot avoid his primary responsibility in this area, to be involved and to provide the overall leadership and contact. As indicated above, the pastoral responsibility toward the Word would also include the responsibility to see that opportunities are provided for formal religious education for youth and adults within the parish. This responsibility is translated into specifics by the coordinator and the Board of Education, but it is still the responsibility of the pastor to see that the faith community grows in its awareness and understanding of the Gospel (adult education) and shares this knowledge (*know* in the Scriptural sense) with their children and with others.

Discern   In addition to preaching the Word, the pastor has a responsibility to discern the work of the Spirit in reference to the Word within the parish. This is generally translated into a specific practice by the pastor's support of ideas and programs which others originate.

In a more formal sense, it would mean that the pastor has the veto power over the work of the Board of Education. This pastoral veto may be exercised through a Parish Council which reviews the decisions of the Board of Education and relates them to the total work of the parish. The Parish Council may exercise the actual veto over the Board of Education, but in the last analysis the pastor still has a veto over decisions of the Parish Council. Thus, it is the responsibility of the pastor to discern that the decisions which the Board of Education and the coordinator make in reference to the educational mission of the parish are authentic; that is, in keeping with the Gospel of Christ and the *magisterium* of the Church which flows from that Gospel. This does not mean that the pastor, in an authoritarian way, tells the Board of Education and the coordinator what to do or bluntly vetoes their decisions. Ideally, the pastor should be involved with them in their deliberations and attempt to point out through questioning and "homily" where he believes their deliberations are deviating from the Gospel and the magisterium. In other words, he should attempt to demonstrate throughout the deliberations what the application of the Gospel and the magisterium offers to the decisions that are being made. In this regard, the pastor can ask the coordinator to show this relationship in what is being proposed also. In the end result, however, if the Board of Education and the coordinator have gone a direction which the pastor does not believe in keeping with the Gospel of Christ and the magisterium of the Church, he has a responsibility to veto their decisions. Obviously, this type of veto should be used very infrequently, for the Spirit of God is not at conflict with himself, and the pastor and the coordinator and Board all in prayerful openness to the Spirit should be able to arrive at a working consensus regarding what should be done with the educational mission of that parish. If such consensus cannot be attained, perhaps the openness to the Spirit is not present either.

In a more practical manner, in reference to discerning the Spirit, the pastor should not over-ride the decisions of the parish coordinator on a day to day basis. He should exercise his pastoral responsibility toward the educational mission by participation on the Board of Education and by his veto either directly or through the Parish Council over decisions of the Board of Education. The coordinator is responsible to the Board and the Board is responsible to the whole community of whom the pastor is the presbyter or leader.

Affirm   In a more informal way, it is the responsibility of the pastor as leader of the parish community to give personal and professional affirmation to those working within the educational mission. It is his responsibility, in other words, to assist these people in their efforts to remain faithful to the Gospel of Christ in their personal lives and also in their professional work.

This affirmation begins, first of all, on a very human level. It is important that the pastor take the coordinator into account, as described above, and affirm that what the coordinator is doing is important for the work of the whole parish and important to the pastor as leader of that parish. The same applies to the pastor's human relationships with the Board of Education. This is simply a translation in a specific way of what is actually being preached in the Gospel itself at the Sunday liturgy; namely, love your neighbor, take him into account, see his worth and the worth of what he does. The pastor cannot avoid practicing what he preaches in this regard.

In addition, it is a pastoral responsibility to provide opportunities for growth in faith on the part of the persons who are leading the educational mission: the Board of Education, the coordinator, and the teachers. Being present at their formal and informal meetings and offering prayer and testimony is one way in which this can be done. Individual counselling and the sponsorship of retreat type sessions for those in the education mission would be another way in which this responsibility could be met. Many avenues are possible, but the responsibility to affirm the worth and work of those persons in the educational mission is a definite pastoral responsibility and one quite important to the realization of the education mission in that faith community.

SUMMARY

The working context between the coordinator and the pastor at the present time is emotionally charged. It is tense for both personal and professional reasons. The personal reasons are related to the current wave of renewal within the Church and to the threat which this makes to the personal life styles of pastor and coordinator, especially if the coordinator is a sister. Professional problems are inherent in any working relationship, but since the role of the coordinator is new within the parish educational mission, these problems are especially acute at this time and make the working relationship particularly sensitive. The problems between the coordinator and the pastor highlight the importance of the preparation process within the parish before a commitment to a religious education program led by a professional is made. They also highlight the need for the full commitment on the part of the parish to the coordinator who is hired. When there is a full commitment on the part of pastor, parish, and coordinator to an effective realization of the educational mission of that parish, this commitment can over-ride the difficulites which arise or at least provide the strength out of which solutions can be found. The pastor, the Board of Education, and the coordinator and, to a certain extent, the teachers must achieve a working relationship which is in effect a model for Christian community. This working together in the Spirit of Jesus will teach more than any of the formal programs which the educational team will offer. It was mentioned above that the Christian community is always in the process of becoming. This is not an argument, therefore, for a working ideal which is unattainable. It is, however, an exhortation to begin striving for that ideal, while realizing that in the Spirit of Jesus all things are possible.

In the words of St. Paul, "I appeal to Evodia and I appeal to Syntyche to come to an agreement with each other in the Lord" (Phil 4:2).

NOTES FOR CHAPTER 4

1) Yves Congar, OP, "The Church: The People of God," The Church and Mankind (Glen Rock, N.J.: Paulist Press, 1965), Concilium 1, pp. 11ff.

2) "Functional" here should be seen not as an expression of functionalism, but rather as a highly personal response to the covenanted relationship between persons in the faith community. Cf. Hans Urs Von Balthasar, *Church and World* (New York: Herder and Herder, 1967), p. 105ff.

3) Cf. Walter M. Abbott, ed., *Vatican Council II, Decree on the Pastoral Office of Bishops in the Church* (New York: Guild Press, 1966), especially paragraphs 18-271. See also discussion of these paragraphs by Karl Rahner, "Observations on Episcopacy in the Light of Vatican II," *The Pastoral Mission of the Church* (Glen Rock, N.J.: Paulist Press, 1965); also in *Concilium* 3, pp. 15ff.

4) Hans Kung, *The Church* (New York: Sheed and Ward, 1967), p. 377.

5) *Ibid.*

6) Walter M. Abbott, ed., *Vatican Council II, Constitution on the Church, The Documents of Vatican II* (New York: Guild Press, 1966), especially paragraphs 23, 24, and 25 for an understanding of the relationship of the Apostle to the People of God.

7) John L. McKenzie, *Dictionary of the Bible* (Milwaukee: Bruce Publishing, 1965), pp. 694ff.

8) The discussion of the role of the prophet by Hans Kung in his more general discussion of the ministries within the Church is most helpful (Kung, *The Church*, pp. 388-411). See also the note accompanying Acts 11:27 in Alexander Jones et al., *The Jerusalem Bible* (Garden City, N.Y.: Doubleday, 1966).

9) Earl S. Johnson, "The Human Dimensions of Supervision," *Supervision: Emerging Profession* (Washington, D.C.: ASCD, Association for Supervision and Development, NEA 1969), p. 119.

10) Drucker, *Effective Executive*, p. 71.

11) Walter M. Abbot, ed., *Vatican Council II, Decree on the Missionary Activity of the Church, The Documents of Vatican II*, (New York: Guild Press, 1966), paragraph 21.

12) Abbott, *Constitution*, paragraph 25.

Chapter Five

WORKING WITH
THE BOARD OF EDUCATION

Catholic people have always been involved in some measure with Catholic education. Parishioners have sacrificed for years to build Churches and schools in which Catholic education could occur. Parents have centered their lives around the workings of the parochial school or have planned their weeks to include the religious education program. A limited number of parishioners have been more intensely involved in one or another phase of the parish educational program. Some parents work closely with the school athletics; others teach in the CCD Program; still others help with a variety of tasks: involvement is not new. Participation in the decision-making processes regarding parish education, however, is a recent development in Catholic education.

CCD EXECUTIVE BOARDS

The goal, "every child in a Catholic school," has never been attained. Well over half of the Catholic parishes in the country do not have a parochial school. In parishes with schools, the school seldom enrolls more than fifty to sixty percent of the total youth potential. Thus, parents have relied on the Confraternity of Christian Doctrine (CCD) to provide opportunities in religious education for the majority of the Catholic youth of the country.

The CCD was organized in Milan, Italy in 1560, and became one of the few Church organizations that must be established in each parish by Church Law. In 1902, the CCD was introduced in the United States as an organization by Bishop M.S. Corrigan and it has since spread rapidly to nearly every Catholic parish in the country(1).

The CCD has always relied upon time and talent volunteered by the people of the parish. Organizationally, it has followed the format and implicit goals embodied in the various manuals which have been produced by the National CCD Center, and to a greater or lesser degree endorsed by the Bishops of the country. Throughout the late 1950's and during the '60's, the organizational design has called for the establishment of a CCD Executive Board. This Board was to be composed of the chairmen of the various groups organized for specific programs — Fishers, Helpers, Teachers, etc. In effect, therefore, it served as a planning committee or ad hoc action committee rather than a policy board which would establish goals and directions for the parish program. These were implicit in the CCD Manual or were to be found in program designs emanating from the diocesan CCD Office.

Some original programming arose out of these

Boards and in a few parishes they actually achieved the *de facto* status of Boards of Education. A few even evolved into parish councils. In general, however, the CCD Executive Boards met with frustration and anxiety for they seldom had the complete support of the pastor and were frequently in direct competition with the school efforts of the parish where a parochial school existed. Hence, they had to operate with marginal human and material resources and were viewed as temporary measures needed until a Catholic school could be established. It is no wonder the Greeley-Rossi Study on Catholic education could note: "At their present level of success, not only are CCD classes not a functional alternative to Catholic schools, they do not seem to accomplish very much at all"(2).

To its credit the parish CCD organization, relying upon volunteer time and talent, has kept alive and demonstrated again and again the responsibility of the whole parish community to be involved in preaching the Word.

PARISH SCHOOL BOARDS

Since 1965, the National Catholic Education Association has been active in promoting parish and diocesan boards of Education. The NCEA notes that there were some 4,000 parish Boards in 1968, with a forty percent increase expected in 1969(3). These efforts have been spearheaded largely by the Superintendents Committee on Policy and Administration, led especially by the late Rt. Rev. Msgr. O'Neil C. D'Amour. Msgr. D'Amour believed strongly in Catholic schools and the role of the school in contributing to the reconstruction of a new American society. He saw the Vatican Council's Declaration on Christian Education as a mandate for renewed efforts to achieve the goal of all Catholic youth in a Catholic school for at least part of their educational process.

The logical conclusion from the principles promoted by Msgr. D'Amour, which are to a large extent incorporated in the thinking of the NCEA's movement toward Boards of Education, would be the following:

1) The Bishop has the chief responsibility for Catholic education within a diocese. He, in turn, delegates this full responsibility to a diocesan Board of Education (Msgr. D'Amour ideally did not wish to see the Bishop have a veto over the diocesan Board of Education's work).

2) The diocesan Board of Education would organize the parochial schools into a diocesan system, run by the Board and the School Office. Parish and regional Boards of Education would be extensions of the diocesan Board of Education, for their chief responsibility was implementing, at the local level, the policies of the diocesan Board. This would even extend to separating school property from the parish.

3) The diocesan board and parish Boards would have full jurisdictional control over the educational program in Catholic schools, catechetical centers and other formal religious education courses. As indicated in the suggested Constitution for a Diocesan Board of Education, "all decisions of the Board of Education shall be binding upon the Superintendent of Education, the Office of Education, all subordinate Boards of Education and the pastors, principals, and staffs of the schools and catechetical programs within the diocesan system"(4). This view of religious education makes it an extension of the school model in catechetical centers and with formal classes.

4) As a separate corporation, much like the Canadian separate school system, the diocesan Board of Education and its subsidiary regional and parish boards

and the educational system which it controls would be receptive to governmental and private assistance, especially since these Boards would be composed of representatives of family, Church, and state; that is, persons representing the people or parents, the priest, religious, and representatives from the public sector.

5) Lastly, Msgr. D'Amour and the Superintendents' Committee strongly insisted that Catholic schools become *the model* of Catholic education. "They (the Fathers of Vatican II) not only accepted the Catholic school but in strong language insisted that every effort be made to provide Catholic schools at the elementary and secondary levels for all children throughout the Catholic world"(5).

This general philosophy puts the Board movement as an extension of the Bishop (pastor) into a representative style of organization. It also separates the educational work of the Church from the Pastoral Mission, since ideally (and in practice, if government aid is to come) the parish or diocesan Pastoral Council does not have a veto over the actions of the Board of Education. The government cannot give aid to parochial schools when the Bishop can veto the basic goals, policies, and directions which those schools take; that is, as long as the schools are Church controlled, for then aid is truly aid to a Church.

This is a basic inconsistency in the thought of Msgr. D'Amour. While on the one hand, giving the Bishop absolute responsibility for Catholic education within the diocese, he delegates it completely to a diocesan Board of Education which functions autonomously from the Bishop.

To simplify the movement concerning Boards of Education in the United States at the present time in history, it might be said that there are two trends headed on a collision course. On the one hand, coming out of the CCD background, there are people who see Boards of Education as an embodiment of the responsibility of the whole community for preaching the Word. They see these Boards of Education as a community of people who seek to answer the pastoral question: What shall the Church accomplish in education at the parish, regional and diocesan levels — in that order? On the other hand, coming out of a school tradition, leaders see Boards as an extension of the responsibility of the Bishop for education, beginning with the diocesan Board and delegated to the regional and parish Boards. The Coordinator movement is caught in the middle between these two directional thrusts. Some coordinators believe strongly in working with Boards; others prefer to work with the Parish Council, and still others would prefer to work with just a cooperative pastor or as part of the pastoral team. Ideally, however, the coordinator is an agent of the Board and people, not of the pastor.

PARISH BOARD OF EDUCATION

As discussed earlier, the *whole* Christian community is charged with the responsibility of proclaiming the Word of God, of celebrating in Liturgy and of ministering to the needs of one another and of mankind. This is termed the Pastoral Mission of the Church. Since the Church is the believing people whose lives are animated by the Spirit of Jesus and who live within a given cultural context (time and space), this Pastoral Mission must always be evolved in terms of the present with a vision of the future and with the perspective of the past. This Pastoral Mission is the responsibility of the Church at all levels. As the theology of the local Church develops, we will see more how the local faith community is proportionately the whole Church and has a local Pastoral

Mission which, of course, must be in harmony with the Pastoral Mission of the larger faith community in a diocese, the Pastoral Mission of the national Church and of the international Church(6).

Catholic education, that is, the educational mission of Christian people, has no reason for existence apart from the general educational work of man himself in the public sector save as it relates to the Pastoral Mission of the faith community (Church). To look at it a different way, the only reason for bringing education and religion together lies within a broader reason for the existence and mission of religion itself. Christian people are different from other people precisely in their belief. They believe in the Spirit of Jesus and this belief carries with it a mission. Catholic education as the educational aspect of that larger mission exists for a purpose and is contained in the broader Pastoral Mission of the whole faith community in any given decade or place.

The Pastoral Mission of the faith community at the local and Diocesan levels is determined by the dynamic interaction between people and Bishop or their extensions. The Parish Council is the organizational extension of the larger community of people. In a formal way, it translates the responsibility for education, liturgy, and social mission into practical terms in that given parish. The Board of Education is that group of people who, in a communal fashion, determine the educational mission of that parish. This is their primary concern. How the educational mission relates to the liturgical aspect and the social action aspect of the parish is determined in the interaction between the committees or commissions representing those concerns and the **Board of Education by the Parish Council** (see Chart 4:1). Hence, the parish Board of Education is an extension of the people of the parish and not of the Bishop through the pastor or the diocesan Board of Education.

Responsibility (Constitution) of Parish Boards This general philosophical difference about Boards of Education (the CCD tradition versus the school tradition) can clearly be seen when the responsibility of the parish Board of Education and its relationship to the diocese is spelled out in a Constitution. Chart 5:1 presents a suggested Constitution and by-laws for a parish Board of Education adopted by the NCEA and published in

CHART 5:1   *PARISH ORGANIZATION*

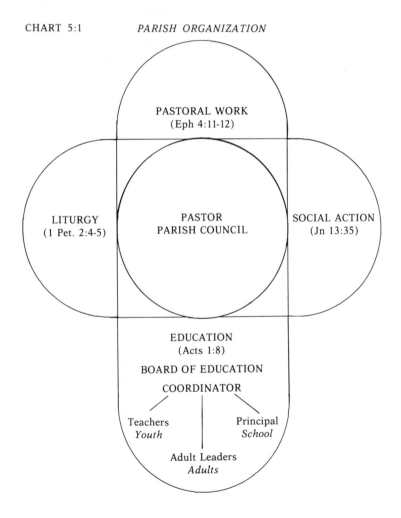

CHART 5:2

NCEA MODEL
SUGGESTED CONSTITUTION AND BYLAWS FOR A PARISH BOARD OF EDUCATION
("Voice of the Community" NCEA, used by permission)

ARTICLE I
Title

The name of this body shall be _____ Parish Board of Education.

ARTICLE II
Nature and Function

Section 1. This Board is a regulatory body operating educational programs at _____, subject to such regulations that proceed from the Diocesan Board of Education.

Section 2. Duties and Functions. The Parish Board of Education shall be responsible for all aspects of the formal educational program of the parish, schooling, catechetical and adult. In the development of its policies, it must insure that these follow the intent and spirit of the policies laid down for the Diocesan system by the Diocesan Board of Education. It shall have as a most important duty implementing at the local level the policies of the Diocesan Board of Education. A partial list of other duties and functions follows.

1. The coordinating of parochial educational activities.
2. Acting as a liaison body with appropriate public authority.
3. Seeking a better understanding and wider support of Catholic education within the local community.
4. Interpreting policies of the Diocesan Board for the local administrative officers and in matters wherein the Diocesan Board has not promulgated policies, creating such policies under which administration shall operate.
5. Having responsibility for determining whether policies are being carried out according to the will of the Diocesan Board.
6. Having responsibility for evaluating the adequacy of its policies and the effectiveness of their implementation.

7. Determining local policies relating to the planning, operating and maintenance of facilities and equipment.
8. Being responsible for the approval of the annual budget and for securing adherence to the budget.
9. Being responsible for such fiscal matters as are not determined by the Diocesan Board of Education.
10. Serving as a local committee in the planning and building of new educational facilities.
11. Retaining personnel according to defined policy.
12. Having responsibility locally for approving the educational aspects of new facilities.

ARTICLE III
Membership

Section 1. a. Members of the Parish Board of Education shall be the pastor (ex officio) and ____ elected representatives.

b. This Parish Board shall have a single executive officer responsible to the Board for carrying out its policies and responsible administratively to the Diocesan Superintendent of Education. This officer shall not be considered a member of the Board.

Section 2. Each lay member shall serve a term of three years, with the exception that the original members shall serve terms varying from one to three years with approximately one-third serving a one-year term, one-third a two-year term, and one-third a three-year term, to be determined by lot or other means.

Section 3. Nominations for new members shall take place before the May meeting of the Board and elections shall be held before the June meeting. Terms shall expire June 30 each year.

ARTICLE IV
Officers

Section 1. The officers of the Board shall consist of President, Vice-President and Secretary-Treasurer, all of whom shall be elected annually by the Board membership at the first regular meeting of July.

Section 2. All members of the Board are eligible for any office.

Section 3. The duties of the officers shall be as follows:

1. The President shall preside at all regular and special meetings of the Board.
2. The Vice-President shall perform all the duties of the President when he is absent or unable to act.
3. The Secretary-Treasurer shall maintain a written record of all acts of the Board; conduct, receive, and dispose of all correspondence as directed; preserve all reports and documents committed to his care; and maintain a record of all financial transactions which are proper to the Board.

ARTICLE V
Meetings

Section 1. The Board shall meet regularly on the ____ day of the ____ week of the month at a publicly designated room. Special meetings may be called by the President as needed or by a majority of the members.

Section 2. Quorum. For the purpose of transacting official business, it shall be necessary that a majority of the total members be present and voting.

Section 3. A simple majority of those present and voting shall carry the motion unless otherwise specified in the constitution.

Section 4. All meetings of the Board are to be open meetings unless designated as being Executive. Decisions made in Executive sessions must be presented and voted on at open sessions before becoming effective. The right of non-members to address the Board shall be limited to those whose petition has been approved for the agenda in advance of the meeting.

Section 5. A written record of all acts of the Board, maintained by the Secretary, shall be preserved in the archives.

ARTICLE VI
Conduct of Meetings

Section 1. The rule of parliamentary procedure as contained in Robert's "Rules of Order" shall govern meetings of the Board.

Section 2. The ordinary order of meetings shall be:

1. Prayer
2. Calling of Role
3. Approval of Minutes
4. Administrator's Report
5. Unfinished Business
6. Reports of Committee
7. Approval of Reports
8. Communications and Petitions
9. New Business
10. Adjournment
11. Prayer

ARTICLE VII
Amendments

Section 1. This constitution may be amended by a vote of two-thirds of the total membership subject only to regulations of the Diocesan Board of Education.

Section 2. Amendments must be presented to the Board at least two weeks prior to voting on such.

Section 3. By-laws may be amended by a vote of one more than a simple majority of the members present at any regular meeting, providing there is a quorum and providing the amendment has been presented at the previous meeting of the Board.

CHART 5:3

RELIGIOUS EDUCATION MODEL
CONSTITUTION FOR PARISH BOARDS OF EDUCATION

PREAMBLE

The people of God of _____, recognizing the dedication and sacrifices made by our predecessors under the guidance of wise and zealous clergy since the beginning of this Parish in _____, (and recognizing the unending labors of the Sisters of _____, in the educational program of this Parish beginning with the establishment of the School in _____) do hereby establish this Board of Education in order to continue that work of facilitating growth in faith and Christian life through quality Christian Education.

ARTICLE I
Title

The Title of this body shall be THE_____BOARD OF EDUCATION.

ARTICLE II
Nature and Function

Section 1: This Board of Education is a regulatory body having jurisdiction over the Christian Education Program of _____ Parish. It is charged with providing quality Christian Education opportunities, both religious and secular for the youth and adults of the Parish Community.

Section 2: In fulfilling this charge, this Board of Education shall be limited only by the policies of the Parish Council and/or the Pastor (in the absence of a Parish Council) and the Diocesan Board of Education in the manner prescribed in this Constitution.

Section 3: The function of this Board shall be:
1. To establish the objectives of Christian Education for this Parish Community.
2. To establish policies for the educational programs designed to achieve those objectives.
3. To provide the necessary resources to implement those objectives and policies, i.e. professional staff, educational facilities, budget and instructional materials.
4. To evaluate the effectiveness of the Parish Program for Christian education.

Section 4: In executing these functions, the Board of Education shall seek to meet the educational needs of the Parish Community and the community at large and to augment the goals and policies of the Parish Council and the Diocesan Board of Education.

Section 5: The Board of Education shall submit to the Parish Council (or Pastor, in his absence) for approval its yearly goals, policies, program and budget. In the event that these are not in harmony with the total goals of the parish, it shall be the responsibility of the Parish Council (or Pastor) to veto them and to explain in writing where the discrepancies lie.

Section 6: This Board of Education shall submit its annual goals, policies, program and budget to the Diocesan Office of Education. In the event that these are not in harmony with the goals and policies of the Diocesan Board of Education, it shall be the responsibility of the Diocesan Office of Education to present to the Parish Board of Education and the Parish Council (or Pastor, in its absence) a written report of where the discrepancies lie, along with recommendations for bringing them into harmony.

ARTICLE III
Membership

Section 1: The Board of Education shall be composed of ___members. These members shall be elected by the Parish Community and shall serve in the manner prescribed by the Guidelines of this Board of Education.

Section 2: The Pastor and the President of the Parish Council (should he be other than the Pastor) shall be Ex-Officio, non-voting members of this Board of Education.

ARTICLE IV
Officers

Section 1: The Officers of the Board shall consist of President, Vice-President and Secretary-Treasurer, all of whom shall be elected annually by the Board membership at the first regular meeting of July.

Section 2: All members of the Board are eligible for any office.

Section 3: The duties of the officers shall be as follows:
1. The President shall preside at all regular and special meetings of the Board.
2. The Vice-President shall perform all the duties of the President when he is absent or unable to act.

3. The Secretary-Treasurer shall maintain a written record of all acts of the Board; conduct, receive and dispose of all correspondence as directed; preserve all reports and documents committed to his care; and maintain a record of all financial transactions which are proper to the Board.

Section 4: The Board of Education shall have an executive officer responsible to the Board for the administration of the educational program of the Parish. This officer shall not be a member of the Board.

This officer shall provide the Board with the necessary assistance in performing its function as described in Article II.

ARTICLE V
Operations of the Board

Section 1: The operation of this Board of Education regarding such matters as its meetings, conduct of business, etc., shall be prescribed in the Board's Guidelines. These Guidelines shall be presented by the Board to the voting community of the parish on a yearly basis for approval. They shall be approved by a simple majority of the voting community.

Section 2: Any member (registered) eighteen (18) years of age or over shall be considered a voting member of the Parish Community, and shall be eligible also for membership on the Board of Education.

Section 3: This constitution may be amended by a vote of two-thirds (2/3) of the Parish Community. The manner of presenting and voting on such amendment shall be determined in the Board's Guidelines.

ARTICLE VI
Conclusion

Section 1: The existence of this Board of Education bears tribute to the concern of the People of God of _____ Parish for providing opportunities for quality Christian Education for the parish community.

In its work, this Board of Education and the Parish Community shall be mindful of the following:

1. That every Christian is entitled to a Christian education in order that "he may grow daily more conscious of the gift of faith

which he has received; that he may learn to adore God the Father in Spirit and in Truth, especially through liturgical worship; that he may be trained to conduct his personal life in righteousness and in the sanctity of truth according to his new standard of manhood (EPH. 4:22-24): (Vatican II: Declaration on Christian Education.)

2. That parents are primarily responsible for the education of their children and thus the opportunities provided by this Board are designed merely to facilitate that role of the parent.

3. "By their Baptism, all Christians participate in the apostolate or mission work of the Church. It is therefore obvious that those who supervise Christian education are also bound to offer training for the apostolate." (Vatican II: Decree of the Apostolate of the Laity)

Thus, this Board and this Parish Community shall be mindful of the total mission of the Church in fulfilling its role in developing its policies seeking to contribute through education to building the earth and the brotherhood of man.

In all we ask the guidance of the Holy Spirit that our efforts may fulfill the mission of Christ Our Lord in the service of our Eternal Father.

the Report of the Superintendents' Committee on Policy and Administration in 1967. Chart 5:2 presents a different model designed to articulate the CCD tradition in Constitution form.

The differences are clearly evident in Article II which in both cases speaks of the nature and function of the parish Board of Education. The NCEA model gives the parish board responsibility for all formal education of the parish, stressing especially school and terming the rest catechetical or adult. It specifically charges the parish Board to implement the policies laid down by the Diocesan Board for the "Diocesan system." The other duties which pertain to the local problems are secondary in nature and the majority of them could be handled by an efficient principal working in close harmony with the diocesan School Office and the diocesan Board of Education.

The religious education model, on the other hand, gives the parish Board of Education full responsibility for all education within that parish, terming it directly as Christian education, both religious and secular. The Board's responsibility is limited only by the Parish Council and the diocesan Board of Education. As indicated in Section 6, the parish Board would submit its annual goals, policies, program and budget to the Diocesan Office, which would then see if these are in harmony with the directional goals and policies set by the diocesan Board of Education. If they are not in harmony, the Diocesan Office would point out the discrepancies to the Parish Board and make recommendations for bringing them into harmony with the diocesan thrust. The decision as to whether or not to accept these recommendations is left with the parish Board of Education.

To take a practical example, following the NCEA model Constitution for parish Boards of Education, the decision to open or close a Catholic school rests with the diocesan Board. Following the religious education model, that decision rests with the local parish Board of Education and not with the diocesan Board. The diocesan Board may make policies regarding the standards which schools should meet, but the local Church, through its Board of Education, following the religious education constitution could take exception to these and continue to maintain its own school.

Other important differences can be seen between these two constitutions. The NCEA model constitution does not give the pastor or the Parish Council a veto over its decisions. The religious education model constitution does. It indicates in Article II, Section 5 that the parish Board of Education shall submit to the Parish

Council (or pastor in its absence) its yearly goals, policies, programs, and budget for approval. The Parish Council then has the responsibility to see that these are in harmony with the total efforts of the parish and to set parish priorities, taking into consideration the proposals from those representing the liturgy aspects of the parish and those representing social action concerns. The NCEA model limits the actions of the parish Board in Article II, Section 2 by placing it directly under the diocesan Board of Education.

An additional difference is extremely important to parish coordinators. The NCEA model constitution calls for a single executive officer, responsible to the Board for carrying out its policies. This could be the school principal or the parish coordinator, depending upon local policies in this regard. In parishes without a school, it would obviously be the coordinator. In parishes with a school, that decision must be made as to whether the principal or the parish coordinator becomes the executive officer of the Board. In either case, following the NCEA model constitution, that person is also responsible administratively to the diocesan Superintendent of Education (schools). The religious education model constitution calls for a single executive officer also—the parish coordinator—who is responsible to the parish Board of Education for executing the educational program of that parish. In this latter case, the coordinator is not responsible administratively to the Diocesan Office. The Diocesan Office would offer service, guidelines, suggestions, and assistance to the coordinator, but these need not be accepted by the coordinator as the coordinator answers solely to the parish Board of Education.

One other difference can be seen between these two model constitutions. The religious education model places many details that are contained in the NCEA model into guidelines to accompany the constitution.

These guidelines can be written out for local circumstances and do not carry the same weight as the constitution itself. Details like how the meeting shall be run, when and where they shall meet, the keeping of written records, etc., are better handled by the local parish and should not be part of a model constitution.

Strengths of Boards of Education The Board of Education movement is not a luxury. It has many pros and cons but the need for the people of the parish to be involved in the decision making relative to the future of education in that parish is an essential need today that cannot be by-passed. Some of the strengths of Boards would include the following:

1) The Board represents the people. This is perhaps the chief strength of the parish Board of Education. Since it is composed of representatives of the people, this Board can represent the educational needs of that parish. In effect, the Board becomes the parish in microcosm. The coordinator and the pastor may wish to make progress quicker since they can see the direction in which education ought to move. However, if they cannot convince the Board of the validity of that direction, then chances are they will never convince the whole parish either. Coordinators are often fearful of working with Boards that have come out of a school tradition, for the majority of the Board members will think of all education in terms of schools. If the coordinator can change the thinking of the members of the Board from a totally school-oriented perspective to a broader approach to parish education, chances are the coordinator also is in the process of changing the mentality of the whole parish.

2) The Board of Education broadens the base of concern and involvement. Since the Board is representa-

tive of the parish, the kinds of concerns which the Board members share at meetings are carried back to other members of the parish. Hence, the base of support and concern regarding the educational mission is broadened. Instead of a few people attempting to work out a program and interest, the Board becomes a form of communication and a frame of reference for program planning.

3) By the act of choosing the Board participates in the act of learning. The Board of Education in choosing between alternatives presented to it by its executive officer (principal or coordinator) is engaging in one of the most significant forms of education—the act of choosing is the act of learning. Choosing between alternatives and the rationales connected with these informs the Board members about the nature of Church, religious education, parish, the times, youth, adults, and so forth. Because the Board represents the people of the parish and is a form of communication, working with the Board is adult education of a very significant form.

4) The Board provides continuity. The Board of Education provides continuity in ideas and direction for that faith community. The coordinator and the pastor may be changed, and at the present time with the CCD Programs, when a new pastor arrives, a whole new program is launched. With a Board, a new pastor or a new coordinator would provide new ideas, direction, and insight, but these would always be integrated into the educational work which has evolved within the parish rather than be totally new and unconnected.

5) The Board provides a forum for educational beliefs. The parish Board representing the educational mission of that particular group of people can, with the pastor and the coordinator, articulate the implications of their mission both within the faith community (now-already eschatology) and within the larger com-

munity (yet-to-be-realized eschatology). This is especially true for public school curriculums like sex education, value education, and religious studies.

Weaknesses of Parish Boards of Education There are also many weaknesses inherent in a Board of Education. These would include the following:

1) Boards are slow. Parish Boards, like boards anywhere, are a slow means to achieving action. When one person is in charge of an activity, action can be implemented quickly. When it must be approved by a Board, debate, reflection, and study are necessary before action is taken. This sometimes is a blessing in that hasty action can be prevented, but more often than not, it is one of the drawbacks of parish Boards of Education.

2) Boards seldom innovate. Another weakness of a parish Board of Education is that like so many corporate groups the Board will seldom be an innovator for programming. Generally speaking, however, it is the responsibility of the coordinator to assist the Board in choosing alternatives; this allows the coordinator to present innovative choices. Boards typically, however, are slow to innovate and are more apt to conserve the past by following precedents.

3) Boards compromise action. With the style of operation that accompanies a Board, good ideas and programs are frequently amended, changed, or altered in such a fashion as to become a compromise action. It is a wise Board that can grapple with plurality and uniqueness of ideas without tempering them according to its own predispositions. Generally speaking, Boards will amend and alter original proposals to such an extent that they often come out vastly different from what was originally proposed.

4) Boards have no legal base. One of the chief weak-

nesses of parish Boards of Education whether they follow the NCEA model or the religious education model is that they lack any genuine identity in law. This can be seen both as a weakness and a strength, but most frequently it is viewed as a weakness. The parish is a legal corporation through the Bishop. This is why the pastor as a representative of the Bishop must sign legal documents. The Board of Education does not have a similar legal identity. Hence, its decisions have no binding force within the community. Boards are in effect, therefore, a consensus body; a group which tries to articulate the opinions of the larger group it serves and bring these into some harmony and focus. It can enforce nothing except by persuasion. By way of contrast, public Boards of Education can use legal action to enforce decisions, when necessary. Even within the Canon Law of the Church, parish Boards of Education have no legal existence at present.

RESPONSIBILITIES OF BOARDS OF EDUCATION:

The general responsibility of the parish Board of Education, following the religious education model (Chart 5:2), is to provide quality Christian education opportunities, both secular and religious, for the youth and adults of the given faith community. To say it using other language, in this conception, the parish Board of Education recognizes that the parents have a formal authority for the education of their children and that adults have the responsibility for continuing their own education. The Board of Education, representing the whole community, assists parents in exercising their formal authority and adults in fulfilling their responsibility.

Following the philosophy articulated above concerning the religious education model constitution, parents could refuse to cooperate with the parish in the Christian education of their children just as the parish could refuse to cooperate with the diocese. Faith is always an act of choice. The parish community, however, like the diocesan community, has a responsibility to point out to parents their responsibility and to show ways in which it can be met. Thus, the parish Board of Education has a responsibility to provide opportunities for quality Christian education. Whether or not these opportunities are utilized is the decision of the parents or individual adult. This general responsibility of the parish Board can be seen more clearly in looking at the specific duties which it fulfills.

Develop Goals and Policies The chief way in which the Board of Education fulfills its responsibility is through the development of goals and policies which govern the educational work of the people concerned with the educational mission of the parish; namely, the coordinator, the principal, the teachers, and so forth. Obviously, the Board usually does not sit down and work out the goals itself. In the process of setting goals, the Board considers an analysis of the local situation plus a conceptualization of the direction or nature of religious education. Out of the interaction of these two is evolved a specific goal which ought to be achieved by that parish in its educational mission. The coordinator as the executive officer of the Board assists the Board both in the situation analysis and in understanding the conceptualization or the aim of religious education. He presents to the Board, therefore, appropriate goals for adoption for the educational mission of the parish, and policies which flow from these.

At this point in history, when a Board of Education comes into existence in a parish, it already inherits a

certain number of implied goals and policies. It is important that, with the help of the coordinator, the Board
think these through and articulate them more clearly
in definite goals statements and policies. By this process,
the Board will come to a realization of where it is; that
is, of the past out of which it has come. It is important
to realize its present position before carving out a future
for the educational mission of the parish.

Part of the way in which the Board carves out a
direction for the educational mission of a parish is the
establishment of *goals*. A goal simply states "we ought
to move in this direction" or "we ought to strive for
this accomplishment." Boards are familiar with the
idea of a policy regulating certain practice; for example,
a school Board will establish a policy that there should
not be more than thirty children in a classroom. The
goal toward which this policy is aimed is left implicit.
In this case the goal would be to "establish a teacher-
student ratio most conducive to learning" or something
similar to that. Goals, in other words, provide the rationale for policy. They say why a given regulation is
established. Since parish Boards of Education are non-
jurisdictional, that is, have no legal base, it is especially
important that they state the educational mission which
they wish all of the members of the parish to attain in
terms of goals. Sometimes, simply stating the goal a-
chieves a certain kind of movement because the members
of the parish know that is the direction in which their
educational mission can be fulfilled. Formal and informal
groups alike can align themselves with that goal without
even the force of a policy being necessary.

Goals ought to be well worded and concise. They
can be started with an introduction, stated briefly, and
then references given as needed. Usually in the statement of goals, references to writings such as the Declara-

tion on Christian Education or the Constitution on the Church or the Scriptures themselves are incorporated to show in what way this goal is an aspect of the educational mission of Christian people. As a general rule, it might be appropriate to state that policies should never be established by a parish Board without first an identification of the goal toward which those policies are directed. Even in situations of crises in which implicit goals are already operative, if the Board strove to sort out its own purpose for a policy that is being proposed, that is, the goal, the policy would be given a clearer perspective and might be more effective than if it were simply stated on its own.

Policies are regulatory and must be implemented by the personnel under the jurisdiction of the Board of Education. As indicated above, policies should be tied in with goals. The reverse is not necessarily true; the parish Board may establish a goal and leave the policy area open until difficulties arise in moving toward that goal. In time of difficulty specific policies can be established which will remove whatever is impeding movement toward the attainment of that goal. Goals simply call attention to the "why," policies regulate the "how." Both ought to be formulated with care but, in particular, policies should not be formulated until necessary as they tend to provide a precedent for action and for later Board members which is often difficult to overcome.

In the place of actual regulatory policies which must be implemented by the coordinator, teachers, and others, under the auspices of the parish Board of Education, *policy statements* could be prepared at the same time as the adoption of a specific educational goal. The policy statement would simply attempt to show in more concrete form how the educational goal will be achieved. Policy statements, in effect, are a prelude to the actual adoption of a policy itself. A goal might be established by a parish Board regarding sex education for the children and adolescents within the parish. The simple establishment of this goal calls attention to the fact of this need. The communication of this educational goal to the whole parish community can set in motion a variety of efforts toward the achievement of that goal. Without an actual mandate, various organizations within the parish sensing the need for sex education, as highlighted by the Board of Education's recently adopted goal, may undertake informal programs to do their part. In addition to the adoption of the educational goal, the Board could attach a policy statement. This policy statement would indicate that the parents ought to be involved in any sex education programs for children or adolescents where appropriate, that any materials used by the educational programs should not offend the local mores and that the Christian perspective on the value of love and its implications in sexual behavior should be clearly emphasized. A policy statement something like this sets the tone for the educational work but does not force it into a given mold before the most effective ways of achieving the goal can be evolved. Later, after the educational personnel of the parish have had experience in working toward that goal, the need for regulatory policies may arise and at that time they can be adopted.

Structure Educational Organization and Board Operations A second area in which the Board of Education works deals with the structuring of the educational organization needed to achieve the goals which the Board establishes for that given faith community and the internal workings of the Board itself.

The Board of Education in the Church has come into existence with an educational organization already present; namely, the school and/or the CCD Program. In this case, the responsibility of the Board is to do the re-structuring necessary to bring the present organizations into effective harmony with the achievement of the educational mission of that parish. Frequently, there is conflict and competition between those working within the school and those in the CCD Program. It is the responsibility of the Board to minimize this conflict and to bring about cooperation. Schools and religious education programs are generally hamstrung by archaic organization. The Board, therefore, should re-structure these organizations so that they are responsive to the educational needs of the parish and effective in the achievement of the parish's educational mission.

In the same fashion, the Board sets its own style of operation. Following the religious education model constitution presented here, the Board would establish — with assistance perhaps from the Diocesan Office or a coordinator — guidelines for its own operation. These guidelines would include when the Board will meet, where, the number of Board members necessary for business, the officers of the Board, and similar details. In some places there will be diocesan guidelines; the Board, in that case, need not create all of these.

Generally, the Board can facilitate its own movement through the passage of *resolutions*. A Board member may resolve, for example, that the Board contact a lawyer to get an opinion on some of its actions or perhaps contact an accountant for advice on financial matters. The resolution is then voted on in parliamentary fashion and, if passed, simply becomes a guideline for the operation of the Board's action — a guideline which either the President of the Board or the coordinator will implement. Resolutions simply handle the business of the Board in consensus fashion where consensus is needed.

Secure Top Education Staff and Provide Compensation It is also the responsibility of the Board to secure the chief executive officer. In the religious education model, he would be the parish coordinator (it could also mean the school principal). The coordinator (or the principal) secures subsidiary staff personnel and sets salary schedules for such personnel, but it is the responsibility of the Board itself to secure the top person and to determine his salary.

With the modernization of religious communities, this principle also applies to brothers and sisters as well as lay personnel. In the very near future, a parish will not ask a religious community to send "a sister" or "a brother" but will specify a particular person whom that Board wishes to hire. The contract will be with that person as parish coordinator rather than with the community that sent him. As this trend develops, Boards will be fulfilling their responsibility of securing the top executive officer. The procedures described in Chapter 2 regarding the securing of a coordinator are the practical ways in which this responsibility of the Board is implemented.

Approve Program Design and Budget The most important responsibility felt by the Board of Education is approving the educational program design with its accompanying budget and providing the necessary resources to implement it. The coordinator presents a projected program for children, youth, and adults for a given year (see Chapter 6). The Board discusses this program in light of its understandings of the parish and its knowledge of what is possible, asks for alternatives or corrections, and eventually approves the projection with budget. If this program and budget is not vetoed by the Parish Council (and/or the pastor) it then becomes the working mandate for the coordinator for the given year. The Board also has to provide the necessary resources to implement that program and budget. This may mean, in practice, that the Board discusses with the Parish Council and/or the pastor the needed funds or establishes committees to raise the same through a variety of means.

Establish Board Relationships and Representatives
An additional practical responsibility of the Board is to establish relationships between itself and other groups; namely, community organizations, diocesan groups, other parishes, other churches, and the like. The Board would send as many representatives to meetings as needed to keep informed and to represent its point of view. In a given diocese, the Board may send a representative to a regional Board and/or to a diocesan committee. It further may appoint a representative to the local school Board within the community or a representative to the Council of Churches Education group. The number of these relationships and the need for a representative is a decision for the Board to make in consultation with its chief executive officer.

Relate to Whole Parish Community   The chief duty of the Board is always to the whole parish community. The coordinator has a responsibility to assist the Board with "public relations" or with the process of communication to the whole parish. But it is the Board's own responsibility and not the coordinator's to see that such communications occur. This communication can occur in many ways. The Board may write a special letter to the parish, distributed at Sunday Liturgy or by direct mail. The Board can actively recruit participation at meetings; the Board can issue a newsletter through the educational program or school and so forth. The extent of interest in the election of the Board members is a good measurement of the effectiveness of the communication between the Board and parish. If the parish community as a whole shares the concerns of education with which the Board grapples, then there will be interest on the part of the community in who are members of the Board. On the other hand, if the Board has a difficult time in generating attendance at meetings and in generating interest in the election, this is a sign that the chief problem to be solved before any of the above responsibilities can adequately be carried out is to re-establish representation and communication.

RESPONSIBILITIES OF THE BOARD MEMBERS:

In addition to speaking of the responsibilities of the Board of Education as a whole, it is helpful to talk about the responsibilities of the individual Board member. In general, he shares all of those mentioned, but they can be viewed in a more particular way by looking at how each Board member would operate in reference to the actions of the Board.

Represent the Community Like the Board as a whole, the chief responsibility of the individual Board member is to truly represent the larger parish community. Even if the Board member is at first appointed, he or she has a responsibility to seek out community opinions on the educational efforts of that parish. This is generally done quite informally by the Board member talking over things with his immediate friends. But if the Board member does not find himself reaching out to a larger group of people to gather opinions and reactions, then he can be sure he is not completely fulfilling his responsibility to adequately represent the community.

Be Prepared   When coming to the meetings, each Board member ought to be adequately prepared. The Board member should read over all of the data pertaining to the action items to be voted on at that particular meeting and should know what the issues are. Then he should seek out the opinion of the people around him whom he is attempting to represent, asking their opinions about the various alternatives or issues under consideration. When coming to the meeting, therefore, the Board member is ready to vote on the action items. He has a general consensus in mind and unless the other Board members can present significant information or opinions, the Board member knows how he will vote before the meeting. This does not mean that he cannot change his mind. It simply means that he is prepared on the issue before the meeting begins and is not apt to be swayed by a momentary feeling and to vote without reason.

Ask Discerning Questions   The chief tool of the Board member is a discerning question. Frequently, Board members complain that they are not experts on education. This is their chief advantage and not a disadvantage. Because the Board member is not an expert on education, he must rely upon the expertise of the executive officer, the coordinator, to answer the questions and to give reasons why things should be done. It is the responsibility of the coordinator to convince the Board member of the validity of actions proposed. The Board member need not have a knowledge of religious education. Frequently coordinators wish that the Board members would go to summer school or read certain magazines in order to become informed on what ought to happen in the parish religious education program. This is a fallacy. Each Board member has a native intelligence, a knowledge of the local community, and faith. The Board member should rely upon these and use questions to the executive officer or other Board members to pull out the wisdom of the actions under consideration. If a jury of citizens can decide the life or death of an accused man, certainly members of a faith community can decide the wisdom in an educational program.

Vote on Convictions The Board member has a responsibility to vote on conviction, that is, to vote on his judgement regarding the opinions of the persons whom he represents and the wisdom of the actions proposed by other Board members or the coordinator. Too frequently the Board attempts to arrive at a consensus and vote unanimously on actions and, in practice, this becomes a matter of reducing the action to the lowest common denominator or mediocrity. Consensus is frequently good but the main consensus should be that the Board intends to vote for what is best for that faith community. There will be differences of opinion by Board members about how this goal is to be translated into specific practice and programs. If there is not a difference of opinion, there is perhaps a lack of ideas. Given the present problems of religious education in parishes, a lack of ideas about how the educational mission of the Church can be achieved is a sure sign of decay.

Insist on Evaluation The individual Board member has a responsibility to insist that the Board evaluate its actions and decisions and that the work of the coordinator or principal be evaluated. Such feed-back is necessary if the Board member is to return to the community whom he represents and adequately show how their opinions have been translated or not translated into action. As indicated in the discussion above on Supplement A, the Board can ask that the coordinator present a yearly evaluation of the success or failure of the program that was proposed and approved. An accurate assessment should be given before a judgement is made. These two steps need to be separated. The first step is the summation of the strengths and weaknesses or the successes and failures of the year's program. The second step is a discussion or the judgement about why. The Board member may wish to take the assessment back to the community whom he represents for the judgement.

Annual evaluation is a good way to get out of the shot-gun, band-aid approach to religious education and to achieve planned growth.

THE BOARD IN OPERATION

The precise way in which the Board of Education operates in a given parish can and should vary considerably. The NCEA recommends that the Davies-Brickle System be used by school Boards. The Davies-Brickle System is deeply rooted in the experience of public school Boards, even though part of the system that is recommended for Catholic schools is based upon an analysis of Catholic school data. This is precisely its limitation. The Davies-Brickle System is based on a *school model*. The parish Board of Education must function partially on a school model and partially on a broader, more flexible religious education model. The educational mission of a parish must not be confused with a school. The school is a means, perhaps even a primary means, for the attainment of the educational mission of the faith community, but it is not the only means and, hence, a system of operation which applies solely to schools cannot be stretched to encompass the broader religious education work of a parish.

Some things can be learned, however, from the Davies-Brickle System and applied to the operation of the parish Board of Education, especially regarding the style of the meetings and the manner of handling records.

Board Meetings   The Board needs to establish a regular meeting date. The majority of the Boards of Education in public school systems in the country meet on a monthly basis. Those which meet more frequently are for the larger systems encompassing more responsibilities. In a parish it would seem that a monthly meeting for at least ten months of the year would be sufficient.

The *agenda* for the meeting is a particularly important item. The agenda for any given meeting ought to be worked out, by the President of the Board and the executive officer, that is, the coordinator. Usually, action items carried over from the preceding meeting form a basis for the agenda, along with new work. The agenda is then mailed to the members of the Board in advance, along with all background material necessary to understand items for voting. Following the suggestions of the Davies-Brickle System, the agenda ought to be divided into two main sections, namely, *Action Items* and *Information Items*. The more traditional parliamentary form of old business and new business can be incorporated into these. The action items need to be taken care of by the Board first, before moving to more routine matters such as information about long range plans and programs, communications, and other such business.

It is suggested that persons attending Board meetings should not be allowed to speak without prior written notice to the Board of Education. This is a good general rule of thumb. However, the Board should be politically sensitive to the fact that persons who come to Board meetings should be given an opportunity to be heard if they have a pressing concern. At least the Board can listen to them briefly and respond by taking the matter under consideration, if action is not necessary. Few items, however, are of such a crisis proportion that they cannot be handled in writing by prior notice to the Board and be considered for a month by the Board and their constituents before action is taken.

The President of the Board   The President of the Board of Education is its most significant officer. He should be elected by the members with care and serious deliberation since he can impede or enhance the work of the Board to a great measure.

The President of the Board has a number of duties, in addition to the responsibilities which he holds as a general member of the Board. These would be as follows:

1) Preparation of the agenda: As mentioned above, it is the responsibility of the President of the Board to work with the chief executive officer, that is, the coordinator, in the preparation of the agenda for each meeting. It is also the responsibility of the President of Chairman of the Board to see that the agenda and the necessary materials pertaining to it are mailed to all the members of the Board in time for their consideration. The coordinator may provide the expertise concerning what items ought to go on the Board agenda, but the President of the Board *with* the coordinator can decide the priority of the items. The President, also, should see to it that the agenda is prepared in a logical and clear fashion which will effectively communicate ideas

to the Board members. Using himself as a criterion in this regard may prove beneficial.

2) Adequate preparation of proposals: It is the responsibility of the Board President to see that items coming up before the Board are adequately prepared and researched. He should see all materials before a presentation is made to the Board by the coordinator or other persons and judge on their completeness. This is a delicate area as the President in seeking to upgrade the quality of what comes before the Board might, in effect, be vetoing material which ought to get to the Board. Nevertheless, it is his responsibility to insure that proposals are well thought out, clearly stated, researched in depth, and appropriate for the Board's consideration. The coordinator is not the best judge of this and needs the President to assist him in such discernment.

3) Keeping the meeting moving: During the meeting it is the responsibility of the Board President to keep the meeting on the track. It takes particular tact and skill for the President to help Board members clarify their questions and points and to sum up where the deliberation is at any given time. The President may wish to ask the Secretary of the Board (the formal secretary, not the stenographer) also to be parliamentarian and to rule upon points of procedure when the need arises. This would free the President to concentrate more directly on the meeting itself. The President needs a knowledge of parliamentary procedure, to be sure, in order to assist him in sorting out the movement of the meeting as do all the members of the Board, but his chief responsibility in this area is to see that the meeting progresses; that is, that the action items are handled in the best fashion and that the priorities for any given meeting are met.

4) People tact: It is especially important that the President of the Board have an ability to work with people. Bringing out a point of humor at the right time can lighten a discussion. Noting the seriousness of a deliberation can also change the tone of the meeting. But, perhaps, the most important area of people tact which the President needs is the handling of the perennial dissenter at the Board meeting, whether that dissenter is a Board member or one of the guests. As indicated above, there is no need for the Board to strive for unanimity. Hence, the President need not attempt to silence a dissenter or bring him around to the point of view of the majority. The President's role is simply to help the dissenter articulate his point of view as concisely and clearly as possible for the consideration of the Board. The President then encourages the dissenter to accept the opinions of other members of the Board, that is, to allow them the freedom to express contrary views. Frequently, dissenters have strong feelings on a subject and pursue their viewpoint vigorously. People tact is necessary to bring out the point of view and yet not impede the movement of the meeting.

5) Being informed: In order to function effectively, the President of the Board of Education must be informed about the agenda items in more depth than other Board members. As a Board member, he has a responsibility to represent the community. This responsibility may suffer a bit, however, if the time which he would ordinarily spend seeking the views of the parish community on the proposals is used to adequately study the proposals themselves, so that he can point out to the Board members the various alternatives and implications of the items appearing before them for decision.

The President of the Board also needs to be careful that he remains a member of the Board and does not become an assistant or co-worker of the coordinator. While working closely with the coordinator on the preparation of the agenda and while learning in depth what the proposals are about, the President may build up a strong identity with the point of view of the coordinator. He needs to guard against a lack of moderation in this regard. The President is still a member of the Board and his responsibility is to assist the Board in its operations and not to sell the point of view of the coordinator. The coordinator, as executive officer of the Board, stands alone before the Board.

Special Sessions and Interim Operations   In addition to the regular meetings, the Board of Education may on occasion want a special indepth briefing on a given subject, for example, sex education. The coordinator then could schedule a special session for the Board and present to the members a comprehensive briefing. This type of session should be used with care and only when necessary. The Board does not need to learn all of the details and background which the coordinator knows about a given proposal. That is why the coordinator is hired. Some proposals, however, are controversial and may cause such a reaction among the larger parish or public community that the Board will need a special briefing in order that the members may establish effective two-way communication with their constituents.

Between Board meetings, the President, Vice President, Secretary and Treasurer may form a type of executive committee which can meet with the coordinator to help him see which course of action is in keeping with the decisions or goals of the Board. Again, caution is necessary that these executive committee meetings do not become action meetings. No action should be taken by the Board except at public meetings when the majority of the members are present. Interim meetings between the officers of the Board and the coordinator are simply for the purpose of seeing that the action is on target.

THE BOARD AND THE COORDINATOR

The relationship between the parish Board of Education and the coordinator is an extremely important one. As discussed above, the working relationship between the pastor and the coordinator is emotionally charged. The relationship between the coordinator and the Board is quite different. Coordinators—most are presently sisters—are inclined to work alone or solely with the pastor rather than develop a close and effective working relationship with a Board. To neglect such a working relationship is fatal for a coordinator. As described above, work with the Board is work with the Parish in microcosm—it is a very special and effective type of adult education. In addition, the Board provides the coordinator with a "reality" view in contrast to the "ideal" religious education which the coordinator has learned in his own preparation. Presently college programs in religious education prepare coordinators with a generalized religious education theology background which the coordinator in turn must translate into practice on the home front. Boards help the coordinator do just that and, hence, are vital to the success of the total educational mission of the parish.

Judging both from the point of view of the data available to Project Coordinator and from administrative theory, it is important and appropriate that the coordinator be directly responsible to the Board of Education for his work, rather than to the pastor. The Board represents the whole parish community and becomes a particular focus for that community's responsibility to preach the Word. The hiring of the coordinator, with the approval of the Parish Council and/or the pastor, is a further concretizing of that larger responsibility. In other words, the coordinator has a definite role in reference to the parish community and to preaching the Word apart from the role of the priest who represents the Bishop (Apostle). It is the dynamic interaction between apostle and people which provides much of the uniqueness of the Roman Catholic tradition of Christian community. The people are not the sole determiners of the charisms of the parish. They do not hire their priest although they should have some voice in the appointment process. The faith community, therefore, operates with a delicate interaction between the priest as representative of the Bishop (Apostle) and the people represented by groups such as the Board of Education and the Parish Council. The Board of Education and the coordinator represent the local faith community. To look at it another way, the coordinator is not an extension of the pastoral team but rather an embodiment of a charism pertaining to preaching the Word, which is part of a larger responsibility of the whole people of the parish to preach the Word. Hence, the coordinator should be directly responsible to the Board and not to the pastor. The working relationship between the Board and the coordinator will be effective if each sees his part clearly.

Policy versus Implementation   The chief responsibility of the Board of Education is to determine the goals and policy for the parish's educational mission. The chief responsibility of the coordinator is to implement these for the Board. This distinction between policy and administration is a subtle one and a necessary one that has to be worked on, if the Board and the coordinator are to get along. Frequently the enthusiasm of a Board member leads him to push for definite programs and actions. For example, the Board may wish to set up a program to educate young adults. One Board member may have a very definite idea about the kind of program that ought to happen. This idea should surely be communicated, but it is the responsibility of the coordinator to determine the best way to implement that goal of the Board and not the responsibility of a Board member. The Board may wish to set up a program of sex education, as another example. Precisely what materials are used and how the curriculum and instructional aspect of the program is effected is the responsibility of the coordinator (see Chapter 6 for further discussion of this point). Basically, the Board keeps before it the question "what" and "why." The coordinator, while assisting the Board with these questions, is chiefly concerned with the question "how."

Capitalize on Strengths, Augment Weaknesses In hiring a coordinator, the Board may wish to find a person of many talents and skills. This is to be expected. Such ideal people, however, are never available. At the present time, the personnel available to fill the role of coordinator have a generalized theological background and are lacking in "executive" skills. This need not deter the Board from hiring such a person. It simply means the Board has to find a way to augment the weaknesses of the particular person hired. For example, the coordinator may not have skills relative to the preparation of a budget. The Board, therefore, must see to it that a person from the faith community who is knowledgeable regarding budgets assists the coordinator with his work in that regard. The coordinator himself may look for help. The main point here is that the Board should be aware of the strengths and weaknesses of the coordinator and assist the coordinator in augmenting his weaknesses.

In return, the coordinator does the same by assisting the Board with the questions "what" and "why," as indicated above.

Managing Conflicts   In an era of change and diversity, conflict can hardly be avoided. Board members should not expect the operations of the parish Board of Education to proceed smoothly. If they do, it might be a sign that the Board is completely out of touch with both pastor and people. Conflict is inevitable, given the immense problems and challenges facing Christian people in their educational mission. The closing of a parish school which has served the parish for a long period of time, for example, cannot be accomplished without conflicting opinions and sentiments. The Board of Education, therefore, should not seek to eliminate conflict but rather to manage conflict. Once again, effective communication between the Board and the larger faith community is essential for the best resolution of conflict. Some problems facing Christian people in their educational mission today cannot be "answered," but only "resolved." There is no answer to some questions, especially about whether or not a given educational program will achieve the goals for which it is designed. The Board must be cognizant of the fact that working in a climate of conflict, people tend to look for a person to blame when things go wrong. The Board should protect the coordinator in this regard, being very careful that the coordinator is only accountable for his failures and negligence that can be demonstrated. Opinion and rumor thrive in an era of conflict and demand a scapegoat. The Board cannot afford to fall into this trap.

Create an Environment   On the positive side of managing conflict, the Board needs to create an environment in which the educational mission of that faith community can be achieved. This may mean the removal of obstacles impeding it, the provision of resources and personnel to achieve it, and similar items. For example, a chief obstacle to the achievement of an effective educational program may be the sense of loss or failure on the part of the people accompanying the closing of the Catholic school. This is a definite "climate" type of problem which can plague the educational programs being provided with a coordinator to replace the school in that parish. In this case, the Board should actively work to build enthusiasm and support on the part of the community for the new educational program, seeing it as a continuation of the past efforts into a new form. Each individual Board member in communicating to his constituents informally provides the means whereby this creative environment is fashioned, in addition to the more formal actions which the Board as a group takes itself. Simply making an effort to communicate to a lot of people the reasons for actions of the Board and the direction in which education is moving in that parish can do much to create a climate in which achievement is possible.

FUTURE OF PARISH BOARDS

Msgr. Victor Gallagher frequently says "A parish gets the priest it deserves." The same might be applied to the Board of Education. If the Board is truly elective, then it represents the people. The decisions which it makes should reflect the mentality and desires of the people it serves. Hence, the quality of education within a given parish cannot be blamed upon anyone but the people themselves. Too often, people hide behind the phrase "if only the pastor would . . ." or "if only the Board of Education would . . ." rather than making

known what they believe to the pastor or Board. This
appears to be a general malaise of older members of a
parish, as well as society itself; younger members have
simply lost trust in organizations and make their concerns known by actions, either positive or negative.
The Pope, the bishop, the pastor, or the diocesan Board
of Education are not to blame for the quality of the
educational program of the parish. The parish itself
through its Board of Education can celebrate its achievements or lament its failures, but the burden of responsibility is with them. No national committee or diocese
in another part of the country will work out a precise
and successful solution to the educational programs of
any given parish. The parish itself must do that. It can
be assisted, to be sure, by ideas and models from other
places, but these are only aids and never substitutes for
the actual facing of responsibility of executing programs
in the parish.

Adjusting from a period in which the pastor dominated the activities of a parish to a time in which there
is a dynamic interaction between pastor and people will
not be achieved without great frustrations and anxieties.
The educational mission of a parish can contribute
greatly to the realization of this interaction, both by
the vision which it communicates and a style of operation which it adopts. If the Board of Education fully
assumes its responsibility, functions as a pluralistic
community, learns to work with a professional coordinator, and chooses to reach out into innovative new
areas, it can set an educational example for other groups
and for the whole parish itself. This is part of the challenge for the future for parish Boards.

The educational mission of a parish, however, also
involves reaching out to the larger community of man —
the yet-to-be-realized eschatology. In the future, the
involvement of the faith community, the workings of

the public school and adult education through the Public Forum will greatly increase. The role of the Board of Education in this regard will increase also. The Board of Education may need to make statements of reaction to public school programs, such as value education, sex education, and allied fields. It may need actively to campaign for or against decisions of the community school Board since these affect a large number of Catholic youth attending the public schools. The parish Board can fulfill a role in reference to the media and adult education. The war in Vietnam can serve as an example here. Sensing the importance of this decision, the parish Board can instruct the parish coordinator to initiate a program pointing out the Christian stance toward peace and war. More frequently the coordinator will be asking the Board to endorse such a general program, but on occasion the Board itself may initiate such an endeavor. The president of the Board in a statement to the news media can highlight the reasons for such a program in the parish and thereby do much toward broadening the base of concern of the whole community to such an issue. The parish professional is expected to be involved in such activities. When a Board of Education as the representative in an official body undertakes such actions it has considerable value for the whole community.

In summary, the Board of Education does not have responsibility for what happens in a public adult education or in public schools. It does have the responsibility, however, representing the educational thinking of the faith community to respond to what happens in the public sector from a Christian educational perspective. This work also lies in the future for parish Boards of Education.

Pastors, coordinators, Diocesan Offices and others debate the pros and cons of parish Boards of Education.

They see strengths and they see weaknesses and, hence, some hesitate to establish such Boards or to work seriously with the Boards which are in effect at present. These are legitimate concerns but they seem minor when compared with the overwhelming need on the part of people today to be involved in decisions which affect their lives. Many organizations no longer serve the objectives for which they were created. Parish Boards of Education are still too new to be so hamstrung by tradition and precedent and the general ineffectiveness of past organizations should not be predicated to them before they have a chance to produce.

NOTES FOR CHAPTER 5

1) Manual of the *Parish Confraternity of Christian Doctrine* (Washington, D.C.: National CCD Center, 1961), p. 54ff.

2) Greeley and Rossi, *Education of Catholic Americans,* p. 191.

3) *Catholic Education 1969.*

4) Superintendents Committee on Policy and Administration, *Voice of the Community* (Washington, D.C.: NCEA, 1967), p. 14.

5) *Ibid.,* p. 4.

6) Msgr. Charles Moeller, "Postconciliar Perspectives in Theology and Catechetics," *Lumen Vitae* 22, no. 1, (1967), p. 110ff.

Chapter Six

PLANNING A PROGRAM
AND BUDGET

Translating the dream or vision of what the faith community should accomplish in their educational mission into reality is a technical skill which the parish professional should be able to offer.

Some parish coordinators see this task as administrative and not part of their work. And many do not actually have the necessary skills to assume this task. This, however, does not remove the responsibility, and the parish has the right to expect a professional religious educator to be able to assist them not only in formulating the vision of what they ought to do in education, but also in translating that vision into a practical program and budget. This is especially true if the coordinator is hired to be the chief educational leader of the parish under the Board of Education.

Since this skill is unfamiliar to many coordinators, a rather detailed sample *Program and Budget Projection* will be presented here, along with general remarks about the process itself. Coordinators can adapt this schema to local patterns or use the description of program and budgetary procedures more fully.

WHY A PROGRAM AND BUDGET PROJECTION?

The *Program and Budget Projection* which follows places the decision for the actual religious education program which will be offered to the youth and the adults of the parish in the hands of the parish Board of Education rather than in the hands of the parish coordinator. The coordinator, to be sure, greatly influences the decision of the Board by what he presents, but the Board makes the decision and authorizes the coordinator to implement the program.

The other alternative is to assign a designated sum of money for youth and adult religious education and then charge the coordinator to plan and implement a "suitable" program. This would place the full responsibility for the kind of program offered in the hands of the coordinator and/or pastor.

The reasons why the first alternative (placing the decision with the Board) is advocated are manifold but include particularly these following.

The responsibility for the type of religious education offered in a parish belongs with the people of the parish. Parents are the primary educators of their children and should be. Adults determine the way in which they will grow in faith and understanding, since they have to be held accountable for their own lives. The pastor is charged with preaching the Word to that faith community, but he cannot be held accountable for the acceptance of the Word by adults or for the way in which children are raised in the faith. The coordinator, like the pastor, does have a responsibility to provide leadership to both parents and adults regarding how they can best grow in faith and understanding, but should not get into the position of expecting the members of the parish community to bow blindly to his authority for religious education.

As was explained above, *all* the members of the faith community are given the gift of the Spirit and the challenge of celebrating the liturgy, proclaiming the Word, and building the earth and the brotherhood of man. Hence, they have the ability and the responsibility to decide upon the course and the implementation of the educational mission of that faith community. Usually this is done through the parish Board of Education, which is the elected extension of the larger community.

The parish professional has the role of service. The call to religious education work is a call of service to the People of God. This is true for both religious and lay persons serving as parish coordinators. Translating this service into practice in education means placing the decisions for education in the hands of the people and assisting them to make those decisions and to implement them.

Educational opportunities are planned (or at least the ability to respond to a range of unexpected events) and educational priorities must be set. A "good" religious education program does not just happen: it is planned in advance. Even with life-centered religious education, the ability to respond to the needs and life-events of individuals and of the larger community can be the result of a flexible plan and of the availability of appropriate resources. In preparing the Projection, the coordinator is forced to look ahead for a year and set up the basic directions of the youth and adult programs and the ability to meet unexpected opportunities.

When presenting the many programs possible to the Board of Education for decision, the coordinator is also asking the Board to establish educational priorities for the faith community. Frequently the conflict of priorities between the coordinator and the members of the parish is never articulated. The coordinator may be attempting to achieve "his" priorities while the parish is wondering why he is not achieving what "they" thought he would be doing. It is no wonder conflict arises. Placing the decision in the hands of the Board lessens the possibility of such conflict.

Funding should always be in relationship to programming. Lastly, the Projection presented here is based upon the idea that the budget for religious education is in direct relationship to the services or programs desired by the parish. Spending should always be for a purpose, and this purpose is what the program presents. It also assists the coordinator and the teachers to see the financial implications of their educational decisions.

These principles will become clearer in the discussion of the specific plan of the Projection. Afterwards we will return to the long-range reasons for this process which, when viewed in the short range, appears to be unnecessarily complicated.

THE PLANNING PROCESS

While the coordinator is responsible for the final production and presentation of the Program and Budget Projection, many persons should be involved throughout the process, if it is to become a real tool for the religious education program of that parish. Who will be involved and in what way each coordinator will need to decide in his own particular situation. The following general aspects of the planning process, however, appear to be valid for most situations:

Decide upon the specific format and process. The coordinator, with the advice of a businessman or an accountant (possibly someone from the Board), should decide upon a format and preparation process workable in that particular parish. That format presented here in Chart 6:1 may be used if suitable, as might the uniform accounting system of the Diocese. The Parish Council may already have developed common accounting guides for the whole parish, and these should be incorporated into this Projection. Whatever system is used, it will need to account for the items presented in Chart 6:1 in some way. An accountant can offer valuable advice here as well as assisting the coordinator throughout with the process of arriving at the costs for the year.

Go over the budget system and projection process with the principals. The coordinator next would gather together the principals or leaders of the various phases of the parish religious education program and go over the projection process and the budget system to be used. The principal with the teachers from the elementary religious education program will plan with the coordinator what they will do next year and how much it will cost. The coordinator could do this alone or perhaps simply with the principal, but the involvement of the teachers could be quite beneficial in the long run, as they would learn the implications of their decisions and would also be able to spread support for the program throughout the total parish community since it has

CHART 6:1

PROGRAM AND BUDGET PROJECTION FORMAT

GOAL:
The goal for the proposed program should be stated first and it should be indicated whether this is a new program (*developmental*) or a *continuing* goal.

NEED:
The practical or sociological reasons for the goal and program are given; e.g., there are X number of children from the parish attending public elementary schools.

RATIONALE:
Here the theoretical reasons why the above need should be met by the following program are presented and documented as needed.

IMPLEMENTATION:
The overview of the program and the broad steps which will be taken to implement it are presented here.

BUDGET:
The costs for the program are presented here according to suitable categories. The following may be used:
#10 Salaries (or stipends for the regular teaching staff)
#20 Employee benefits (where applicable)
#30 Office supplies and equipment
#40 Curriculum resources (the learning resources to be used)
#50 Instructional services (the aids and machinery to be used)
#60 Travel (for the coordinator and/or teachers or projects)
#70 Utilities (phone, lights, heat, etc.)
#80 Maintenance (including fees for janitorial service)
#90 Capital and fixed (insurance, new major purchases)
#100 Miscellaneous (petty cash, and unexpected small items)
#110 Research and development (special aspects or programs)
#200 Income related to the program (should be divided into a number of suitable categories for the kinds of income)

| TOTAL BUDGET FOR GOAL: |

become "their" program instead of just "a" program. The teachers would also know the total budget for the elementary program and would not think that the coordinator is favoring one teacher over another or one program over another. The principal will lead the particular group of teachers involved and therefore should be briefed in depth before actually meeting with the teachers, in order that she can assume the leadership role with them.

The principal (or leaders) and the teachers for that area meet and project their program. The coordinator may need to meet with them the first time and assist them in this process, but as much as possible the principal and the teachers should project their own program and budget in various areas of the parish religious education program in order to learn how and why. But the coordinator is not really helping the people to become capable of filling *their* educational mission if he pushes them to adopt *his* program.

In working out this Projection for their particular area, the principal and teachers will need to answer the following basic questions and then translate them into a common format, such as the one presented in Chart 6:1 :

1) Goal: What do we want to do? This should be an administrative goal and not simply a theoretical goal. A theoretical goal for children, for example, might be stated: "We want the children to grow in the knowledge and love of God as Father." This is only half of the goal. Adding the administrative side to the above, it might be stated as follows: "To provide through weekly classes the opportunity for children to grow in the knowledge and love of God as Father."

After stating the goal the first time, wait until the

full implementation is projected, and then it can be re-stated including a phrase which summarizes the *need,* the *rationale,* and the *implementation.*

2) Need: For whom? This question is an integral part of the one above, but it can be separated for planning and presentation. The particulars about the group for whom the program is being planned form the need section. This should be as specific as possible. Often, as this section is being defined, the goal will change; it becomes obvious that what is being projected is not suitable. This is particularly true for adults. Not all adults can be presented the same opportunities. The unique character of different groups of adults must be defined closely before an effective program can be presented.

3) Rationale: Why is this goal and program important? Why should a religious education program be presented to this particular group defined above? At first it might look as if this question would apply only to adult education. In this coming decade, however, we will need to give better reasons for our youth programs also. Some of them just may be invalid. At any rate, in this discussion, the principal and teachers attempt to come to a good, clear synthesis of their thinking about why they are offering this program to this group. The synthesizing that goes on here also provides a common frame of reference for the interaction with the coordinator throughout the year in catechist education (see Chapter 7). In the case of youth programs, it can further provide the basic content for parent-teacher interaction.

4) Implementation: How are we going to do it? Given the validity of the goal; that is, if there is a good reason for attempting to do what we have stated for this

particular group, then how will we accomplish it? Should we have weekly classes? Should there be a lecture series? discussion clubs? weekend trips? retreats? or what other type of program? To a certain extent, the goal and the need will set the tone for the type of program suitable. But there are many ways to achieve the goal. The tendency to do what has been done before should be seriously re-examined. The principal and the teachers can "brainstorm" the possible programs which could be presented to achieve the goal, throwing them all out on the table first before asking which are possible to implement in terms of the human and material resources. If several good ideas emerge, perhaps the teachers can break into groups and further define one of the ideas. The groups can present their ideal program to the whole group. Finally, the principal and catechists judge from among these ideas which program they deem best for achieving the goal.

5) Budget: What do we need to implement this program? What kinds of human and material resources do the principal and teacher need to implement the program designed? In discussing this question, all the variety of curricular and instructional resources should be considered. In effect, the discussion becomes, therefore, a type of in-service catechist education. If several of the catechists for the adolescent program, for example, want a flexible multi-media program for the coming year, and several do not, then the principal (and the coordinator) will have to work toward a consensus by leading the catechists to judge which kinds of resources will best achieve the goals for the groups they are designed for. The goal, which is based upon the need and the rationale, becomes the main criterion for the selection of the learning resources — textual materials, audiovisual aids, etc.

6) Evaluation: How will we know if we have achieved what we set out to do? This is a question that does not become part of the actual Projection to the Board. It might come up in the oral discussion with the Board about the rationale of the program. Even if it does not, the question should be answered as far as possible by the principal and teachers, as it provides part of the basis for the total review of the program at the end of the year, a review which will also be given to the Board (and the parish) before another year's work is begun.

PROGRAM AND BUDGET PROJECTION

After these questions have been discussed and the basic program idea projected, the principal and the coordinator can work out the translation of these ideas into a common format for inclusion in the total Program and Budget Projection which will be presented to the Board of Education. Chart 6:2 gives a sample of how this might be done. In this sample, the adult leaders have projected meeting with engaged couples and assisting them to understand the meaning of the decision to marry which they have made.

"Adult Education Goal III (developmental): to provide opportunities for engaged couples to explore the meaning of a marriage commitment." Several things should be noted in this sample. First, it is listed as "developmental," which means that such an opportunity was not provided in the previous year. The Board will need to decide if it can adopt this recommended goal in the light of the total program projected. Secondly, stating the goal in terms of "opportunities" leaves the decision of whether or not to participate with the couples. And lastly, the adult education is around a life event.

CHART 6:2

PROJECTION
(Sample)

ADULT EDUCATION GOAL III (developmental): To provide opportunities for engaged couples to explore the meaning of the marriage commitment.

NEED: In St. Agnes Parish each year approximately 85 couples marry. With the exception of the required pre-marriage pastoral sessions, they have no opportunity to consider the full meaning of their decision to marry.

RATIONALE: The Church has always stressed the sacredness of marriage and the seriousness with which couples approach this important decision. The various *impediments* to marriage which must be checked by the pastor before he witnesses to a marriage in the Church are an example of the seriousness with which marriage is approached. (confer Canon Law 1012-1143). In Mark's Gospel we read: "But from the beginning God made them male and female. This is why a man must leave father and mother, and the two become one body. They are no longer two, therefore, but one body. So then, what God has united, man must not divide. (Mk. 10:6-9)." Since, therefore, the decision to marry is a life commitment which must be made with full knowledge and freedom (see also Pope Pius XI's encyclical *Casti Connubii* and the Vatican Council's statements in *The Constitution on the Church in the Modern World*, par. 47-52), the parish must be concerned with assisting engaged couples to weigh the implications of their decision so it can truly be a free and life-long commitment. The following program of small group interaction is presented rather than a class which emphasizes knowledge about marriage because adults learn best in discussion when the knowledge must be related to their particular life decision. "Learning cannot take place unless and until the student translates and incorporates the knowledge in relation to his questions and his problems . . ." (*How To Teach Adults*, Adult Education Ass., 1955, p. 7).

IMPLEMENTATION: The following general plan will be followed:

1) A team of four or more couples will be selected to serve as leader couples for the sessions.

2) The coordinator will meet with these couples throughout the month of October to assist them in deepening their own understandings of marriage and to plan with them for the sessions to be offered to the engaged couples.

3) Couples who are engaged and who plan to marry in the months of April, May, June, and July will be identified, invited to meet with

a group of couples with similar plans, and those accepting organized into a group with a leader couple.

4) The group will determine the place, hour, and number of sessions to be held. At least six sessions are anticipated.

5) The basic discussion materials will consist of the book, *Love and Sexuality: A Christian Approach,* by John and Mary Ryan (Image Books, 1969) and mimeographed excerpts from other sources. The audio-visuals will consist of the film, *Engagement: Romance or Reality,* when available from the library; and the tapes, *Young Adult Enrichment Program,* as appropriate.

6) The leader couples will make efforts to work with the parish Liturgical Commission in assisting the couples to plan the options for their marriage celebration.

7) After their marriage, an effort will be made to keep in touch with the couples, especially those who will remain within the parish. At six-month intervals, they will be asked to evaluate the preparation sessions and the marriage celebration.

BUDGET:

#10 Salaries ($25 for each leader couple)	$100.00
#30 Office	
31. Basic supplies	20.00
#40 Curriculum materials	
41. Textual materials (*Love & Sexuality,* 95¢x100)	95.00
42. Mimeo supplies (5¢x100x6)	30.00
#50 Instructional services	
51. Stipend for guest speaker	50.00
52. A-V purchase (Youth Enrichment tapes)	32.00
53. Film rental	5.00
#60 Travel	
61. Coordinator (150mi.x10¢)	15.00
#70 Utilities	
71. Bell Telephone Co.	10.00
72. Power Company	5.00
73. Gas Company	15.00
#80 Maintenance	
81. Janitorial services (extra clean-up)	25.00
#100 Miscellaneous	
101. Hospitality	30.00
SUBTOTAL	$432.00
#200 Income	
201. Donations from couples (65x$5.00)	325.00

TOT. BUDGET REQUEST FOR ADULT ED. GOAL III $107.00

"Need: In St. Agnes Parish . . ." The relevant socio-logical data is given for that particular parish. Boards of Education typically want to know for whom the program is being planned. The coordinator and the teachers will also find that the closer they define the audience for whom they are offering educational opportunities, the more relevant and effective the program is apt to be. This is particularly true for adult religious education. The spectrum of "adult" needs, interests, and experience are considerably greater than a similar spectrum for adolescents. A young married mother sees life and faith different than does a retired widow. Both might profit from a quality educational experience. The need section of the Program and Budget Projection seeks to focus on the particular group for whom the program is being prepared and demonstrate why a program is being prepared for them.

"Rationale: The Church has always stressed . . ." Here the theoretical reasons why the above need ought to be met and in what manner are given. As religious educators we have had little experience in bringing concep-tions to bear upon actual programming. We find it easy to state theological or anthropological principles but often simply transpose these statements as content into our educational settings without actually applying the principles to the setting itself. In stating an educational goal in the Projection the coordinator will find it neces-sary to relate what he has learned to both the educa-tional setting and to the content which will be included. The decision to offer week-end youth sessions in place of classes, for example, will need to be justified on the-oretical grounds to the Board. The Board would under-stand (or would allow the decision without understand-ing) a change to a new textbook more readily, unless that textbook is controversial, because the implied as-

sumption that young people should receive schooling
in religion is not being challenged.

Education and schooling should not be confused.
Schooling hopefully is a process for education but there
are many flexible and creative ways in which education can occur. As the coordinator begins to plan such
opportunities, he will also see the need to convince the
Board of the validity of these in the rationale. Try explaining the reasons for spending $500 on a film festival,
for example.

One other thing ought to be said about this rationale
section before moving on. The rationale also is a form
of adult education. Assuming that the Board of Education is elected and therefore fairly representative of the
total faith community, if the coordinator can convince
them to change to new forms and content for religious
education, then he is also educating the larger parish
community. The coordinator may see why the classes
for pre-school youth should be dropped. And if he had
the decision about which programs would be offered in
the parish, they would be discontinued. Placing this
decision in the hands of the Board, however, means
that the coordinator needs to convince them (perhaps
in the rationale section and in the oral presentation
with it) that *they* should take this step. If they agree,
real adult education has occurred, especially if the Board
members have to go back to friends and parishioners
and explain to them why they voted to drop the program.

"Implementation: The following general plan . . ."
It should be noted that in this sample the implementation steps are specific yet flexible. From this plan the
coordinator can see what he will need to do and can estimate the amount of time and preparation that should go
into it. In looking over all of the proposed programs, the
coordinator will need to be careful to allow time for the

unexpected events, for study and on-going research, and for finding ways to begin to move into new educational opportunities.

"Budget" This section will prove to be an "Excedrin headache" for most coordinators but the agonies will eventually be worth it if the first trials can be endured and the skill learned. Money is energy to accomplish worthwhile goals. The availability of money from almost any group is directly in proportion to the value they place upon that for which the money will be spent. Within the Church we have tried for decades to spread a little amount of money over many worthwhile educational projects with the result that we have done poorly in most of them. Parish religious education has been poorly financed because most of our human and material resources have gone into Catholic schools which are themselves now facing financial crises. Hence the present financial limitations upon all forms of Christian education demand a serious re-examination of what it is that we really ought to do in education in the Church. Priorities must be set and funded accordingly. Projecting costs in relationship to goals facilitates the process of setting priorities. It also points out the financial implications of the program decisions.

"Salaries" In this section for adult education, the only salary listed is for the stipends to be given to the leader couples. If a teacher were to be hired solely to work with these engaged couples, her salary would be placed into this program projection. If the Board decided that they did not want this program, the teacher would not be hired. This is simple enough to understand. It becomes confusing for coordinators when they begin to list their own salary. The coordinator's salary should be spread over the major continuing programs for children, adoles-

cents, and adults. If the coordinator will spend one-third of his time planning, coordinating, and assisting the teachers of the adolescent program, then one-third of his salary is placed under that goal and program projection. In other words, the coordinator is not simply hired and given a salary and then funds for program-ming. The coordinator is hired for a specific purpose and that purpose should be reflected in the budget al-locations.

Suppose, for example, a parish hires a religious education coordinator to work out a quality elementary and secondary religious education program. Adult educa-tion is left with the parish priest. In presenting the Projection designed to implement that mandate, the coordinator would place half of his salary under the continuing elementary program goal and half under the adolescent program goal. This shows where the coordinator will work. The following year the coordina-tor might be requested by the Board to head the adult religious education program also. In the Projection (first draft) the coordinator would place one-third of his salary under the elementary goal, one-third under the adolescent goal, and propose placing the remaining third under the adult education goal. If the Board ap-proves this, then the coordinator has received a man-date to spend a third of his time and energy on adult education. Relating the money to a definite program requires that priorities be set.

In an average parish religious education program, the coordinator is apt to spend about one-fourth of his time with the Board of Education work, one-fourth with the elementary program, one-fourth with the sec-ondary program, and the remaining one-fourth with the adult religious education. In a very large parish, a full-time catechist might be hired for the elementary pro-gram and another for the secondary program. The coordinator could then spend more of his time with adult education, Board work, and other areas not yet developed.

"Office" In this sample goal (Chart 6:2), very little is projected for office supplies and equipment. The majority of office expenses are under the administrative goal—working with the Board. Mimeograph paper and such supplies are related to specific programs and placed under either #40 or #50 depending upon their use.

"Curriculum Materials" This section is for the textual materials, library books, magazines, teachers' references, student references, and other such curriculum materials. In other words, in this section the coordinator places all the learning resources which he or the youth and adults will use.

Various subsections can be used; #41, for example, could be used for library materials, #42 for textbooks, #43 for teacher reference, and so forth. Keeping similar categories from year to year in both the budget and the record-keeping can greatly assist the coordinator to see where funds are spent over a period of years.

"Instructional Services" In this section the people, things, and other resources which are directly utilized in the teaching process are indicated. This might include the rental of a hall for a lecture, the stipend and travel for the lecturer, a movie projector, film rental, and similar items.

"Travel" The coordinator's travel related to this goal and program are projected along with other travel expenses involved in the program. All travel expenses could be placed here in subsections—food, lodging, gasoline, insurance, and so forth.

Summary In educational work the Board has the responsibility to set goals and decide upon policy and broad program design. The coordinator has the responsibility to assist the Board in these areas by preparing goals and programs with accompanying budgets, and in implementing these once they have been adopted.

With this in mind, it might be objected that the sample goal and program described above is too detailed; it gives the implementation steps including curriculum materials to be used which are ordinarily professional decisions for the coordinator to make. This might be true in general education or in business work with boards. In parish religious education, however, Boards are very new, and the ability of Board members to distinguish between education and schooling (classes, lectures, etc.) is limited. Hence the more they can see the reasons for and the extent of an educational decision, the more they will grow in their ability to assume their full responsibility for leadership in the educational mission of the parish.

PROGRAM AND BUDGET PROJECTION: SUMMARY PAGES

After all the goals and program projections (with budgets) are finalized for the first draft, the coordinator (perhaps with the help of an accountant) prepares the summary pages. Samples are presented here in Charts 6:3, 6:4, and 6:5.

Program Summary (Chart 6:3) The program summary shows the total scope of religious education for that parish for the year, together with the budget. It also distinguishes between what is being spent on *continuing* programs and what is being spent for new areas or

CHART 6:3

RELIGIOUS EDUCATION PROGRAM SUMMARY
(Sample)

| CHILD EDUCATION | *Continuing* | *Develop.* |

Goal I   Primary grades—classes (p.) $
Goal II   Intermediate—classes (p.) $
Goal III First Communion program (p.) $

Total continuing $
Total developmental $

| TOTAL CHILD EDUCATION BUDGET $ |

| ADOLESCENT EDUCATION |

Goal I   Junior high classes (p.) $
Goal II   Adolescent week-ends (p.) $
Goal III Senior trip (p.) $

Total continuing $
Total developmental $

| TOTAL ADOLESCENT $
EDUCATION BUDGET |

ADULT EDUCATION

Goal I	Lecture series	(p.)	$	
Goal II	Discussion clubs	(p.)	$	
Goal III	Engagement sessions (p.)			$107.50
Goal IV	Senior adults weekend (p.)			$
	Total continuing		___	
	Total continuing		$	___
	Total developmental			$

TOTAL ADULT EDUCATION BUDGET	$

ADMINISTRATION

Goal I	Board work	$
	1971-72 Total Continuing Budget	$
	1971-72 Total Developmental Budget	$

1971-72 TOTAL RELIGIOUS EDUCATION BUDGET	$

developmental programs, for children, for adults, and for adolescents. The goals are numbered and given a phrase-title and page number, to help board members find the detailed projection as needed. This page in the total Program and Budget Projection becomes one of the main pieces for the verbal discussion at the Board meeting.

Summary of Categories (Chart 6:4) This summary page shows how the full projected budget will be spent according to the budget categories. The majority of the funds will be under the sections on *salaries, curriculum materials, instructional services,* and perhaps *office* or *travel,* unless, of course, rent or a mortgage is being paid and is listed in #90, *capital and fixed.* This summary page could also divide the totals according to the continuing and developmental columns. It should list, as in Chart 6:4, the variance between this year's projected budget and last year's actual budget (when such figures are available).

Explanation of Variances (Chart 6:5) After the Summary of Categories, the page explaining the increases and decreases is presented. The Board members will want to know why more is being spent or less is being spent in each of these areas of the budget. In the discussion and in the explanation of variances, the coordinator also refers to the projected goals and programs as needed to show the reasons for the differences.

PRESENTATION OF THE PROGRAM AND BUDGET PROJECTION

After the various groups have projected their year's program and the coordinator has completed the sum-

CHART 6:4   RELIGIOUS EDUCATION BUDGET—SUMMARY BY CATEGORY
(Sample)

Budget series:	Child Ed.	Youth Ed.	Adult Ed.	1971 Tot.	1970 Tot.	Variance
#10 Salaries	$	$	$	$	$	$
#20 Benefits	$	$	$	$	$	$
#30 Office	$	$	$	$	$	$
#40 Curriculum materials	$	$	$	$	$	$
#50 Instruc. services	$	$	$	$		$
#60 Travel	$	$	$	$	$	$
#100 Research & Develop.	$	$	$	$	$	$
#110 Miscell.	$	$	$	$	$	$
TOTAL	$	$	$	$	$	$
#200 Income expected	$	$	$	$	$	$
TOTAL 1971 Budget	$	$	$	$	$	$

CHART 6:5

EXPLANATION OF VARIANCES
(Sample)

#10 Salaries:
   The salaries will increase with the 1971-72 program because
   of . . . in Youth Goal I.

#20 Benefits:
   The benefits will increase because of the new federal ruling
   that . . .

#30 Office:
   Office expenses are lower this year because no new equipment
   is required. This year's budget includes continuing maintenance
   on the equipment purchased last year.

#40 Curriculum materials:
   This years budget is only slightly higher because of the addition of the tapes to be used in Adult Ed Goal III. This is
   an expenditure over and above the usual yearly allotment
   for audio-visuals.

#90 Capital & Fixed:
   The 1971 budget is substantially larger than last year's in this
   category because of the curtains which will be purchased to
   darken the audio-visual room for film use. (see use of films
   in Youth Ed Goals I, II, & III; Adult Ed Goal III).

#220 Income:
   This year's estimate of income was placed substantially lower
   than last year's because of the experience with poor payment
   of fees and because it is unknown whether or not donations
   can be expected from young adults (see Adult Ed Goal III).
   The estimate is realistically low. The quarterly reports will
   reflect whether or not they are accurate.

NOTE: Special notice should be given to the long-range plan
   which is being begun with Youth Education Goal IV. This could
   set a precedent which the Board may not want to establish.
   The ultimate cost of these trips might make them prohibitive.
   This year's Goal will be experimental to see if that is so.

mary pages, the first draft of the total Program and Budget Projection can be put together in a folder and an appointment for a presentation to the Board of Education requested.

The coordinator with the others as needed presents the total projection to the Board at their regular meeting. It is discussed and questions are answered. Frequently there will also be a spirited exchange between the coordinator (and the principals, if involved) and the Board, especially over new and innovative programs that are proposed.

The Board should not vote on the projection at that meeting. Instead the members should study the projection for a month, calling upon the coordinator for further clarifications and upon members of the parish for discussion of the pros and cons of the proposed programs before voting. This is a risky process — some people might be against what is proposed — but a highly educational one. If the projection has been done well, it will be meeting real needs and will be showing the value of what is projected. Hence there should be moderate negative reaction. Any reaction, however, is good, as it is beginning to awaken the total parish to the nature and scope of their educational mission. Asking for their criticism also firmly places the responsibility for the educational mission in their hands.

At the next meeting — or later if serious opposition arises — the Board can vote on the projected programs. There are two decisions to be made: Do we want this program and can it be achieved with less cost? The Board should be very sensitive about the second question. It may be possible to drop items from the projected budget and achieve much of the goal with less cost; e.g. not paying a stipend to volunteer catechists. The total effect of that decision should be weighed and not just the economic factor.

When the Board of Education has agreed upon which programs it wishes for the parish, then a recommended ranking according to priorities should be made for the *developmental* goals. This selection of priorities becomes important for the next step in this process, namely the presentation to the Parish Council (or pastor).

The Parish Council seeks to look at the total movement of the faith community, and with this total picture in mind, it listens to all concerns and judges all projected programs — liturgical, educational, and charitable (or social action). The Council may see greater priorities in other parish areas and hence return the Program and Budget Projection to the Board of Education with the suggestion that none of the *developmental* goals can be achieved this coming year. Or the Council may ask the Board to see if it can reduce the projected costs for all the goals by a certain percentage. In either case, the Parish Council takes the recommended Program and Budget Projection from the Board of Education and weighs it against the similar projections from other areas of the parish and against the total anticipated income for the parish. The Council members then have to sort out which goals from which groups will receive attention that year. The Board may be asked to re-examine the projection to find less expensive ways to achieve the same goals, but the recommended goals of the Board should be accepted; i.e., the Council has no business devising their own educational goals and forcing these on the Board. The Council simply adopts the recommended goals presented by the Board of Education unless they are in conflict with other aspects of the parish's Pastoral Mission or unless there is a lack of funds. If there is a conflict, the goals are sent back to the Board with recommendations for revision. The Board and the coordinator would then revise them seeking to incorporate the recommendations and bring the goals into harmony with the total parish thrust.

Once the Parish Council and the Board of Education have adopted the goals for the educational mission of the parish, the coordinator can begin to implement the programs involved. First, however, the Projection should be finalized into an *Annual Program and Budget for 197___*. This is a statement of the actual program and budget to be implemented. Suggestions will have been made about achieving the desired goals with less cost, about the implementation of the program, and about other aspects of the projected program and budget. Goals will have been clarified especially in their statement and meaning. All these suggestions and changes should be incorporated into an actual statement of what the parish will seek to accomplish in education in that year or in an *Annual Program and Budget*. This becomes the guidebook for the coordinator and teachers and a source-book for parents, the Board, and adults who are interested in the educational mission.

Spread Sheets   One addition should now be made to the budget summaries, namely, a spread sheet showing when the money will be spent (see Chart 6:6). This chart is usually arranged according to quarters and gives both the monthly and quarterly totals for spending. Such a chart is presented to the Board; the Treasurer of the Board then knows when and how much the parish must deposit throughout the year to activate the educational program.

A separate account should be maintained for the educational work. The coordinator can be authorized to sign the checks for this account with the Board Treasurer's signature required for large items. The Board (and the pastor) already know where the money is going through the projected budget. Hence they need

CHART 6:6

BUDGET SPREAD SHEET
(Sample)

ITEM	Quar.	Jan.	Feb.	Mar.	Quar.	Apr.	May	June	Total
#11 REC	2125.00	708.33	708.33	708.34	2125.00	708.33	708.33	708.34	4250.00
#20									
#30									
#40									
#50									
#60									
#70									
#80									
#90									
#100									
#110									
#120									
Subtotal									
#200									
Total									

not be involved in each transaction as it occurs. The pastor or the Finance Committee (or whoever signs the checks) simply makes out a check for the projected total for each month's budget. The coordinator adjusts spending accordingly. If the income (#200) is lower than anticipated, the coordinator either presents to the Board the need for increasing the budget for the next quarter or adjusts the program spending to keep it within the approved figures.

Program and Budget Reports At the end of each quarter the coordinator presents to the Board a summary of the program and budget showing where it is going well and where it is failing thus far. These provide the basis for evaluation of the total educational mission, the financial aspect of the programs, and the work of the coordinator. An annual report should also be submitted by the coordinator showing whether or not the program was achieved as projected and where the funds were actually spent. This annual report and the Board's reaction to it provides the data for projecting the next year's program and budget.

LONG-RANGE PROGRAM PROJECTION

A certain measure of the coordinator's time should go into planning a long-range planning program. The data from the yearly program as it progresses can provide part of the picture for the long-range. Other sociological facts will also need to be gathered. The following questions may assist in this long-range planning.

What was the parish like five years ago? How has it changed? What has caused that change? While it is not possible to identify all of the reasons for the changes, it is possible to select many, and these causes may be quite indicative of the general health and movement of the parish. Perhaps the coordinator was hired because the pressure of the parish's deterioration was beginning to be felt. In this case, is the coordinator to assist the priest in presiding over the funeral, so to speak? Or can the trend be reversed? This usually cannot be answered until it is known why the parish is declining.

On the other hand, if the coordinator was hired as the result of a continual growth in the total parish mission, what has accounted for this growth? What causes can be seen and supported?

Included with this general question, of course, is the educational picture of the parish five years ago. These facts will be available from the Board of Education if it has been in existence that long or from the Diocesan Offices and/or parish records. How many children were enrolled in educational programs? How about adult education? Why has the school closed or stayed the same or grown? Or why hasn't the parish built a school?

What was the community (city, suburb, town, etc.) like five years ago? How has it changed? In what ways? Why? The impact of the total community upon the faith community is great. The rise and fall of national ghettos is an example of this impact. The mission of the faith community to the public community depends also upon what that community is like, needs, and is becoming.

The power or telephone companies usually have sociological data about the growth of the community. The town government should be able to provide information about the changes and the direction of growth. Frequently the city or town budget is available in the city hall and contains much information about the priorities of the community. Public school personnel also have data to share with the coordinator in this long-range planning.

What is happening today in the parish (and in the community) that is likely to shape the future? For example, a community may be building a large shopping-living complex in the southern section of the parish territory. This could become a new sub-community in which the natural flow of life and work would be centered for the people involved. To ask them to participate in the educational opportunities offered in a parish which is "far-away" in miles perhaps and especially in its different life style, is an endless frustration. The coordinator may see that the faith community should rent the social room of an apartment complex and hold general adolescent educational events there rather than to expect them to participate in weekly classes at the parish center.

This is an example of the impact of present trends when they can be "seen." Before they can be seen, facts have to be gathered by the coordinator without translating them into program possibilities. After the facts are assessed, they can be translated into program projections.

Other questions might be: can the public school facilities be used for educational purposes? Is it possible to hold ecumenical educational programs for all youth? What is the average age of the parish now in comparison with five years ago? How many young families are moving into the parish? How many leaving? Is there a shortage of priests developing in the diocese? What impact will that have for this faith community? What is the diocese doing? What is happening to the Church nationally? What is public education doing? What kinds of decisions and plans are being made?

What is the Church? What is revelation? What is the

Pastoral Mission of the Church in this decade? What is the educational mission (or the purpose of Christian education)? This is the theoretical aspect of the long-range planning. While these questions could each be answered by a book in itself, nevertheless the coordinator should attempt to formulate a synthesis or select some concise quotations which best express what he is coming to understand as a workable answer to these questions. Again no attempt should be made to draw out originally the implications of these syntheses for the educational mission of the faith community. This will come later.

What should this faith community be like in five years? What should be their Pastoral Mission, their educational mission? This is the first step in judging the above and synthesizing it into a long-range projection. The coordinator can do some of this work originally himself. He should review the data gathered for the above questions and brainstorm what it means for the future in reference to these larger questions above.

Next, it is advisable that the coordinator take the summaries of data from the above questions to the Diocesan Office or to one or more respected coordinators in the area and ask them to brainstorm with him about the implications of this data for the future of the faith community which he serves. With this input in mind the coordinator (with the pastor) can then gather together some of the catechists of the parish and/or Board members and brainstorm with them about the future of the faith community in general and especially in reference to the educational mission. At this point specific planning steps and programs should be left open. The discussion can too easily get off on these details and their merits and lose the focus on the broad direction. The coordinator will need to search out people who are capable of such brainstorming; many people have never had the experience of projecting broad ideas toward the future rather than making immediate practical decisions.

A day could be spent with these people brainstorming where the parish should go (in light of the data gathered), discussing, praying, probing, seeking, and in general focusing on tentative answers to these broad questions. The coordinator may secure a capable secretary for that day to take notes as needed in order to free the group for free thinking. A tape of the proceedings would also be valuable for future reference.

How would we proceed? After the brainstorming, one or more general strategies for the movement of the faith community in the educational mission over the next five years can be formulated. More than one might be necessary and even desirable as the Board and the Parish Council should have reasoned alternatives for decision.

A small group of practical planners can be gathered together by the coordinator to translate the data and general dreams into full strategies for the five year future leading back to the kinds of decisions that will need to be made each year as the plan unfolds. A tentative budget projection should be included after the strategy is formulated.

Should we proceed? In what direction? Once formulated, the strategies can be presented to the Board of Education for consideration. The Diocesan Office should also see the long-range plans and the Board should ask them for a formal reaction with recommendations. The long-range plan should also be given to catechetical leaders, ecumenical leaders, and other specialists as available for their reactions. The reactions can be summarized and become part of the consideration about which way to proceed. The Board then makes its own recommendations about the direction to be taken and presents these and the general strategies to the Parish Council and the entire parish for consideration. Eventually a general consensus will evolve and the coordinator will have a general sense of direction for the formulating of the *Annual Program and Budget.*

WHY ALL THIS?

The reactions of coordinators to this process of planning a program and budget annually and for the future are mixed. Some frankly admit that they do not have the skills to do this type of work. This may be true. Effectiveness, however, can be learned. The coordinator can develop many of these skills involved by himself or at least he can find persons who can compensate for his weakness to achieve this necessary planning.

Other coordinators question whether this type of planning is really necessary. They emphasize that we live in an era of rapid change and that the religious educator simply has to respond as events happen. This would seem to be a denial of the faith covenant which stresses both election and response. The challenge to preach the Word and build the earth also is a challenge to become involved actively as the leaven to the process of growth with people. We do live in an era of rapid change and this is precisely why tentative plans must continually be made about what to do now, in the immediate future, and in the long-range future. These plans will be changed regularly as the events of life occur, but changing from one plan to another response is a mature step compared with simply reacting with the changes that arise. Change is movement from one thing to another; growth is movement in a direction. The planning process allows the coordinator and the parish to see where they are and why, before moving on, and they must move, if growth in faith and community are to occur.

The planning process described in this chapter is also a very effective form of adult education. One of the purposes of education in general and particularly Christian education is to free people to see who they are, what they can become, and the implications of their decisions. The planning process can provide part of this. It is not enough to speak about these things in content terms in classes or lectures. They often make a vital life decision and its meaning a simple content principle to remember. This does not affect a change in a person's life style. Facing decisions, gathering insight into the nature and effect of those decisions, and living with the impact of that decision is a humanizing process of adult education. The "sense of doom" which many coordinators feel about the future of the parishes for which they work impels them to push adult education with a vigor. They become frustrated when the adults do not respond. Frequently they do not respond to "adult education" because it has little to do with their lives except as an information luxury. Facing decisions about the education of their children and their own growth in faith and about the future of the parish will involve adults if they are really given the decision to make. The coordinator, if he is not careful, can take over the responsibility for the education of children and of adults from the people themselves. This only furthers a dependency which is the opposite of the freedom which Christian education should provide. Helping people see and face decisions is helping them to become free to decide how they will live and why. A planned program and budget can contribute to this growth process.

Chapter Seven

ASSISTING TEACHERS

Of all of the responsibilities assigned to a parish coordinator perhaps the most important is working with teachers. No other factor so greatly affects the quality of parish religious education for youth and adults as the catechist. "Superior teaching is the first prerequisite of providing an efficient educational program of good quality, for the teacher, while not all of education, is nevertheless most of it"(1).

There is widespread agreement among parents, pastors, publishers, and coordinators that the teacher is central to the success of parish religious education. And most will agree that catechist education is vitally important. There is, however, great disagreement about what constitutes "good teaching" and how catechists are best prepared.

WHAT IS A "GOOD TEACHER"?

Each of us has had considerable experience with teachers in our education and in the back of our minds we have a model of what makes a good teacher. This model may have been reinforced by our reading and preparation in religious education also. These models persist despite the fact that there is very little conclusive research—especially in catechetics—to verify the characteristics and methods of a good teacher. Philip Jackson, who has spent much of his career researching teaching, notes that "almost all of the noble crusades that have set out in search of the best teacher and the best method—or even the better teacher and the better method—have returned empty-handed. The few discoveries to date are pitifully small in proportion to their cost in time and energy"(2). N. Fattu concurs(3) and Arthur Combs does also(4).

In religious education, there is very little research on catechists. What books and articles there are usually describe the ideal catechist in reference to a theoretical conception of religious education. Thus we are faced with the fact that coordinators have little objective data to utilize in preparing catechists for their participation in the educational mission.

This need not be alarming. If we look back over our own educational experience, we will soon realize that we have had one or more "good teachers" and that some things can be said about them. What research there is also would support these rather general conclusions that a "good catechist" or the "better catechist" is: (1) a unique person, that is, one who is alive as a human being; (2) a person filled with faith and knowledge of Christianity; (3) a person who has developed an effective teaching style; and lastly (4) a person who is deeply interested in learners.

A Unique Person Arthur Combs states quite simply that "a good teacher is primarily a unique personality"(5). He says "(we) may define the effective teacher formally as a unique human being who has learned to use himself effectively and efficiently to carry out his own and society's purposes in the education of others"(6). This fact of the impact of the personality upon the learners is demonstrable from research although the research is not able to link precise personality traits with definite responses or results. It simply documents the impact of the personality of the teacher on the learners(7).

Dr. Beryl Orris, director of the Divine Word International Centre, explains that "every active mind has its effect on some other human being" and that, once a person has made the basic decision to live life rather than exist, he is able to walk hand in hand with others seeking a fuller life(8).

Perhaps the most demonstrable "proof" for the impact of the personality of a good teacher lies in our own experiences. We can look back over our education and pick out the teachers who have a profound impact upon us and it was not so much their techniques—these are in effect extensions of self anyway—as the force of their personalities. There is little doubt that life generates life and that an alive catechist has an impact(9).

A Person Filled with Faith and a Knowledge of Christianity Research and our personal experience again will show us that the effective catechist has a deep faith and an in-depth understanding of Christianity. Our experience with good teachers most frequently produces an excitement for the teacher's field. The teacher's own enthusiasm comes from a depth understanding and appreciation of the relevance of what he is teaching. This is contagious.

Gabriel Moran has consistently pointed out that catechetics is based upon rather superficial understandings of theology and has pleaded for more theology at a time when catechists have tried to shed the dominance of knowledge in religious education. Moran explains that "(what) is needed in not to strip away more theology but to begin to develop a more adequate theological foundation for the catechetics movement"(10). The kinds of decisions which a catechist has to make, if he would do more than follow the text, demands a criterion for decision-making. This criterion comes from sound theology.

So much has been written about the need for a solid faith in catechists and for a deep understanding of Christian revelation, that this aspect of a good catechist need not be discussed further here. The relationship of the in-depth understanding of the "content" to decision-making in teaching will be discussed later.

A Person Who has Developed an Effective Personal Teaching Style There is considerable research on teacher-centered versus learner-centered teaching techniques. Much is written in religious education journals about the pros and cons of methods of teaching. The more serious research simply shows, however, that certain techniques work well for certain purposes and poorly for other purposes, and that some techniques work well for certain teachers with certain learners and others do not. Lectures, for example, are effective for communicating knowledge to some people and not to others. The latter people may receive new knowledge more effectively from personal reading or through discussion. Discussion groups appear to be more effective in assisting most people to integrate new knowledge into what they already know but they are also shown to be poor means for communicating new knowledge(11).

Robert Strom and Charles Galloway explain that it is futile to attempt to define "good teaching" in terms of a definite method. "The traditional aim of trying to identify 'good' teachers and 'good' teaching has failed.

Essentially, it has failed because a single set of criteria has been used in an impersonal way. Until recently, the complexity of accepting each teacher as a unique person with a unique set of intentions for a classroom of unique children has been deferred"(12).

While it is important and effective for coordinators to discuss various teaching techniques with catechists, it should be remembered that each catechist, much like an artist, will have to discover his own idiom for effecting his intentions in leading a learning situation.

A Person Who is Deeply Interested in Learners Once again our own educational experience will tell us that we learned most effectively from a teacher who respected us and who cared. Research will also demonstrate this.

A number of people have begun to research the nature of the helping relationship that occurs between people in teaching, counselling, and general interpersonal relationships. One of the more well known researchers is Carl Rogers. Rogers sees the "facilitation of learning as the aim of education . . ."(13). He also described three key attitudes on the part of the teacher which best promote the facilitation of learning. First of all, he notes that when the teacher (or facilitator as he calls him) "is a real person, being what he is, entering into a relationship with the learner without presenting a front or a facade, he is much more likely to be effective." Secondly, he explains that the teacher needs to prize the worth of the learners, that is, to genuinely care about them. Thirdly, Rogers notes that to be effective in a relationship a teacher needs to have an empathic understanding, that is, "the ability to understand the student's reactions from the inside . . ." When this is present, he explains, "then again the likelihood of significant learning is increased"(14).

This ability to care, to see things from the point of view of the other person, to value him irregardless of whether or not we share common beliefs, aspirations, and experiences, is a quality that promotes effectiveness in many fields. Sales personnel(15), teachers(16), ministers(17), and executives(18) all find that this human quality transcends particular techniques and makes them effective if the aims of the people involved are compatible and the affection felt genuine.

At first, these four characteristics or qualities of a "good" teacher may seem evident but they are like the pearl of great price, for although simple in theory, they are difficult to achieve in practice.

Even though it is difficult to speak in exact terms of "the good teacher" when preparing for catechist education, coordinators should not drop the whole issue. It is possible to speak of catechist education in terms of conceptualizations about religious education and in terms of assisting individuals to become "better" catechists. "Saying all teachers can become better states something quite different from urging all teachers to be good; 'better' suggests an emerging condition emphasizing the process and growth of becoming rather than an established state, a finished stability of being"(19).

Jackson distinguishes between "pre-active" and "interactive" teaching. Applying this distinction to catechist education can provide a basis for preparation programs. "Interactive" teaching refers to the personal range and style of responses which a teacher develops out of the interaction with learners. Each particular group of learners may evoke a different response. Over a period of time, the teacher learns, by trial and error so to speak, a certain range of effective teaching behavior which helps him to achieve his intentions in the educational process.

"Pre-active" teaching refers to the kinds of things

which the teacher does in planning for and in evaluating the interaction. Here the basic understandings of the teacher about the nature of teaching, the teaching model, are brought into decision-making. Catechist preparation can deal with these conceptions. Virgil Herrick notes that "the conception the teacher has of her role sets the way in which she will tend to handle many kinds of routine situations in her teaching. Perhaps role conception is the basis of teacher style"(20).

THE ROLE OF THE CATECHIST

In addition to the more informal conceptions which pastors, parents, and catechists have of what a "good" teacher is like, there are the actual role expectations which accompany (1) the various areas of the total educational mission of Christian people, and (2) the curricular and instructional materials designed to achieve the goals of these.

The Areas of the Educational Mission The work of Catholic people in education has traditionally been divided into administrative categories: Catholic schools, Confraternity of Christian Doctrine, Newman, and so forth. Perhaps it would be better to distinguish the various areas by the generic terms *catechesis, religious education,* and *Christian education.*

Catechesis: In this book, *catechesis* refers to the educative experience between a chatechist (priest, religious, or lay) and learners (adult or youth) which transforms their faith perceptions. Catechesis, in other words, is a faith experience in an educational setting. It is a prayerful happening in which the personal witness of both the catchist and the learners and the presence of the Spirit transcend the "content," originally the focus of the educational setting. Because catechesis is an opening to the dynamic of the Spirit, it cannot be planned or programmed precisely; it simply happens. In fact, only by realizing that catechesis cannot be planned are we free to allow the Spirit to overcome us and for this faith experience to occur.

In catechesis, personal metanoia occurs. The perceptions of the individual regarding self, others, the world, God, and faith are altered by the impact of the experience. Knowledge of previous life experiences and the "content," both of that session and of previous religious educational experiences, are re-oriented along new or deeper patterns of life style. Abraham Maslow speaks of such occurences as "peak experiences" and further explains that "it looks quite probable that the peak experience may be the model of the religious revelation or the religious illumination or conversion which has played so great a role in the history of religions" (21).

This kind of faith experience—catechesis—can be found in all phases of the faith community's educational work: Cursillo, retreats, discussion clubs, Cana conferences, and more structured classes and sessions. The catechesis experience appears to differ from the similar faith experiences in liturgy or prayer sessions largely in the source out of which it has arisen. Catechesis is the desirable outcome of religious education but it cannot be programmed to happen. Furthermore, religious education has other purposes apart from this catechesis experience.

Religious Education: Religious education is supportive of catechesis but different from it. Catechesis aims directly at a living faith relationship much like the radii of a circle aim at the center of the circle. Religious education is more inclusive; it occurs between the radii, so to speak. Religious education builds toward and reflects upon the catechesis experience and all life experiences. Thus, religious education is not only person-oriented but also content-oriented, whereas catechesis is totally *Person*-oriented.

The content of religious education is the reflections of men of faith — past and present — upon life, man, God, Church, and so forth. These reflections are formalized into the Scriptures, teachings of the Church Fathers, Popes, Councils, and the magisterium. This revelation, faith doctrines and facts become the focus for the structured religious education learning experiences. These experiences can be programmed and involve definite curricular and instructional materials and teaching-learning roles.

Perhaps, Ian Ramsey's distinction between commitment and discernment will clarify further the difference between catechesis and religious education; catechesis leads to commitment.

"Ramsey begins by describing the kinds of situations in which the use of religious language is appropriate. These are principally of two kinds; namely, those of discernment and those of commitment. Discernment situations are ones in which a fresh and unexpected disclosure occurs yielding a new insight into the depths of meaning in experience. Commitment situations are ones in which a person is grasped by a sense of the intimate worth of something (or someone) to which he is willing to dedicate himself"(22).

There is another term which should be discussed very briefly here; namely, *religious studies*, or the *study of religion*. Public schools especially will be working with this area in the coming decades. The chief difference between the study of religion and religious education appears to be the perceived relationship to faith and the catechesis experience. The study of religion probes for its content the religious phenomenon of man; religious education probes this and the experience of God with the purpose of fostering growth in faith. "The object of the study of religon is the universal phenomenon of human religiousness, or 'religion.' . . . Thus, unlike theology, the object of the study of religion cannot be 'God' nor even 'the sacred' *per se*, but only the sacred as universally experienced and expressed in . . . 'religion' which may be defined formally as a universal mode of being human"(23).

Christian Education: Christian education refers to the circle — to continue the image used above. Catechesis is a faith experience in an educational setting; religious education reflects upon this and upon the content of other faith and life experiences; Christian education embraces all the other educational work undertaken by the Church. This can be spoken of as direct and indirect Christian education.

Direct forms of Christian education would include all educational programs not dealing with religious content (and, therefore, religious education) but which are under the auspices of the Church. Catholic schools are an obvious expression of Christian education. There is no such thing as Christian biology or mathematics, but there may be a Christian reason for the Church sponsoring classes in biology and mathematics. Furthermore, the total curricular and instructional pattern of a Catholic school ought to be designed to achieve objectives deemed valid from a Christian frame of reference.

Indirect forms of Christian education are all of the activities of the Church in the public forum regarding education. These would range from the Church working for quality public education to public legislative policy relative to the study of religion in public schools. It would also refer to the educational work in public adult education through media and social action.

Lastly, the term *'catechetics'* should be described briefly. Brother Gabriel Moran has noted that "the problem of catechetics is that it exists." As he put it later in the same talk to the Catechetical Forum (1968), "My trouble with the field of religious education is that I am doubtful that it ever had or should have had an identity. Theoretically, I see no difficulty in religion and education being brought together; but, the existing models seem to be strange hybrids."

There is a reason, however, for the existence of catechetics if it is understood as the process of synthesizing conceptions about the catechesis experience, the mission of the Church, the signs of the times, and knowledge of learners into a projection of the purpose of the educational mission of Christian people in a given era and cultural context. This projection becomes the curriculum priority out of which general goals and specific program objectives are created.

Summary: It is important to speak of the area of work for which a catechist is being prepared, because this determines part of the role expectation which in turn affects the actual interactive teaching style the individual adopts. Defining a catechist as man of faith involved in teaching, we can see that the preparation which a volunteer needs for weekly parish religious education sessions differs considerably from that which a professional teacher needs in a Catholic or public school. The parish coordinator should be involved with both.

Theories of Religious Education The other source from which catechist role expectations are derived is the theories of religious education(24). A theory of religious education is a mental model encompassing what ought to happen in religious education, why, to whom, how, and with what results. As with education in general, we have only a scant attempt at theories of religious education and so we all too frequently rely solely upon moral maxims by some religious educator or upon some generalizations from our own or others' successful experiences. These have their place but with the increased thrust toward quality parish religious education dictated by the demands of our times, more embracing and valid theories of religious education are needed. Coordinators in their work in parish religious education need not wait for scholars to develop such theories either. Coordinators who have developed a research attitude will be able to gather data, devise hypotheses, test programs, and evaluate results on their own as part of their on-going educational leadership.

Jerome Bruner speaks of the importance of such theories of education. He notes:
"We do a greater part of our work by manipulating our representations or models of reality than by acting directly on the world itself . . . We know now that theory is more than a general description of what happens or a statement of probabilities of what might or might not happen . . . It entails, explicitly or implicitly, a model of what it is that one is theorizing about, a set of propositions that, taken in ensemble, yield occasional predictions about things"(25).

Out of a theory of religious education, implicitly or explicitly understood, program planners, curriculum designers, and others project an expectation of the way in which the catechist ought to act. This is popularly viewed as the role of the catechist. Catechist preparation programs are designed to introduce the prospective teacher into this theory of religious education and the expected role behavior. Armed with a teaching model, so to speak, the catechist interprets the data of his inter-action with learners into a format which ultimately becomes the range of his interactive teaching style. Hence, it is important to discuss the roles of the cate-chist in relationship to a theory of religious education however poorly worked out.

Curriculum Design: A curriculum design makes known the relationship between the theory of religious education and the expected role of the catechist. It also becomes the frame of reference for catechist preparation programs.

Following the Conference on Curriculum Theory at the University of Chicago in March of 1950, the concept of curriculum design became widely discussed and researched in educational circles. Most coordinators will have had little exposure to curriculum design, how-ever, as these concepts have been introduced into few religious education master's programs.

"Curriculum design is a statement which identifies the elements of the curriculum, states what their rela-tionships are to each other, and indicates the principles of organization for the administrative conditions under which it is to operate . . ."(26). Virgil Herrick further explains that "Any adequate structure or design of curriculum defines the important components or aspects of curriculum, determines the pattern of their relation-ships to each other and to the curriculum jobs to be performed"(27).

In whatever definition is used, a curriculum design does the following:
1) identifies all the major elements of the educational program.
2) shows the relationship of these major elements to one another.

3) establishes priorities for curricular and instructional decisions.

4) becomes a criterion for the defining of objectives, the selection of learning resources, and the evaluation of outcomes.

5) serves as a criterion for introducing change.

6) and provides the rationale for the daily administrative and instructional decisions, especially through the projection of roles.

For all of these reasons, it is important that a coordinator become familiar with curriculum design. The last point, however, is the reason for the introduction of curriculum design here, for catechist preparation largely depends upon what the catechist is expected to do.

The curriculum design for religious education is presented here (Chart 7:1) to serve as a model for coordinators in their interactive work with catechists. Eventually, they can evolve their own theory of religious education and curriculum design to provide the basis of their work with catechists.

In a religious education class or session, there are a number of elements present: (1) an aim, (2) a catechist, (3) learners, (4) content, (5) process, and (6) evaluation. The expected roles for the catechist and the learners, the particular aim, content, and process, and the evaluation are presented in terms of a more basic curriculum priority or the expressed purpose of religious education. A few examples will make this clear.

Baltimore Catechism Theory of Religious Education: Behind the Baltimore Catechism approach there is a definite theory of religious education which, because of the thinking in the curriculum bases (see Chart 7:1), states the objective of religious education

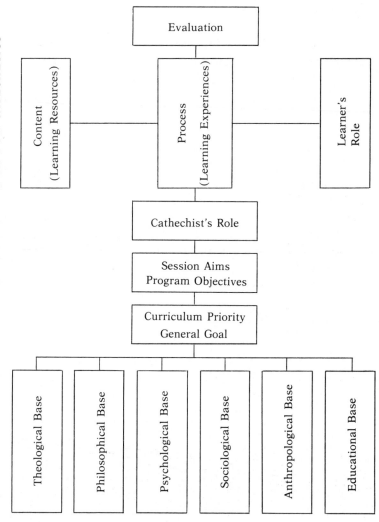

CHART 7:1   *A CURRICULUM DESIGN FOR CATECHETICS*

Evaluation

Content
(Learning Resources)

Process
(Learning Experiences)

Learner's
Role

Cathechist's Role

Session Aims
Program Objectives

Curriculum Priority
General Goal

Theological Base

Philosophical Base

Psychological Base

Sociological Base

Anthropological Base

Educational Base

as "the art of imparting knowledge of religion together with its practical application to children and adults"(28). Religious education can be concerned about many aims but "its main interest is the efficient and fruitful presentation of Christian doctrine to others"(29). The catechist is expected to impart the doctrine objectively and efficiently, aiming for "a certainty of information"(30) on that particular subject.

Catechist preparation, therefore, seeks to give the teacher sufficient authoritative background so she can teach with confidence, correctly explaining the content and answering questions. Collins notes:
"It is necessary for the catechist, therefore, to have a good grasp of the subject, much more than is actually needed for teaching. This additional background gives the teacher confidence in his ability to provide out of his surplus of information accurate explanations to difficulties not found in the text"(31).

If the coordinator were working with this theory of religious education in the parish, he would see to it that the catechist had an in-depth preparation in the official teachings of the Church and had learned ways of communicating these clearly to youth and adults. The catechist preparation program would stress the content which the catechist would be expected to teach.

Eichstaett-Bangkok Theory of Religious Education: After the International Study Weeks on Mission Catechetics held in the early 1960's in Eichstaett and Bangkok, a great revival occurred in religious education in North America. This was due largely to the presentation of a new theory of religious education which was the result of advances in the fields of Scripture, liturgy, psychology, and other fields then being brought into catechetics. In particular, the content for teaching changed. The theological outlines of questions and answers which provided the basic content for the catechisms were replaced by the *kerygma.*

"The Greek word, *kerygma,* means message and in the New Testament kerygma means specifically the Good News of Salvation that Christ preached and commissioned his Church to proclaim"(32). The *kerygmatic* approach to religious education has as its objective "the transmission of God's message to man for the purpose of evoking a commitment and faith in the one to whom we give the message"(33). This approach is similar to the catechism approach in some ways and considerably different in most others. It still places a great deal of emphasis upon the message to be transmitted, but there is also a great deal of emphasis given to the importance of the catechist.

The catechist is expected to be concerned about the students "as persons"(34), should give them a "sense of community"(35), and be a "herald of the Good News"(36). In all, the personal witness of the catechist is of prime importance.

Catechist preparation programs for this approach are aimed at (1) giving the catechists a thorough background in Salvation History and the kerygma, (2) assisting them to learn the Munich Method which accompanied the Eichstaett-Bangkok movement, and (3) assisting the catechists to develop a mature faith and active Christian life style in order that they may be good witnesses of the Good News in their lives(37). Audio visual aids, liturgical celebrations, group singing, Salvation History, New Testament study—these and many more items—were introduced into catechist preparation in comparison to the programs accompanying the Baltimore Catechism era and theory of religious education.

Most of the education which coordinators themselves have received has dealt with the Eichstaett-Bangkok Theory of religious education in one form or another.

Only since 1968 have college and diocesan programs of preparation for catechists begun to change substantially to a different theory.

Post Vatican Theory of Religious Education: A great deal of time could be spent differentiating the many kinds of theories which have begun to develop toward the end of the 1960's. The impetus of the Second Vatican Council brought to the foreground many of the developments in the disciplines which provide the base for catechetics and helped develop a new life-centered approach to religious education.

In the Baltimore Catechism theory of religious education the emphasis is largely upon the content to be taught. In the Eichstaett-Bangkok approach the emphasis is still largely upon the content — the kerygma — but with much more attention given to the learners and the process. In the Post Vatican approach, the prime emphasis is upon the learner who, in the company of a community of believers, is led to reflect upon his life experiences in light of the saving words and deeds of Jesus as understood and taught by the faith community.

Gabriel Moran explains that "Christian revelation is a personal communion of knowledge, an inter-relationship of God and the individual within a believing community. God's bestowal and the individual acceptance are both indispensable to the process. The human partner is not a recipient of "something" called revelation. Humanity stands within the process and not outside of it, and revelation is not a 'thing' at all but exists in present, continuing, conscious experience of people . . ." (38). Therefore, the purpose of religious education in this approach is stated quite differently:"The purpose of catechesis is to explore reality in the light of God's action in the experience of men"(39).

Basically, the expected role of the catechist in this approach is to facilitate the process of exploring life in relationship to faith. Believing that the basic search of man for meaning in life is fulfilled by Christ, the catechist seeks to remove the barriers which impede man from seeing life and self in relationship to God and from building a life style upon the perspective which faith offers. Babin, in writing about the role of the catechist, states: "He will help his students have basic principles and insights that the students themselves can use to perceive and evaluate the situations they are in. He will, thus, have to adopt a pedagogy of invention (teaching which opens the student to search for meaning) rather than one of teacher transmission (one in which the teacher hands down a collection of truth formulated and defined). Finally, he will have to train his students to approach this world in terms of ultimate meaning, and not to stop at the organizational or functional level of life"(40). Catechist preparation for this role will be considerably different than in either of the above two cases. Since teachers learn much about teaching by the way in which they are taught, catechist preparation will focus on the catechists themselves as believers in addition to preparing them for fulfilling a role in religious education. This will be explained in more detail later.

Summary: This very superficial introduction to theories of religious education and curriculum design is *given to assist the coordinator* with teacher preparation.

It was noted at the beginning that each catechist must develop his own interactive teaching style much like an artist. Some assistance can be given to improve his teaching style, but only the catechist can develop effective teaching behaviors for *himself.*

The way in which the catechist thinks about what he is supposed to accomplish in religious education and the particular aspect of the educational mission which he chooses—these do affect the type of teaching style which the catechist will develop.

Therefore, it is important that the coordinator begin to work out for himself clear understandings about the teaching model or the theories about religious education. These can provide a definite sense of direction for the interaction with catechists in the preparation program. The simple introduction of new techniques will not suffice. Unless each catechist has a rationale for them, rooted in a basic sense of direction, and can perceive the difference between what he wishes to become as a catechist and what is expected of him, new techniques will not become integrated into an effective teaching style(41).

CATECHIST PREPARATION PROGRAMS

As the coordinator begins to plan for fulfilling his responsibility for catechist education, a number of questions arise which should be resolved. These can only be discussed in general terms here, but they are basic to planning in most every situation.

Who Should be Involved? Should the coordinator work with all those engaged in educational work in the parish at the same time? For purposes of this discussion, we will limit this section to those catechists who will work with catechesis and religious education for youth. Catechists for adult religious education and professional teachers in other phases of Christian education will be discussed in the next section.

What type of people should be selected for working with youth as catechists? Are there some criteria possible for selecting the best people for becoming catechists? The problem of catechist preparation starts with selection of the persons to be prepared, for first of all the "better" catechist is a unique human being, alive with faith. Faith cannot be taught to people; such persons can only be found. How does one discern the "teaching charisma" in a person? The importance of selection must be faced. A survey on who teaches in CCD programs revealed that the majority of catechists were drafted or accepted without any reference to qualifications and were allowed to work in religious education with little or no preparation(42).

This question cannot be resolved here. More research must be done on the kinds of "charismatic" qualities which should be sought in prospective catechists and some criteria must be prepared to assist in decision-making in this area (keeping in mind that no standard model of a "good" catechist will ever be found).

What Should the Catechist Preparation Program Seek to Accomplish? Unless we wish to mistake activity for accomplishment, the definition of goals for catechist preparation programs cannot be avoided. The coordinator needs to determine what it is that he seeks to accomplish with this group of catechists in this preparation program using more precise goals than are usually given. This question is answered from several "sub-questions":

What does this particular group of catechists need for their particular situations? What are their personal faith concerns? The introduction of new information will not be effective unless it is given personal meaning and this is done in terms of personal goals and meaning(43). A process early in the preparation program should be used to assist the particular group to articulate what they expect to learn, and what their particular faith concerns are. This sets the perspective through which the rest of the program will be viewed(44).

This process is not simply a means to achieve information. The process of setting goals is a skill which the prospective catechists need to learn, especially for their interaction with older youth. Religious education programs based upon a life-centered approach will involve the learners in the process of setting goals for their own learning. In an era of change, the Christian needs to be able to shape his changing life style into a direction he deems valid. Cox notes that "the child or adult who is equipped by his education merely to find a place in the society, to fill his niche in the culture, is not prepared for the secular world. He must learn from the outset to accept responsibility for fashioning the values and images of the culture and for shaping the institutions of his society"(45). To a certain extent, this skill of "fashioning the values" can be learned in the teaching-learning situation through the goal-setting process, if the catechist allows this to be part of the curriculum. Snygg explains that "fundamentally, the curriculum aids the student, not by giving him answers to problems that he does not have, but by helping him to discover new and more fruitful objectives in his personal campaign for feelings of greater worth and value" (46).

Another sub-question related to the objectives for the catechist preparation programs is what are the needs of society and of the Church. If the educational mission of Christian people is integrally related to the Pastoral Mission, then the Pastoral Mission, that is, the Church's response to the needs of man in that era and place, must be taken into consideration as part of the goals for catechist preparation. Ideally, if the catechist is a believer rooted in the times in which he lives, the catechist's own personal concerns would reflect part of the same needs. The perspective of the larger faith community, however, needs to be brought to bear upon the goal setting process between the coordinator and the catechist in preparation. To use an example, a particular group of catechists may be concerned about authority in the Church and may wish to teach this to the youth with whom they will be working, and yet the issue of the day to which the faith community must respond may be war and peace. To prepare catechists to handle authority in the Church and not to confront the Christian stance on war is to prepare them to be a "sounding brass or a tinkling cymbal" (1 Cor. 13:1) rather than a herald of the Good News.

In other words, it is not a simple task for the coordinator to say this is what you need to know in order to be a good catechist. What they need to know has to take into consideration their personal concerns, the concerns of the times and of the Church, as well as the Christian message.

What Content Will Best Prepare Catechists for their task? The goals which have been established for the preparation sessions will dictate the scope and nature of the content. There simply is so much known about Scripture, liturgy, theology, and allied fields that it cannot all be presented to catechists with the expectation that they in turn will teach it to the youth with whom they will work.

Since the catechist preparation programs involve both the personal concerns of the catechists themselves and the message they expect to communicate to others, this balance will need to be reflected in the content. Simply relating the content which the catechists need for their own faith growth is not sufficient. That is adult religious education and not catechist preparation. The content will need to deal with this, but also with (1) the educational mission, (2) the curriculum design and the role expectations, and (3) the theologic and anthropic disciplines related to the educational mission and the expected concerns of the youth whom they will be teaching.

1) The Educational Mission: As was mentioned above, the catechist needs a strong sense of why he himself believes in order to be a witness to faith. He also needs a sense of what the educational mission of Church is about in that era — a sense of why he should be teaching and what that teaching should accomplish. This sense provides the parameters for his teaching decisions about what kinds of learning experiences and content are valid.

2) Curriculum Design and Role Expectations: By understanding how the proposed programs expect to achieve the educational mission described above, the catechist has the parameters for the development of his interactive teaching style. This may sound very academic, but it is really quite simple and true. Catechists have an image of what they *should* do in teaching religion. Often, this image is in conflict with what they think they *would like* to do. A large portion of a coordinator's work with them is one of simply providing a climate of support in which the catechists can bring the role expectations and their personal hopes together.

A discussion of curriculum design — especially in specific curricular and instructional materials to be used by the parish — and the role of the catechist has a definite place within the content for catechist preparation sessions. Formerly, this was called "applied catechetics" or "methods" but the term, "curriculum design," means more than either of these, as was explained above.

3) The Theologic and Anthropic Disciplines: The structural elements in theology, Scripture, liturgy, and

related God-oriented (theologic) disciplines and those of psychology, sociology, anthropology and the other man-oriented (anthropic) disciplines obviously are part of the content to be included in catechist preparation programs. The question is really one of how much of which discipline? This has to be answered in terms of the particular goals and objectives of that group of catechists being prepared. It is not simply a matter of bringing in new information. "Any item of information will affect an individual's behavior only in the degree to which he has discovered its personal meaning for him"(47). The persons present at the training sessions, their existential context in the parish, and the demands which will be placed upon them as a catechist in a given situation—these shape the relevance of content and become part of the criterion for the selection of what will be included in catechist preparation programs. The other part of the criterion comes from the structural elements of the disciplines themselves. Each of the disciplines or fields related to catechetics has an internal set of concepts or an internal structure around which the major themes or clusters of information are patterned. Consequently the coordinator, as a curriculum specialist, ought to "direct his efforts toward identifying the large principles and generalizations, the cognitive structures, which undergrid a subject"(48). These, then, are the other part of the criterion for the selections of the content for catechist preparation programs. In this context, the continual stress of Gabriel Moran on a more "adequate theological foundation for the catechetics movement" (49) makes a great deal of sense.

How are Catechists Best Prepared? "One learns to teach partly by being well taught"(50). Most catechists have learned their own faith by one style of teaching and in the new religious education program they are asked to teach by a different style. Hence, it is vital that their preparation program be in a style similar to that for which they are being prepared.

Instead of trying to describe the vast variety of instructional strategies and techniques which may be helpful in catechist preparation—a process that would require a book itself, a rough model will be presented in summary form, based upon research on teacher education, data from Project Coordinator, an experimental teacher education program, and a variety of experiences with parish and diocesan teacher education(51).

The Consortium(52): The consortium is like a seminar for catechists. It is led by the coordinator who assumes the role of facilitating the growth of the catechists themselves. Basically, the facilitator (coordinator) serves as a support person. He seeks to help the catechists sort out their own role expectations, their own personal and professional (teaching) concerns, and introduce them to knowledge and skills which will help them more effectively realize their aims in religious education. The coordinator as facilitator is a creator, sustainer, and mediator. He creates a climate of discovery and concern for the improvement of teaching behavior; he sustains the efforts and attempts of the catechists; and he brings knowledge and skills to their attention in their process of improvement.

Pre-service: Before the catechists begin to teach, the consortium is formed by the coordinators. Through a process of definition, the catechists articulate their expectations and needs. From these and from the coordinator's understanding of the nature of teaching religion and the particular challenges which will be faced in that given parish with youth, goals for the learning sessions are tentatively established. It may be found later that these first goals are not essentially valid.

The establishment of goals — what we shall attempt to do together — is important as it provides a basic frame of reference out of which the catechists and the coordinator can shape their interaction. "It would be indeed strange to purport that one is assisting a teacher without knowing something of the direction in which he hopes to achieve"(53).

From these goals, the coordinator and the catechists work out the content and the learning style for the pre-service consortium and for the religious education program. They also determine a reasonable length of time to meet, taking into consideration the situation of that parish. This pre-service period may only be for two months and in effect it sets the tone for the on-going in-service consortium by setting up some general role expectations against which the catechist can interpret the interactive data from teaching. Basically, this pre-service period may answer the following questions — depending, of course, upon the particular objectives set: (1) What does it mean to believe? (2) Why should I become a catechist? (3) What is the purpose of religious education today? (4) What are the learners with whom I will be working like? (5) What do they need? (6) What is available to assist me in this parish? (7) What kinds of teaching techniques are possible and effective? Gradually, the consortium group will have developed a common sense of direction — even though it may be multifaceted — and gain some general ideas about what they wish to do and try with the learners.

In-service: After the religious education program has started, the consortium takes on a slightly different supportive role; namely, feed-back on what is happening and where it is going to go from there. The consortium need not continue to meet consistently; rather, the coordinator may work with one or several of these teachers at a time. The identity with the group, however, should not be lost. Liturgical and social interaction also help to build a supportive climate in which the catechists are free to sort out their own faith, their intents for teaching, the possibilities open to them, and gain the courage to try to improve their teaching.

There are many feed-back techniques open to the coordinator. Simply visiting the session and discussing it afterwards with the catechist is one way. Taping a session and then discussing it with the catechist later is a good technique. These individual procedures should be coupled with regular group sessions during which the consortium assesses if what they set out to do is happening and why or why not.

Over a period of time, the consortium becomes a most effective means for growth. In the second year, it may be necessary to start a new group on their own rather than mix new and old members.

How do We Know Catechist Preparation is Effective?
In this approach to parish catechist preparation, there is no need for certification or other external measurements of performance. The success will be measured by the success of the religious education programs. "The success of our professional behavior, as we might judge it personally or as it might be judged by outsiders, depends, first, upon the genuine worth of our aspirations and, secondly, upon our effectiveness and efficiency in achieving them"(54).

The consortium can become a learning community in which the coordinator and the catechists probe the Christian mystery and the educational mission together. As such, it can become the model for the learning community which should develop between the catechists and learners as they probe the meaning of life in faith together. Feed-back, that is, evaluation throughout the learning process, is given by the coordinator to the catechists and by the catechists to one another. If the consortium is successful, a dynamism will be evident and this in turn contributes to the success of the religious education programs. The Good News inspired sufficient enthusiasm on the part of the first disciples that they were accused of being drunk at the ninth hour. If catechists have personal and "professional" belief in Christianity they too will have a contagious dynamism. The coordinator has much to do with the creation of the atmosphere in which this growth is possible.

One other variable for the facilitation of growth in teachers should be mentioned here. The coordinator's role in procuring teaching resources is also important for producing change. Catechists, for example, are more apt to begin using media in the learning sessions if media materials are readily available. The availability of resources has a definite impact upon change in teaching, especially the rate of change.

CATECHISTS FOR ADULTS

Parish adult religious education varies greatly in both format and purpose. Hence, it is difficult to speak of the preparation of catechists or leaders for it. In many places the parish coordinator is expected to become the teacher of adults; other parishes rely upon diocesan or regional center adult programs—frequently of the lecture type. There is a great deal of concern over the importance of adult religious education in general, but few really effective model programs emerge. The rush to learn what the Second Vatican Council was all about is over. Liturgical changes and internal Church problems no longer draw interested adults. The time is at hand for radical change in the approach to adults in the educational mission. But in what direction?

One direction in which adult religious education

will move is called life-centered. To be life-centered means that religious education aims to illuminate with the saving words and deeds of Christ the given context (the time/space life circumstances) and life style of the individuals involved. This is a broad statement which can be translated into reality in many ways, both pastoral and educational.

First of all, it should be remembered that there is a strong educative element in all liturgy. Growing in consciousness about life in relationship to the Lord is a great part of the Liturgy of the Word. Secondly, it should be recalled here that work with the parish Board of Education on the part of the coordinator is a very important form of adult education. And, thirdly, it should be kept in mind that every adult is confronted with numerous informal opportunities daily in which learning occurs—including contacts with the pastor, coordinator, and catechists. The big compulsion to have adults gathered together in classrooms or lectures simply must be challenged. This is schooling and not necessarily education. Education is a life-long and life-centered activity not confined to classrooms or lecture halls exclusively. It occurs especially in the interaction between people and at the times in life in which people have a great deal of themselves invested in what is happening. Abraham Maslow explains:

"The final and unavoidable conclusion is that education—like all our social institutions—must be concerned with its final values, and this in turn is just about the same as speaking of what have been called 'spiritual values' or 'higher values.' These are the principles of choice which help us to answer the age-old questions: What is the good life? What is the good man? The good woman? What is the good society and what is my relation to it? What are my obligations to society? What is best for my children? What is Justice? Truth? Virtue?

What is my relation to nature, to death, to aging, to pain, to illness? What is my responsibility to my brothers? Who are my brothers? What shall I be loyal to? What must I be ready to die for?"(55).

These ultimate questions are value-laden and they are usually asked informally during the events of life. At the times of "peak experiences" (catechesis experience?), a radical re-orientation of the individual's perceptions about self, others, life, and God is made. Entering into an educative relationship leading toward a catechesis experience at the time of these peak experiences is an adult religious education potential that should be investigated much further. Gabriel Moran explains about revelation: "If we speak of revelation as historical events, this can only mean events in the life of a human subject who takes part in and to some degree consciously grasps the meaning of these events as relating him to God"(56).

Let's artificially classify value-laden or meaningful experiences into two categories: primary experiences and secondary experiences — terms used to express the extent of meaning which would be involved. Some of the more *primary experiences* of life which have a potential value for a catechesis experience would include the following:
pregnancy
birth and baptism
entrance of children into school
first reception of sacraments
adolescence
preparation for marriage
marriage or vocation
career beginning
sickness and/or death in family or friends
climacterium or "change of life"
retirement and aging

In a given parish, the coordinator, a core of persons concerned about adult religious education, and the pastor could survey the parish situation and plan short-term rather spontaneous programs that would enrich these value-laden life experiences.

For example, the group could identify the couples of the parish who are expecting their first child. These couples could come together after Sunday Liturgy (or some other appropriate time) in a "humanized" setting (such as someone's living room) and discuss what was happening to them and what it might mean. The whole Old Testament concept of looking forward to the one who is to come, the New Testament eschatology, the Christian sense of person — these and other concepts are integrally related to the child who is to be born. They need not be talked about purely as "content," that is, the coordinator and adult catechists need not go into literary forms about expectancy and a theology of hope except in an informal fashion. If the discussion and human interaction proceeded well, these couples could also come together to celebrate the communal baptisms. An event such as this could become a catechesis experience which would radically alter the perceptions and values of the persons involved. After this experience, they might not "need" to be involved with formal adult religious education for some time.

Some secondary life experiences might include some of the following:
family birthdays
community celebrations and special days
national holidays such as Christmas, Independence Day, Memorial Day — why not combine All Souls' Day and Memorial Day?
a national crisis
purchase of a new home
peace demonstrations, labor strikes, etc.

On certain occasions, such as these regular and extraordinary events, the coordinator and a group of adult catechists could plan situational sessions to clarify the values inherent in the events, relate them to the Gospel, and project with the adults possible Christian responses.

A good example of such adult religious education might be the annual income tax time. The coordinator could arrange for a tax advisor to come to the parish. Fathers could be invited to come and be briefed on the latest tax situation and the best ways of preparing the income tax forms. As part of this session, the Christian principles of social justice could be discussed as they relate to the topic at hand. The people interaction of the session could also contribute toward the development of a communal rootedness among the people of that faith community.

The type of catechist preparation needed for this style of life-centered adult religious education would be quite different from the preparation needed for discussion clubs, lectures, and classes. In effect, the coordinator would need to work with a core of leaders who could be selected for their talents and creativity. Together, over a period of time — after becoming very familiar with the nature of life-centered religious education — they could evolve creative situational adult programs which have the potential of becoming catechesis experiences (peak experiences).

ASSISTING TEACHERS FOR CHRISTIAN EDUCATION

An additional work of the coordinator which will need to be explored much more in the coming decade is assisting the professional Christian teachers both in Catholic and public schools.

The relationship of the parish coordinator to the parish (or diocesan) Catholic school is unsettled. If the parish coordinator is limited to the volunteer catechists in the parish youth and adult religious education programs, then this is not an issue at present. It is the recommendation of this author, however, that the coordinator become the chief executive under the parish Board of Education coordinating the total educational work of the faith community. Hence, part of the coordinator's work in conjunction with the school principal would include the professional religion teachers in the Catholic school.

The professional teachers may or may not have had education preparing them for the teaching of religion. If they have had none, then perhaps a consortium similar to that described for the volunteer catechists could be established by the coordinator for them. Their level of participation should be greater in some regards due to their professional background. It would be more helpful, therefore, if the professional teachers were in a consortium group of their own which could work toward the improvement of religious education within the school.

The Catholic teachers in the public schools are most often neglected within the educational mission of the faith community. This is unfortunate for they are involved in the outward aspect of the educational mission and could be of great benefit to the total faith community's concern about education. The coordinator should gather them together and probe together what they can do to further the educational mission of the Church.

What preparation sessions the catechist actually provides for both of these groups will need to be determined in the local situation. Many of the resources which the coordinator would gather together at the parish learning center would be of benefit not only to the volunteer catechists but also to the professional teachers involved in Christian education and religious education.

SUMMARY

When a parish coordinator begins to plan for fulfilling his responsibility to prepare catechists, a number of questions must be answered. The five general questions presented here, along with the consortium model for catechist preparation, may assist the coordinator in making better plans. If the extent of the information tends to overwhelm the coordinator, he should remember that the same is true for the fledgling catechist.

In addition, just as there is no precise way in which a "good" teacher teaches, so there is no correct way to prepare catechists. The coordinator and the catechist—like the learners and the catechist—will simply have to search and to stumble together down the road toward the catechesis experience. While teaching is a complex task, faith is relatively simple. Religious education is somewhere in between. The ultimate aim in a parish is not for a staff of professional religion teachers; rather, it is to have a Christian community in which there are many roles and one master; "apostles, prophets, and teachers." "And to some, his gift was that they should be apostles; to some, prophets; to some, evangelists; to some, pastors and teachers; so that the saints together make a unity in the work of service, building up the body of Christ"(Eph 4:11-12).

NOTES FOR CHAPTER 7

1) Francis Keppel, *The Necessary Revolution in American Education* (New York: Harper and Row, 1966), p. 90.

2) Philip W. Jackson, *The Way Teaching Is* (Washington, D.C.: ASCD, NEA, 1966), p. 9.

3) N. Fattu notes: "It is commonplace but not very flattering to this commentator to deplore the fact that more than a half a century of research effort has not yielded meaningful, measurable criteria around which the majority of the nation's educators can rally." N. Fattu, New Horizons in Teacher Education, Report of the National Commission on Teacher Education and Professional Standards (Washington, D.C.: NEA, 1964).

4) Arthur W. Combs, *The Professional Education of Teachers* (Boston: Allen and Bacon, 1965), p. 4.

5) *Ibid.,* p. 6.

6) *Ibid.,* p. 9.

7) Cf. J.W. Getzels and P.W. Jackson, "The Teacher's Personality and Characteristics," ed. N.L. Gage, *Handbook of Research on Teaching* (Chicago: Rand McNally, 1963) and *The Wisconsin Studies of the Measurement and Prediction of Teacher Effectiveness* (Madison, Wis.: Dembar Publications, Inc., 1961).

8) Unpublished notes from lectures at Divine Word International Centre, London, Ontario, 1967-68.

9) Cf. Richard Y. Will, "The Education of the Teacher as a Person," *The Journal of Teacher Education* 18 (Winter, 1967), pp. 471-475: "If teaching is an art, it is a deeply personal art. Ideally, it involves open and honest personal relationships with others." See also Arthur T. Jersild, *When Teachers Face Themselves* (Teachers College, Columbia University: Bureau of Publications, 1955), p. 165: "The self is the citadel of one's own being and worth and the stronghold from which one moves out to others."

10) Gabriel Moran, FSC, "The Time for Theology," *The Living Light* 3, no. 2, (Summer, 1966), p. 8.

11) Cf. N.L. Gage, ed., Handbook of Research on Teaching (Chicago: Rand McNally, 1963); See also the continuing research reports in The Journal of Teacher Education of the National Commission on Teacher Preparation and Professional Standards of the National Education Association. See also Herbert Schueler and Gerald S. Lesser's Teacher Education and the New Media (Washington, D.C.: American Association of Colleges of Teacher Education, 1967).

12) Robert D. Strom and Charles Galloway, "Becoming a Better Teacher," *The Journal of Teacher Education* 18 (Fall, 1967), pp. 285-292.

13) Carl R. Rogers, "The Interpersonal Relationship in the Facilitation of Learning," ed. Robert Leeper, *Humanizing Education:*

The Person in the Process (Washington, D.C.: ASCD, NEA, 1967), p. 3.

14) *Ibid.*, pp. 7-9. Also see Carl R. Rogers, "The Characteristics of a Helping Relationship," *Personal and Guidance Journal* 37 (1958), pp. 6-16.

15) Earl Nightingale, *Great Ideas In Selling* Media Pack (Chicago: Nightingale-Conant Corporation).

16) Cf. Herbert M. Greenberg, *Teaching With Feeling* (New York: Macmillan, 1969).

17) A.W. Combs and D.W. Soper, "The Helping Relationship as Described by 'Good' and 'Poor' Teachers," *Journal of Teacher Education* 14 (1968), pp. 64-68.

18) Warren G. Bennis, and Edgan H. Schein, Personal and Organizational Change Through Group Methods, (New York: John Wiley, 1965).

19) Jackson, *The Way Teaching Is*, pp. 12-17.

20) Virgil E. Herrick, *Strategies of Curriculum Development, Selected Writings*, ed. J.B. Macdonald, D.W. Anderson, and F.B. May (Columbus, Ohio: Charles Merrill, 1965), p. 81.

21) Abraham H. Maslow, *Religions, Values, and Peak-Experiences* (Columbus, Ohio: Ohio State University Press, 1964), p. 27.

22) Philip H. Phenix, "Curriculum and the Analysis of Language," *Language and Meaning* (Washington, D.C.: Association for Supervision and Curriculum Development, NEA, 1966), p. 4.

23) Guntram Bischoff, "Some Reflections on the Rationale and Desirability of the Academic Study of Religion in the Public School," unpublished paper presented to the Joint Committee on Religion and Public Education of the Michigan Catholic Conference, Michigan Council of Churches, Anti Defamation League of B'nai B'rith and others, (Fall, 1969).

24) Cf. Harry S. Broudy, "Needed: A Unifying Theory of Education," *Curriculum Change: Direction and Process* (Washington, D.C.: ASCD, NEA, 1966), p. 18ff. Also see Pierre Babin, *Options* (New York: Herder and Herder, 1967) for developments in this direction.

25) Jerome S. Bruner, "Culture, Politics and Pedagogy," *Saturday Review* (May 18, 1968), p. 89.

26) Hilda Taba, *Curriculum Development: Theory and Practice* (New York: Harcourt, Brace, and World, 1962), p. 426.

27) Herrick, *Strategies of Curriculum Development*, p. 17.

28) Joseph B. Collins, *Teaching Religion: An Introduction to Catechetics* (Milwaukee: Bruce Publishing, 1953), p. 4.

29) *Ibid.*

30) Msgr. M.A. Schumacher, *I Teach Catechism* (New York: Benziger, 1946), p. iii.

31) Collins, *Teaching Religion*, p. 42.

32) Johannes Hofinger, SJ, *Imparting the Christian Message*

(Notre Dame: University of Notre Dame Press, 1961), p. viii.

33) Alfred McBride, O. Praem., *Catechetics, A Theology of Proc-lamation* (Milwaukee: Bruce Publishing, 1966), p. 1.

34) Joseph Novak, SJ, "Formation of the Teacher for High School Religion," *Worship* 38, no. 7, (June-July, 1964), p. 410.

35) Sister Mary Verde, BVM, "Pre-Evangelization and the Class-room," *Catholic Educator* (April, 1966), p. 96.

36) Hofinger, *Imparting the Christian Message*, p. 45.

37) There are many sources of discussion about catechist pre-paration and each has a slightly different emphasis. The Eichstaett Congress itself stated: "The training of catechists must impart to them above all a complete grasp of the fundamentals of Christian doctrine concerning man's salvation." Mother Jean Fletcher, *Bearing Witness to Christ* (New York: Herder and Herder, 1964), p. 40. See also William J. Tobin, "Kerygma and Catechesis: A New CCD Cate-chist Preparation Course in the Archdiocese of New York," *The Living Light* 3, no. 1, (Spring, 1966), p. 65ff.

38) Gabriel Moran, *Catechesis of Revelation* (New York: Herder and Herder, 1966), p. 13.

39) Gabriel Moran, Gerard Pottebaum, Mary Ryan, et. al., "Catechesis For Our Times," *Bible Today* (February, 1967), p. 1971.

40) Babin, *Options*, p. 89.

41) Herrick, *Strategies of Curriculum Development*, p. 53.

42) Joseph C. Neiman, "Who Teaches CCD Classes?" *Our Sunday Visitor* 55, no. 21, p. 10.

43) Robert. E. Bills, "About People and Teaching," *Bulletin of the Bureau of School Service*, College of Education, University of Kentucky, 28, no. 2, (December, 1965).

44) Joseph C. Neiman, "Report on Experimental TeacherEdu-cation Program at Traverse City, Michigan," unpublished research report, (Religious Education Office, Diocese of Grand Rapids, Mich.: 1967). Prospective catechists were surprised to discover that others had doubts about faith, that others did not view religious education the same way they did, and that others had different views about what the catechist should be like. From this confrontation of views, a joint search was possible.

45) Harvey Cox, "Secularization and the Secular Mentality: A New Challenge to Christian Education," *Religious Education* 61 (March-April, 1966), p. 87.

46) Donald Snygg, "A Cognitive Field Theory of Learning," *Learning and Mental Health in the School* (Washington, D.C.: ASCD, 1966 Yearbook), p. 89.

47) Combs, *Professional Education of Teachers*, p. 28.

48) J. Cecil Parker and Louis J. Rubin, *Process as Content: Curriculum Design and the Application of Knowledge* (Chicago: Rand McNally, 1966), p. 8. For additional information, see Jerome

Bruner, *Toward a Theory of Instruction* (Cambridge: Balkap Press, 1966).

49) Moran, "A Time for Theology," p. 8.

50) Elmer R. Smith, *Teacher Education: a Re-appraisal* (New York: Harper and Row, 1962), p. 60.

51) See also such articles as Barbara Chambers Arnstine, "Making The In-Service Institute Operational," *Adult Leadership* (Sept., 1966), p. 77ff; Robert D. Strom and Charles Galloway, "Becoming a Better Teacher," *Journal of Teacher Education* 18, no. 3.

52) The term "consortium" and some of the concepts related to it are a development of a seminar report. Cf. Louis J. Rubin, Seminar Director, The Professional Growth of the Educator (Santa Barbara: Center for Coordinated Education, 1966). See also the other related report entitled The Nature of Teacher Growth (Santa Barbara: Center for Coordinated Education, 1966).

53) Strom and Galloway, "Becoming a Better Teacher," p. 39.

54) Stephen M. Corey, *Helping Other People Change* (Columbus: Ohio State University Press, 1963), p. 14.

55) Maslow, *Religions, Values, and Peak-Experiences*, p. 52.

56) Gabriel Moran, *Theology of Revelation* (New York: Herder and Herder, 1966), p. 45.

Chapter Eight

WHAT CAN BE EXPECTED
FROM THE DIOCESAN OFFICE?

The best general answer that can be given to the above question is: it depends. The particular character of a Diocesan or Religious Education Office(1) is determined by the mandate which the Bishop has given to it; upon the philosophy and skills of the Diocesan Director and his staff; and upon the relationship to the School Office. It is difficult, therefore, to make generalizations about what can be expected from a Diocesan Office responsible for religious education.

There are a few general characteristics of the Diocesan Office, however, which can be presented. These influence its potential role somewhat and, thus, it is well for the parish Board of Education and coordinator to keep them in mind when dealing with their particular Diocesan Office.

First of all, most Diocesan Offices are relatively new, are inadequately staffed, and are poorly financed.

The National CCD Survey sponsored by the National Conference of Diocesan Directors(NCDD) of CCD and the National CCD Center in 1968, indicated that 73% of the diocesan directors had been in their present jobs less than two years. In addition, 36% were still part-time directors and 50% described themselves as professionally inadequate for the job(2).

The National CCD Survey further indicated that 71% of Diocesan Offices had annual budgets under $30,000. Many had to raise funds from selling books, from parish assessment, or other sources. However, the majority were financed directly by diocesan funds.

Although the picture has improved considerably in the last decade and even from the date of the Survey, nevertheless, parish Boards and coordinators must realize that Diocesan Offices have had little continuity, and also little experience with professional personnel at the parish level. Generally, they have a limited ability to deliver all the assistance which still accompanies the "diocesan image."

This leads to a second general characteristic. Diocesan Offices are expected to do more than is realistic. The syndrome which was spoken of earlier leads priests, and to a certain extent parish leaders, to expect strong, detailed, and authoritative direction from the Diocesan Office. Even efficient Offices cannot deliver all that is expected of them. A few pastors implicitly expect the Office to run their parish programs for them—although they would never say this directly.

As Diocesan Offices receive more human and material resources, some fall victim to this perceived role. They establish great master plans for all the parishes of the diocese and seek to implement them through committees or professional personnel. Such dioceses frequently seek to employ parish coordinators as extensions of the Diocesan Staff in a region or parish, with

varying degrees of success. Bypassing the process discussed in Chapter 2, and bypassing the parish Board
of Education can lead to considerable difficulties for
both the Diocesan Office and the coordinators hired.
The pros and cons of such plans, however, are better
discussed on an individual basis. It suffices to say here
that some Diocesan Offices have swung from a relatively
powerless position to one of assuming more responsibility for parish religious education than is proper.

A third characteristic of Diocesan Offices that
should be mentioned deals with the professional staff.
While the number of professional persons employed
by the Office has increased in recent years, nevertheless, the persons employed are generally unable to be
of significant assistance to parish coordinators. The
education and experience of diocesan consultants is
quite similar to that of the parish coordinator and,
hence, the specialized assistance which the coordinator
is beginning to need cannot be met by diocesan personnel except in a small number of dioceses. This is not an
indictment of diocesan personnel; rather it is facing
the fact that they too, like the coordinator, are *generalists* in religious education rather than *specialists* in a
given area of competence.

Lastly, it should be stressed that Diocesan Offices
are staffed with persons exceedingly dedicated and concerned about advancing quality religious education.
Often they are the only persons within the Diocese to
whom the coordinator can turn for moral support as
both face great frustrations and anxiety in seeking to
sort out the emerging directions for religious education
and their implications in practice. This coming together
for moral support and "professional" enrichment is extremely important for both the Diocesan Staff and the
coordinator. "Professional" enrichment is questioned
here because the coordinator and the Diocesan Staff

usually have about the same level and style of professional background. Their educational relationship, therefore, is more that of members of a peer group than of specialist and generalist. This relationship has great value, but it should be seen for what it is.

One final remark. Parish coordinators are in effect the "new frontier" of Christian Education. For years, the CCD people have battled the "school establishment" seeking to turn human and material resources from schools to the majority of Catholic youth who attend public elementary and secondary schools — and recently into adult religious education. Now the Diocesan Directors of relgious education find themselves about to become the "new establishment." They have won some hard earned gains and in the process have become defensive and battle worn. For this reason, they are touchy when pressed by newly emerging coordinators who have a rather militant and impatient tone, as they should. This is unfortunate, for the coordinators are partially existant due to the pressures exerted by the CCD people; but more importantly, both the diocesan personnel and the coordinators share much of the same dream for what might be in religious education and can profit from a close working relationship.

Because Diocesan Offices vary so greatly, an ideal model will be presented here which corresponds to the role described above for coordinators and to the model constitution presented for parish Boards of Education. Practical implications will be drawn where possible but each Diocesan Office and parish group will need to draw their own conclusions from this general model.

THE PURPOSE OF THE DIOCESAN REO

The purpose of the Religious Education Office (REO) is to offer authentic and relevant religious educational direction and services to the People of God in the diocese, both through their parishes and organizations and at large (*now-already* aspect of mission); and to offer educational services to the people of the public community, based upon a sound Christian perspective (*yet-to-be-realized* mission).

These directions and services are authentic if they are in keeping with the Spirit of Christ and the Gospel message as taught through the Holy Father, the Councils of Bishops, the magisterium, and the theological community. They are relevant if they assist the People of God in providing quality opportunities for religious education for youth and adults tailored to their needs, to the "signs of the times," and to the particular area in which they are located; and if they assist the People of God in effecting their educational mission to the public community.

In other words, the Religious Education Office is to the diocesan community what the parish coordinator and the teachers are to the parish community. The "clients" or recipients of the educational services on the diocesan level are the parishes, the schools, the diocesan and public organizations, and special groups rather than families, children, adolescents, and individual adults as on the parish level. This relationship is clearer when speaking of the particular responsibilities which rest with the Diocesan Office.

Responsibility to Parishes The primary responsibility of the Diocesan Religious Education Office is to the parishes of the diocese. Recognizing that parents are the primary educators of their children, recognizing the principle of subsidiarity proclaimed by the Second Vatican Council, the Religious Education Office has the task of offering direction, leadership and professional services to the faith communities in order to assist them in fulfilling their responsibilities in religious education.

In other words, it is not the task of the Diocesan Office to provide a uniform plan for the religious education of youth and adults which must be implemented in all of the parishes of the Diocese. Rather, it is the task of the Office to assist each parish in making responsible decisions for their own educational mission. These parish decisions are responsible if they take into consideration both the particular needs of the youth and adults, the larger needs of the diocese and the whole Church, the needs of man in that area served by the parish, and the authenticity of the Christian Gospel.

The Diocesan Office assists the parishes in seeing these responsibilities and in meeting them in a fashion similar to the way in which the parish assists parents and individuals in seeing their educational mission and fulfilling it. The Office does this through the *professional services* which it offers to the people involved in parish religious education, and through the *directional goals* and *policies* set by the Diocesan Board of Education. These set the direction for parish Boards of Education and provide the parameters or outer limits for their decisions. The "jurisdictional" relationship is between Diocesan Board and parish Board rather than between Diocesan Office and parish Board and/or coordinator. The Diocesan Office is responsible to the Diocesan Board as the parish coordinator is to the parish Board.

Responsibility to Schools The Religious Education Office also has a primary responsibility for religious education in Catholic schools. Presently many dioceses place this responsibility in the Catholic School Office, but this is an unnecessary separation and frequently results in a duplication of talents. There are essential differences in the curriculum and instructional style of religious education between parish programs and school programs. The basic goals, learning psychology, and learning materials, however, are similar and, hence, the difference is adaptive rather than substantive.

If with the passage of "parochiaid" bills the schools become a separate system, then perhaps they will need a separate school Board and will function much like a corporation. In that case, the Christian Education wing of the Diocese will purchase religious education services from the school corporation much like the Catholic Social Services might purchase certain social work services. The "Catholicity" of the schools then would be a result of their philosophy, the faith of their teachers, and the inclusion of religious education classes rather than their orientation as an integral part of the educational mission of a diocese. If they wish to remain as a part of the total educational mission of the diocese, then they will need to be organizationally linked to that diocese under a diocesan Board of Education. This Board will be intimately bound into the Pastoral Mission of the total diocese; that is, subject to a veto of the Diocesan Pastoral Council and/or the Ordinary of the diocese.

In this model, it is assumed that schools will become a consolidated system operated by the Diocesan Board of Education through the Superintendent of Schools. Governmental assistance is not assumed except in a form through the parents—tax rebates, vouchers, or some similar means.

Responsibility to the Diocesan Community The Religious Education Office also has a secondary responsibility to the diocesan faith community through its corporate structures and at large. In effect, this means that the Office brings its educational expertise to bear upon the problems and actions which the People of God in the diocese face as a whole, outside of their parishes and through their diocesan organizations.

Recognizing that many individuals and families within the diocesan community have specialized educational needs which cannot be met adequately by a parish alone, the Office has a responsibility to organize educational opportunities to meet these needs. Luncheon meetings for businessmen or doctors is a good example. Other special inter-parochial courses would include: a Christian-Marxist Dialogue, training for Board or Parish Council members, ecumenical courses, and similar educational programs which cannot be met by parishes alone.

In addition, the Office, when requested, should bring its expertise to bear upon the educational aspects of programs sponsored by other diocesan groups and agencies. Assisting the social services with educational programs on abortion or the human relations commissions with its educational efforts against racism or for open housing are examples of ways in which this secondary responsibility can be exercised. The cooperation between the Religious Education Office and the Liturgical Commission, the Ecumenical Commission, and Family Life groups is even more obvious. Involvements between the Office and the Building Committees or the Tribunal are more subtle and frequently precedent and politics militate against cooperative action.

Responsibility to the Public Community The outward reach of the educational mission is neglected on the diocesan level at present as it is on the parish level. The Religious Education Office, however, does have a secondary responsibility to the public community in the part of the state in which the diocese is located. This includes large civic and state bodies and the public at large.

State departments of education stimulate curriculum programs in crucial areas such as sex education, value education, and religious studies. The planning of committees at the state and regional levels should be a concern of the Office and Office personnel should be involved. The Office also can become involved in large scale programs launched by cooperative groups — Anti-Defamation League of B'nai B'rith, Council of Churches, Civil Rights Commission, and similar groups — designed to educate the public community on crucial issues.

The impact of radio and television upon youth and adults is spoken about frequently, but real involvement is scarce. The Religious Education Office should be planning to meet its responsibility in this area in cooperation with other diocesan groups. This does not necessarily mean the establishment of a separate educational channel; this has debatable merits. It might mean, in a particular diocese, offering to the radio, television, and local press a concise Christian perspective or reflection on crucial issues to which people must respond and concerning which basic values are being formed.

These are a couple of the obvious ways in which this secondary responsibility can be translated from vision into reality. Many more are possible, once a Diocesan Office begins to see this responsibility and work toward meeting it. At the start, small things such as mailing a recommended list of good Catholic books to the public libraries within the diocese can be undertaken. This could be done locally by a coordinator, but it is more readily done by the Diocesan Office. The county papers frequently look for "filler" material of interest to their readers. Cooking columns, sports stories, and even novels are put in. Expanded news releases which contain larger portions of talks will often be incorporated by a county newspaper when the more concise version may or may not get into the larger press.

Responsibility to Special Groups The Religious Education Office also has a secondary responsibility to special
groups (whether organized or disparate) within the
diocese. Large senior citizen homes, rehabilitation centers, prisons, and individuals not aligned with any particular group, especially alienated Catholics—these are
some of the special groups who should receive some of
the attention of the Office.

Much of the service extended by the Church to institutions such as prisons and senior citizen homes is
pastoral in nature. Yet educational programs would
greatly improve the impact of the pastoral services on
the persons involved. The rehabilitation of prisoners,
for example, should include education; just visiting
prisoners and bringing them sacramental opportunities
is not enough. An educational program assisting them
to sort out their basic values upon which to build a
new life style is a definite possibility and a responsibility
which could be met by the expertise of a Diocesan Office.

Providing disenchanted Catholics or polarized
groups with educational opportunities to see the reasons
for their views and the implications of them for themselves and the total faith community is a more obvious
example of this secondary responsibility.

ADMINISTRATIVE ROLES AND RESPONSIBILITIES

Meeting the above responsibilities looks impossible.
Considering some of the present organizational plans
and priorities of Diocesan Offices, it is. The present,
however, need not determine the future. When the implications of the present movement toward the parish
coordinator are felt on the diocesan level, radical changes
will be possible and some of these responsibilities will
be attainable.

The model administrative structure which follows is a compromise between what is and what might be. It is presented in this fashion with the hope that Diocesan Offices can begin to move toward meeting the broader responsibilities as they cope with the coordinator movement.

Diocesan Board of Education The Diocesan Board of Education is to the diocesan faith community what the parish Board is to the parish community; that is, the diocesan Board carries the responsibility for the educational mission of the People of God in the diocese. Ideally, the Board is composed of elected representatives from parish (regional) Boards and a representative of the priests and/or the sisters serving the diocesan community. These latter two representatives are included not as professional educators—the professionals are always subject to the Board—but as representatives of special communities within the total faith community.

General Responsibility: It is evident from the discussion in Chapter 5 that there is a considerable difference in the conception of the role of the Board on the part of those in the school tradition (and voiced through the NCEA) versus those in the religious education tradition. The responsibilities presented in this model administrative structure and Board constitution attempt to articulate the religious education tradition.

The NCEA Constitution (Appendix A) gives the diocesan Board of Education absolute authority over all education within a diocese. It envisions the parish and regional Boards as extensions of itself. The constitution further does not exclude Catholic colleges which may be within the diocese from its jurisdiction nor does it establish the relationship between the Diocesan Board and the Newman Campus Parishes.

The religious education suggested constitution (Appendix B) gives the Board responsibility over the educational work of the Diocesan Office, responsibility for establishing *directional goals and policies* to guide the responsibilities of parish Boards, and establishes a working relationship between the Board and Catholic colleges and other educational groups within the diocese (see Article 1, Sections 1, 2, and 3). Furthermore, the religious education constitution gives the bishop and/or the Diocesan Pastoral Council veto power over the Board's decisions. The NCEA model does not. Frequently, it is amended in particular dioceses to include this, but the suggested model *excludes* it and this is the intent of the Superintendents' Committee on Policy and Administration, following the thought of the late Rt. Rev. Msgr. O'Neil C. D'Amour.

As indicated in the religious education model constitution, the Diocesan Board exercises its responsibility in three distinct ways.

1) In reference to the Diocesan Education Office (or Offices): The Board has complete authority over the goals, programs, staff and resources with which the School Office and the Religious Education Office operate. This authority enables the Board to meet its responsibilities toward parishes, schools, the diocesan community, the public community, and special groups.

2) In reference to parish religious education and schools as presently constituted: The Board exercises its responsibility by providing *directional goals and policies* to be taken into consideration by parish Boards in their decision-making processes for their own responsibilities. In other words, seeing the larger picture, the diocesan Board has a responsibility to communicate to parish (and regional) Boards the best understanding of how the Church can meet their education mission in that state or area.

3) In reference to schools, if they become a diocesan system: With the movement of schools toward a central consolidated system, the diocesan Board will have two options. First, if the schools become a system separate from the corporate structure of the diocese and parishes, that is, completely out from under the veto control of the Bishop (pastor), they will have their own corporation board to govern them. Then, the diocesan Board will exercise some responsibility toward this independent school system through recommendations and perhaps purchased services. If schools become a consolidated system under the auspices of the diocese, then the diocesan Board will become in effect a corporation board operating a school system. In this latter case, parish Boards will purchase services from this diocesan system run by the diocesan Board.

To a large extent, which direction schools will move will depend upon the nature and availability of governmental assistance. It is assumed here that schools will become a system under diocesan auspices with or without the passage of parochiaid, since it is essential that schools run by the faith community become part of the educational mission which is always integrally related to the larger Pastoral Mission—hence, the veto power of the Bishop and/or the Diocesan Pastoral Council.

Specific Responsibilities: The specific ways in which the Board carries out its mandate, that is, fulfills its diocesan educational mission, are very similar to the way in which the parish Board operates except that the scope of the mission is different.

1) Development of goals and policies: The Board, largely through the work of the Superintendent of Education, first of all establishes *directional goals,* guidelines for what the Church should accomplish in its educational mission in that decade.

Directional goals are broad and general in their very nature. They are formulated by the Board not to be implemented by all parish Boards or schools but rather to serve as "valid knowledge"(3) to be used by such groups in their own decision-making process to arrive at program objectives. Directional goals are important to the diocesan Board, parish Boards and other educational groups within the diocese for assisting them to see their program objectives in perspective and to establish priorities among them. Such goals point a *direction, but are not directives.*

Directional goals should be formulated out of the interaction of two elements: (1) the Board members and diocesan staff persons—especially the Superintendent of Schools, and the Director of Religious Education; and (2) catechetical experts—persons with in-depth knowledge in fields that will pertain directly to the educational mission of the Church. These might include a theologian, Scripture scholar, catechetical scholar, sociologist, and a psychologist.

The Board members and diocesan staff present what is needed by the parishes and the diocese, what is being done, and why what is being done is deemed important. The catechetical experts come with insight into the nature of catechesis and the mission of the Church (as dioceses acquire specialists in their Diocesan Office, some of these persons might well serve as the catechetical experts). Together the group establishes tentative directional goals for the educational mission of the Church in that diocese. These tentative goal statements are then circulated for reaction among leaders within the diocese (especially coordinators) and the whole Board. After due deliberation and reaction, the amended goals are then established by the Board as directional goals to guide the educational mission of the Church in that diocese.

Directional goals might be better formulated at a provincial level involving Board members, diocesan staff, and others from the several dioceses; and available catechetical experts from the Catholic colleges or sources outside of the province. If this is not possible, then it is important that it be done at the diocesan level. As the national groups fulfill more of their responsibilities, it will be necessary for a diocesan Board to adapt a national statement of the goals for religious education to the diocese and to establish these as the directional goals.

In exercising its responsibilities toward the Diocesan Office, the Board needs to establish *program objectives* to guide the work of the diocesan personnel. The Diocesan Office presents a Program and Budget similar to that discussed for the parish coordinator. These are aimed to achieve specific objectives; e.g., teacher education, inter-parochial adult education, coordinator recruitment, and so forth. The Board reviews these in light of (1) the needs of the parishes and schools which it serves, (2) the human and material resources available to the Diocesan Offices, (School and Religious Education), (3) the directional goals described above. It then establishes the program objectives deemed suitable, and then sets priorities among these objectives. Following this, the recommendations of the diocesan Board are forwarded to the Diocesan Pastoral Council and/or the bishop of the diocese. If the program objectives and their accompanying budgets are consistent with the total Pastoral Mission of the diocese, and if the budgetary requests can be met, then the Diocesan Office begins to implement the programs designed to achieve the approved objectives.

However, if the diocesan Pastoral Council sees greater priorities in the total Pastoral Mission; e.g., the need to launch a special civil rights program, they may send the total Program and Budget of the diocesan Board back with recommendations concerning which priorities can be met. The Board then re-considers and adapts. If the Board's Program and Budget contains objectives that are inimical to the Pastoral Mission, it is the responsibility of the Pastoral Council to point out where the conflict lies and recommend ways by which the Board can bring their projection into harmony with the total diocesan mission.

The Board also will issue from time to time relevant *policy statements.* These are not binding in jurisdiction upon the Diocesan Office or parish Boards (or schools) like policies are, but they do express the intent of the Board in policy areas. They are, in effect, guidelines for the achievement of goals set by the Board for the educational mission of the diocese. They translate these broader statements into model practice. They also are frequently issued to state the mind of the Board in areas not covered by goals or policies but which are becoming a pressing concern to parishes or schools.

In certain limited areas, the diocesan Board will need to establish *policies* that will be binding upon parish Boards, schools, and the Diocesan Offices. These will deal particularly with areas where the responsibilities of subsidiary groups have implications for the total diocesan community. Policies also establish communication networks and modes of operation. A good example of a policy would be the Annual Parish Report. The Board would establish as a policy that parishes must send in an Annual Parish Report concerning their education program. The Diocesan Office then reviews these to see that what is happening is consistent with the goals and objectives of the Diocesan Board; that is, to see if what is being done is complimentary with and developmental of the total diocesan educational mission and not contrary to it.

Like the parish Board, the diocesan Board also votes in *resolutions* which assist it to operate and which expedite business.

2) Structuring the educational organization: In addition to establishing goals and policies, the Board is responsible for structuring (or re-structuring) the Diocesan Offices in such a fashion that they effectively accomplish the responsibilities of the Board. In most dioceses, there is already existant—when the Board comes into being—a Diocesan School Office and a Religious Education Office. The Board, upon recommendations from the Superintendent of Schools and the CCD or Religious Education Director (or Superintendent of Education, where existant), re-structures these into one Christian Education Office of the diocese or at least establishes the nature and mode of cooperative action by the two Offices.

3) Securing the top educational personnel: As with the parish Board, the selection of the top educational leadership, that is, the Superintendent of Education, and the establishment of his salary is a prerogative of the Diocesan Board in consultation with the bishop of the diocese.

It is recommended that the Board set the Superintendent of Schools and the CCD Director as their Executive Offices until an effective cooperation is established. In this way a description of the work of the Superintendent of Education and of suitable candidates can be determined with the help of the School Superintendent and the Director. Ultimately, however, the choice rests with the Board and the bishop.

4) Approving the Program and Budget and the provision of resources: This was discussed above in reference to program objectives and previously in reference to parish Boards.

5) Establishing the Board's relationship with other

bodies: It is especially important that the Diocesan Board establish effective channels of communication with colleges and informal education organizations within the diocese. The religious education model constitution for a Diocesan Board includes this (Article 1, Section 1), but many relationships may not be included in the constitution either because they are temporary or because they are out of the realm of the Board's ability to formally establish a relationship. This is especially true with secular colleges and educational organizations. An in-depth and free-flowing relationship with influential educational groups in or near the diocese is important if the Board would obtain the necessary input of information and perspective to truly fulfill its educational responsibilities.

6) Relationship of Board to diocesan community: There is large scale apathy and depression looming over the educational mission of the People of God in most dioceses in this decade. The closing of schools has given many a feeling of failure. The lack of demonstrable success of parish religious education fills others with the fear that all is lost. It is essential that the Diocesan Board aggressively attack this problem. It is part of the on-going responsibility of the Board to keep in communication with the people whom they represent, but it is an especially important application in this decade. The Board can set a tone which will have great psychological impact on all working with education in the diocese. Such a tone is imperative if the good efforts being undertaken are to have a climate in which they can succeed.

7) Evaluation: Educators are prone to become trapped within their own presuppositions and programs. This is natural when educators become totally involved in what they believe. However, the Board must remain

objective and detached about the programs of the Diocesan Office in order to be constructively critical. Board members should continually seek to know the effectiveness of what is being done by the Office. Even the most nebulous religious education programs are undertaken for a reason. This reason must be made manifest and continuously re-examined in light of new information as the program progresses.

Superintendent of Education The Superintendent of Education is the Executive Officer of the Board. He is to the Diocesan Board what the parish coordinator is to the parish Board in this model administrative structure. The nature of his work, however, is different.

The primary responsibility of the Superintendent of Education is to assist the Board with its work and to coordinate the work of the Superintendent of Schools and Director of Religious Education in reference to implementing the Board's goals and policies. More detailed descriptions could be given but such would not be pertinent to this discussion. Suffice it to say that the Superintendent of Education would work with the diocesan efforts regarding coordinators at the Board level. He may assist with some conferences to share his administrative expertise with the coordinators in helping them function as an executive of parish Boards, but generally even this would be handled through the Religious Education Office personnel.

Assistant Superintendent for Personnel and Publicity: In this model, there is an assistant to the Superintendent (See Chart 8:1) to handle personnel and public relations. He would prepare personnel policies. Some of these would bear upon coordinators. His work might include the preparation of recommended salary scales, professional and personal benefits, and the like. If these

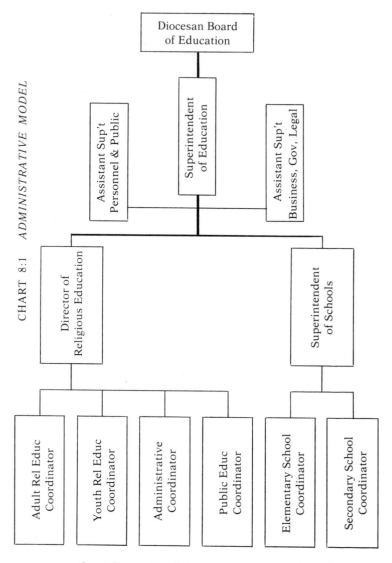

CHART 8:1   *ADMINISTRATIVE MODEL*

Diocesan Board of Education

Assistant Sup't Personnel & Public

Superintendent of Education

Assistant Sup't Business, Gov, Legal

Director of Religious Education

Superintendent of Schools

Adult Rel Educ Coordinator

Youth Rel Educ Coordinator

Administrative Coordinator

Public Educ Coordinator

Elementary School Coordinator

Secondary School Coordinator

Specialists as Needed   Specialists

were adopted by the Board, after consideration by the Director of Religious Education, they would become standards which parishes would use in completing Supplements A and B described above. This assistant would also help the Diocesan Office in the recruitment of personnel for the diocesan and parish work. This would include potential coordinators. The Office, through this Assistant Superintendent and the Director of Religious Education, would assist parishes in finding potential coordinators. The parishes, however, would make the final decision as to the person whom they want and to the specific details of the Supplements A and B. The Assistant Superintendent would only facilitate the search process and establish standards to guide personnel.

Assistant Superintendent for Business and Governmental Affairs: This Assistant Superintendent would again help the Diocesan Offices with information about legal and business matters. Much of his time would be consumed presently with the question of governmental aid to parochial schools, but some work would be done to be of assistance to coordinators in preparing programs for their parish and Boards. The whole area of the involvement of religion and public education, for example, is filled with legal questions about which the coordinator would need precise information; e.g., the use of public school facilities, released time, shared time, baccalaureates, sex education, and so forth.

This Assistant, like the other, would be a *staff* position as compared with a *line* position, to use old distinctions. He provides expert knowledge and service, but the Superintendent of Schools takes it to the schools, the Director of Religious Education to the parishes, and the Superintendent of Education to the Diocesan Board.

Superintendent of Schools Diocesan Boards will need

to take a stand concerning the consolidation of schools. The way in which the schools will be part of the total educational mission of the diocese and, hence, their relationship to the Diocesan Board and through the Board to the bishop and the Diocesan Pastoral Council will need to be solved. The kind of governmental aid to be sought should depend upon the relationship the diocese desires to have with the school system, and not the reverse. If the availability or lack of governmental aid will determine the educational mission of the schools, then why maintain them as Catholic?

Until this problem is solved, the relationship between the Superintendent of Schools and the coordinators will remain vague. In this model, it is assumed that the schools will become a consolidated system operated by the Diocesan Board, under the jurisdiction of the total Pastoral Mission of the Diocese, and in a direct veto relationship with the bishop and/or the Diocesan Pastoral Council. It is also assumed that the coordinator will be the chief Executive Officer of the parish Board of Education. The parish coordinator, therefore, will need to work with the principal of any school located within or near the parish(4). The coordinator may need to advise the Board of Education in the parish about "purchasing services" from the consolidated diocesan system. Regarding such matters, the coordinator will need the assistance of the Superintendent of Schools. What other relationship the parish coordinators will have with the Superintendent of Schools will need to evolve with the changing picture of Catholic schools.

Director of Religious Education The Director of Religious Education is responsible for the work of the Religious Education Office and is the chief catechetical leader of the diocese. The Director's relationship with parishes is different from the relationship of the Superintendent of Schools to schools. In the former, the parishes have the responsibility for religious education and the decision as to how it will be achieved within the broad parameters established by the diocesan Board. The Director, therefore, works with parishes (Boards and coordinators) in an influence capacity with an authority of competence and leadership rather than with a jurisdictional authority. His jurisdictional authority is limited to the work of the Religious Education Office and to those few limited areas in which the diocesan Board has established policies binding upon parish Boards — areas where the work of the latter affects the whole diocese.

The relationship of the Director of Religious Education through his staff to schools will depend upon what direction the consolidation takes. Basically, however, the religious education within schools should be under the leadership responsibility of the Director of Religious Education.

Basic Strategies of the Religious Education Office
Before presenting some model administrative roles for the personnel in the Religious Education Office, it is important to look at some broad strategies for the work of the Office. From these, the specific administrative roles can be derived.

Strategy A — Generalized Services to Parishes: As mentioned above, many parishes expect the Diocesan Office to do more for them than is actually possible or desirable. In effect, parishes frequently want the Diocesan Office to take over their responsibilities.

Even though this is not the intent of the Office (in this plan), nevertheless, it is a "political" reality that must be considered by the Office Staff. A certain number of *generalized services* will need to be maintained to assist parishes and schools until they can obtain the necessary personnel, e.g., a coordinator, to carry out their responsibilities themselves. These services should be maintained both because the "political" support of the parishes is necessary (they will need to see some immediate and direct benefit from the Diocesan Office, if they are going to support it) and, secondly, because future support will be necessary when the Office begins to launch its "new" program designed to meet the responsibilities outlined above. To a certain extent, the Diocesan Office cannot begin to move into the uncharted areas of responsibility described above until it has assisted the parishes in becoming capable of meeting their own responsibilities. For this reason, the Religious Education Office must allot some of its human and material resources to this strategy of assisting parishes with their present efforts.

At the present time, parishes need the following kinds of generalized services:

1) Planning skills: The REO can have each parish appoint a contact person (volunteer coordinator) to assume the leadership, with the parish Board, for developing the total plan of educational efforts in the local faith community. This person will need a great deal of assistance from the Diocesan Office with the details of planning a total parish program for youth and adults; teacher in-service education; Board work; and other administrative work. Eventually, the work may be done by a professional coordinator in the parish or this assistance could be given by a regional consultant rather than the Diocesan Office itself. At any rate, parishes need this kind of service now.

2) Curriculum design: The contact person with the teachers and the Board will need assistance in designing the best instructional program for both the youth and the adults. This includes the total instructional style of

the programs as well as the texts and media materials to be used. Many parish leaders (frequently the priest) have some previous experience with this already. In fact, some do an excellent job. Nevertheless, most parishes need this kind of generalized service.

3) Catechist in-service education: Volunteer teachers feel a great need for on-going support and professional training. The Diocesan Offices generally provide some form of teacher education on an interparochial basis. This generalized service can consume much of the human and material resources of the Diocesan Office and it should, therefore, be watched most carefully in terms of the other basic strategies to be achieved.

The Diocesan Office, in order to appear effective to the parishes which it serves, should meet these present parish needs with generalized services. On the other hand, the Office must begin to make long-range plans to meet both its own larger responsibilities of diocesan education and to assist the parishes with achieving the ability of meeting these general needs themselves. Strategy A, therefore, should be closely defined and regularly assessed, lest the pressure of the present needs compel the Diocesan Office to concentrate all its efforts and become unable to project toward the future.

Strategy B—Development of Specialized Services: Concomitant with the offering of generalized services to parishes, the Religious Education Office should develop *specialized services* to fulfill its long-range responsibility to parishes (and schools perhaps) and to begin to meet the responsibilities to the diocesan and public communities and special groups.

1) Leadership development: The top priority in specialized services should go to the development of local leadership. This would mean assisting Boards of Education to form and operate in parishes, assisting

such Boards in their work, especially in relationship to hiring a coordinator, *and* developing leadership abilities among key teachers, principals, and contact persons.

2) Curriculum models and development of local media: This service is different from the generalized work regarding curriculum which the Office must do in helping parishes. What is intended here is the development of curriculum and instructional models which can be used by coordinators in their work. Also keeping up on the availability of media for religious education and the production of media (especially tapes) from local sources for local use is a specialized service which is increasingly needed as religious education becomes more life-centered.

3) Educational services to the public and diocesan communities, and to special groups: In its strategy to develop specialized services the REO can begin to meet its responsibilities to the public and diocesan communities and to special groups as described above. Adult education for special needs which cannot be met by local parish groups, adult education in the public forum on crucial issues, consultation with other diocesan groups regarding their education efforts, participation in public education crises and planning, are some of the areas in which specialized services can be begun.

Strategy C—Administration:

1) Directional goals and policies: The coordination of the generalized and specialized services into a unified plan of action which can be promoted by the diocesan Board is an area of work or a basic strategy which the Diocesan Office will need to meet. First, the Office will need to convince the Board of the validity of its basic strategies, that is, holding the line with present generalized services in favor of moving toward specialized ser-

vices. Second, the establishment of directional goals and policies which provide the parameters for the movement of local Boards is integrally related to Strategies A and B. If the diocesan Board, for example, adopts a goal relative to sex education in schools and parish religious education, then the Office will need to orient its services toward the attainment of that goal.

2) Innovation and evaluation: Included in Strategy C, which will largely involve the diocesan Board, the Superintendent of Education, and the Religious Education Director, are the areas of innovation and evaluation.

Innovation is used here to refer to the long-range planning and the actual stimulation of change through pilot programs. After the identification of a valid direction in which to move, the Office can closely design a pilot program, e.g., the hiring of a coordinator in a parish. Next, a parish should be selected for the program, a parish which will not only be receptive, but which will also be potentially innovative. This is important because other parishes will look closely at the success or failure in the selected parish and modify their own efforts accordingly. Hence, if the pilot program is successful, change will occur in a number of parishes without intensive efforts on the part of the REO.

The tendency to drop programs presently being used in favor of the adoption of a "new idea" must be carefully avoided by the diocesan Office. The Office has a responsibility, in other words, to subject the plan of employing a parish coordinator to critical analysis. This should not be viewed by coordinators as an opposition, for in the long run, it is a real help.

In addition, the Diocesan Staff frequently follows this pattern and wishes to drop all generalized services in favor of a newly discovered specialized service or some other innovation. By careful internal communi-

CHART 8:2

RELIGIOUS EDUCATION OFFICE JURISDICTION

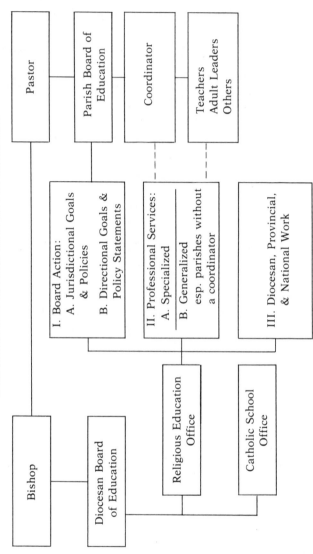

cations in the REO, the personnel can assist one another to see that all services are part of a unified effort. Gradually, present generalized services can be dropped as new innovations are proven workable.

The evaluation applies to the total work of the REO as well as to innovation. The Director with the Board must get together pastors, coordinators, teachers, and others to critically review everything which the diocesan Office is doing. This type of evaluation need not be threatening to the Staff, for it should eventually provide a genuine two-way communication between those looking to the REO for assistance and the types of services by the Staff to aid them.

3) Public Policy: An additional aspect of Strategy C applies to the area of public policy. The Director and the Board (and possibly other staff) need to be working on the public sector with the organization energy contained in a Diocesan Office. The stimulation of new legislation and/or state department guidelines in areas related to religious education, e.g., religion in the public schools, can have long-range benefits for all working within the diocese. It is potentially possible, for example, that a state university or college could offer a teaching degree in religious studies which would provide a large part of the theoretical background needed by coordinators for their work. An expanded Newman parish could offer the additional opportunities for community experience and growth in personal faith. This type of work could change the total climate of possibilities within a diocese and is, therefore, an aspect of the Diocesan Office's work which should be planned even to the partial neglect of some short-term projects or generalized services.

Staff of Religious Education Office Based upon these strategies in this model administrative structure, the personnel of the Religious Education Office would include the following:

Adult religious education Coordinator: This person would coordinate the work of the diocesan adult education personnel—generalists and specialists. The generalists may be area coordinators or persons working out of the Diocesan Office in areas of the diocese. Basically, they help the parishes with the generalized services described above. The exact number of generalists would, of course, depend upon the size of the diocese and the variety and scope of other educational efforts by such groups as the Liturgical Commission and the Human Relations Commission. Specialists will be explained later.

Youth Religious Education Coordinator: For the present, this team might be the largest within the Office as Strategy A is worked out. The Diocesan Office personnel in this group would provide the parishes with the *generalized services* described above, assisting them to effect quality religious education for children and adolescents. The precise number of generalists working in this regard would again vary with local needs.

Public Education Coordinator: This would be a radical step for most dioceses—the establishment of a section within the Religious Education Office which works on public youth and adult education. The primary purpose of this section would be to work with public schools toward the achievement of quality education, especially in such important areas as value education, sex education, comparative religions, and other social studies and humanities. Bringing the Christian Gospel and the educational expertise of the Diocesan Office to bear upon the educational problems and programs affecting public elementary and secondary schools is a proper concern for the Diocesan Office because (1) the majority of the Catholic youth attend such schools and (2) the faith community has an educational mission to man.

The other work of this section of the REO would include public adult education, especially through the mass media. The Gospel can be brought to bear upon the issues of the day through an educational process in the mass media, especially in reference to current problems. This work may also be cooperative with other Diocesan groups and departments.

Administrative Coordinator: Lastly, the REO would have an Administrative Coordinator who would assist parish coordinators with their professional development and involvement in the diocesan efforts. The coordinators may wish to establish a peer group of their own for professional development. In this event, the Administrative Coordinator would represent the Office at their sessions and would spend the majority of his time working with parish Boards of Education. In general, the Administrative Coordinator would bring the expertise of the Diocesan Office to bear upon the parish administrative problems and coordinator development.

Specialists: The specialists in the Religious Education Office would be people with knowledge and skills in fields needed by the coordinators and Office Staff. These persons would be working in-depth in their area of expertise and would not relate to the coordinators or the schools except through one of the above sections: Adult, Youth, Public, and Administrative. These specialists might be employed on a part-time or one-time basis by the REO rather than be full-time personnel.

Some examples may clarify this general concept. A specialist in the area of *media* could be a full-time position. This person would assist the Adult and Youth Coordinators with up-to-date information about films, television, music, and other media materials related to youth and adult religious information. This information would include the nature of these media materials, how to use them, and where they are available. The present efforts of Diocesan Offices to maintain lending libraries will dissipate in favor of such specialized service as the publishers produce more self-contained media kits and as independent groups make media materials readily available. Frequently, public libraries handle some of these materials with competent advice.

The Media Specialist would also work with the Public Education Coordinator in preparing original materials for radio and television use. Original materials for youth and adult education could also be produced, especially those relating to local issues.

Another full-time specialist might be working with the other Office Staff in reference to the *religious education of the blind, deaf, and retarded*. There is considerable difference of opinion about what to do in this area. It is assumed in this model that the Diocesan Religious Education Office should not launch a special school or closely organized diocesan program. Rather, the Special Religious Education Specialist would assist the Youth, Adult, and Public Education Coordinators with their work as it pertains to special religious education. The stimulation of public school efforts for general education for retarded children in cooperation with the Public Education Coordinator may also be one of the responsibilities of this specialist. Another may be to work with parent groups and parishes to assist them to identify and cope with the special religious education needs which they have.

A psychologist, versed in learning theory, could be employed by the Diocesan Office on a part-time basis — perhaps in conjunction with a local college. This person would work especially with the Adult and Youth coordinators in their planning sessions, bringing the understandings of psychology to bear upon their projected programs.

The number and kind of specialists will vary with the given needs of a Diocesan Office. The main point here is that the earlier (or perhaps present) need for basic general religious education work — planning, basic curriculum design, etc. — will wane with the advent of coordinators within a diocese. In its place, a need for special knowledge and skills to augment the general abilities parish professionals will develop. The Diocesan Office should be expected to offer such help eventually.

Specific Staff Roles and Decision-Making Processes: The above administrative model for a Diocesan Office aims to show how the services which the coordinators will need can ultimately be met. It also seeks to point out the nature and scope of the educational mission of a Diocesan Office in a somewhat ideal form. How a particular Diocesan Office meets its responsibilities is another matter.

It was mentioned above that communication between the Office and the coordinators is essential. The same applies to intra-office communication. In order for the basic strategies which a particular office adopts to be implemented, it is necessary that specific roles be established and a process of decision-making be identified *and followed.* Communication between professionals in religious education work today is of a rather low quality. Perhaps this is a result of the syndrome factor described above. It might also result partially from the immense growth pains which dioceses are experiencing

in the transition from a school approach to a total religious education approach in their educational mission.
Nevertheless, the highly emotional atmosphere which
a coordinator experiences when working with the pastor
also is found within a Diocesan Office and between the
Office and the coordinators.

To facilitate communication—although it will
always be problematic—each Diocesan Office should
work out a chart similar to the sample presented here
from the Grand Rapids Diocese (Michigan) in Chart 8:3.
In that diocese, the work of the Office was divided into
three working teams: Central Office, Northern Team, and
Southern Team. The geographical divisions were deemed
necessary to cope with the largely urban character of
the southern area and the largely rural character of the
northern area. Each Team had assigned responsibilities
which they met in the manner deemed most appropriate
by them. The Whole Staff consisted of all of the members
of the three Teams plus a representative of the coordinators' group which had formed in the diocese. The
areas requiring a vote by the Whole Staff were clearly
designated. After decisions and plans were made by
the Whole Staff, they were carried to the diocesan Board
of Education as needed. The decisions of the Board then
became the working mandate for the Office.

Through a means such as this, the internal communications within the Diocesan Office can be improved,
the coordinators know what to expect from whom at the
Office, and the coordinators participate in the broad
decisions which affect them.

SUMMARY

Coordinators and parish Boards will need to assess
the strengths and weaknesses of their own particular

CHART 8:3

RELIGIOUS EDUCATION STAFF
DECISION MAKING PROCESSES
(Diocese of Grand Rapids, Michigan — 1969-70)

*Categories for columns 2 and 3 are: Whole Staff, Central Office, Team
Staff and other (meaning special assignment or ad hoc staff member).*

I. ASSESSMENT OF NEEDS

	Initiated by	*Decided by*
A. Diocesan Assessment	Central Office	Whole Staff
B. Area Assessment	Teams	Teams

II. PROGRAM GOALS

A. Diocesan Goals	Central Office	Whole Staff
B. Area Goals	Teams	Teams

III. DIOCESAN PROGRAM

A. Communication

1. Letters to Pastors	Central Office	Central Office
2. Catechetical News		
Diocesan wide	Central Office/Teams	Central Office
Area releases	Team	Team
3. Associate Bulletins	Other	Other
4. Speakers	Central Office	Central Office
5. Liaison with Groups	Central Office	Central Office

B. Curriculum Consultation

1. Center Displays, etc.	Teams	Teams
2. Parish Visitation	Teams	Teams

C. Instructional Services

1. Teacher Education		
Diocesan Course	Teams	Teams Central Office
Workshops, etc.	Teams	Teams
2. Adult Education		
Diocesan Courses	Teams	Teams Central Office
Area sessions	Teams	Teams
Consultation	Teams	Teams
3. Parish Coordinators		
Placement	Central Office	Central Office
Professional Develop.	Central Office	Central Office
Religious Develop.	Central Office	Central Office
Program Consult.	Teams	Teams

IV. PROGRAM EVALUATION

A. Total Diocesan Program	Central Office	Whole Staff
B. Area Programs	Teams	Teams
C. Special Projects	Other	Whole Staff

V. RESOURCES

A. Staff	Central Office	Central Office
B. Centers (Offices)	Central Office	Central Office
C. Budget	Teams/Central Office	Central Office

VI. RESEARCH

A. Staff Development	Central Office/Teams	Central Office
B. Program Development	Central Office	Whole Staff
1. Coordinator Project	Other	Whole Staff
2. Special Education	Other	Whole Staff

Diocesan Office and work to help that Office attain a capability of offering the kind of assistance which they need. Basically, the Office cannot be expected to provide the general knowledge about youth and adult religious education programming. This, the coordinator should have as a professional. The Office should provide specialized help and educational programs which meet inter-parochial or specialized needs. This, the coordinators have a right to seek — whether or not the Office has the present ability to provide it.

The Diocesan Office should be able to provide leadership through directional goals and the personal vision of the staff members. It should be able to assist the coordinators with skills in the assessment of parish needs and in the decision-making processes which the coordinator can use in helping his faith community assume its responsibilities. It should provide in-depth advice on curriculum and instruction; pilot program research; normative policies to guide local Board actions; access to information not available through the professional media; and public/diocesan community opportunities not attainable by local groups. In short, the Diocesan Office has its responsibilities and the coordinators have theirs. The Office cannot expect the coordinators to be extensions of itself; nor can the coordinators expect the Office to do their work for them.

The growth of the parish professional will have radical impact upon Diocesan Offices and, hence, the transition period will not be smooth. Nevertheless, both parish coordinators (and teachers) and the Diocesan Office are dedicated to quality religious education in an era when both sense the desperate need for a new mission to meet a new age. This dedication to a common educational mission and this unity with a common Spirit should provide the climate in which both can work cooperatively — each in his own sphere of responsibility.

NOTES FOR CHAPTER 8

1) Some Diocesan Offices are still called the Confraternity of Christian Doctrine (CCD) Office; others are termed Religious Education Office; still others are part of a central diocesan Christian Education Office or something similar in name. The general trend is toward becoming a Religious Education Office and towards a closer working arrangement with Catholic School Offices.

2) Census Management, Inc., *National CCD Survey*, submitted by Research Committee of National Conference of Diocesan Directors and CCD National Center (Washington, D.C.: census January-April, 1968), unpublished research document available in the files of Diocesan Offices or at the National Center.

3) Cf. Warren Bennis *Changing Organizations* (New York: McGraw-Hill, 1966). "Valid knowledge makes the distinction between theoretical knowledge for its own sake and theoretical knowledge introduced towards a practical end. It is the difference between pure research and action research, random probing and problem solving."

4) There are studies already made about separating the parochial school property and control from the parish and placing it into a diocesan system run by the Diocesan Board and the School Office. This is deemed necessary to establish a separate school system under lay control in order to be receptive to governmental aid. If such happens, then parish Boards of Education will not control parish schools, for these will become parts of a diocesan system. Parish Boards will then need to consider how much and what kind of services they will purchase from this system for the people of the parish. The present work of the Superintendent of Schools would also become much more complex. He would become more like the superintendent in a large city school system and less like a state level superintendent of public instruction.

Chapter Nine

STAYING PROFESSIONAL

The parish professional religious educator is a new phenomenon, and thus there are few criteria for judging professionalism. In fact, some would question whether or not there really is a validity to the field of religious education itself.

There is validity, however, to the educational mission of the Christian people. The Gospels, the Acts of the Apostles, and the Epistles clearly speak of the teaching role of the followers of Jesus. This responsibility is shared by the whoie Christian community, but especially by those who stand in the place of the Apostles (bishops) and by the prophets and teachers (cf. 1 Cor. 12:28). The Christian Community has the right to look for particular charisms from those who will lead their growth in the Word; that is, the faith community has a right to expect leaders of the educational mission to be "professionals" in the proper understanding of that term.

Webster's *New World Dictionary* defines "profession" in four ways. First, it is seen as an act of declaring or avowing belief in something, usually a religion. Secondly, it is a vocation (calling) or occupation requiring special preparation and generally involving mental rather than manual work. Thirdly, "profession" is defined as a body of persons involved in a particular vocation or occupation. Lastly, "profession" is used to describe the action of formally entering into a religious group.

It would seem, therefore, that a parish coordinator could definitely be called a "professional" if he meets the general criteria: (1) he believes firmly in the faith and religious education, (2) he has special background and talents for leadership positions in reference to religious education, (3) he compares well with others like him who are fulfilling these same general responsibilities, and (4) he has been called (hired) to the task of leadership for the educational mission of a given faith community.

To give these general criteria perspective, let us compare them with what was *not* said. First of all, the coordinator is not simply a technician with specialized skills for educating people, nor is he an administrator who manages defined tasks. Furthermore, the coordinator is not a supervisor who guides a course of study. He is a person called to leadership responsibilities serving the Christian Community in their educational mission. Degrees—those sacred idols—are not necessarily prerequisites for becoming a "professional" religious education coordinator. We simply must stop worshipping the M.A. degree in religious education, religious studies, or theology. Degrees do not guarantee effective leadership. They simply indicate academic achievement according to the standards of the degree-granting institution. In fact, a degree does not even indicate academic competence in all cases.

If we must begin to establish criteria for judging

the "professionalism" of coordinators, then let us begin to state them in terms of the coordinator's ability to know and live the Gospel, his ability to lead people, his awareness of the times in which we live and of the nature of growth and development, and similar criteria. Judging the "professionalism" of a coordinator by the degrees which he possesses is not a good criterion. Seeking to determine academic competence is another story. A person can be academically competent — he can be aware of and able to apply the best thinking of the magisterium and related fields to the challenges facing a faith community — without having academic degrees.

With the above in mind, let us attempt to describe some of the general characteristics of "professional" religious education coordinators and some of the ways in which growth in effectiveness can be augmented.

PERSONAL LIFE STYLE

A coordinator's personal life cannot be separated from his "professional" life in reality, for a large part of who he is stems from what he does and believes. To totally equate them, however, produces problems also. For purposes of discussion, therefore, the more personal aspects of a coordinator's total life style will be viewed first apart from those which are closely related to his contracted (covenanted) responsibilities.

Embrace Life The professional coordinator is a person who has made the basic commitment "to live rather than exist," as Dr. Beryl Orris would put it. And this commitment shows. The people around such a person have the feeling that "something is happening here."

Each of us is raised in a family in which we are taught fundamental attitudes and values for the basic direction of our lives by parents and relatives. As we mature—usually at the end of adolescence—we are confronted with the choice of accepting the responsibility for our own lives. We are forced to decide whether we shall live or exist, whether we will accept what has been given to us by our families and build on it freely and responsibly, or whether we will surrender to another "family" the control over our destiny.

While no one can completely control his own destiny—to attempt to do so is to attempt to play God—nevertheless, each of us has to assume the responsibility for the course which we will take, for the ideas and people in whom we will believe, and for the general style in which we will live our lives.

It sounds somewhat extreme to speak of the coordinator needing to make this basic decision to embrace life as part of his development as a professional religious educator, but this is particularly necessary in our age, when so many people, faced with massive change, have either surrendered their freedom to an organization (secular or religious), have withdrawn into their own little world, attempting to defend it from everything outside, or have simply become apathetic to all change and people.

If the goal of religious education is the development of a sound human being, then the coordinator who will lead the parish in this process must first of all be in the process of becoming a sound human being himself. The first step in this direction is to become aware of who and what he is and to decide to do something about his future growth. The old expression, "Who you are speaks so loudly that I can't hear what you say," is a most apt summary of this first personal characteristic of a professional coordinator. Unless a coordinator has become aware of his aloneness and freedom in the face of life and has decided to live, he is unable to know God and to commit himself totally to a life in faith and hence is unable to take the lead in the educational mission of Christian people.

Believe Firmly It is rather obvious to say that the professional coordinator is a man of faith. But what may not be so immediately obvious are the simplicity and continual growth which real faith demands. Leaving Egypt for the desert or Nazareth to go into Egypt are biblical examples of the total dependence and trust amid anxiety and insecurity which genuine faith implies.

The professional coordinator will be faced continually with the frustration of creative tension — comparable to that between the now-already and the yet-to-be-realized eschatology. He will feel inadequate before the challenge of leadership and yet confident enough in himself to risk trying. This abandonment to the Spirit is a characteristic of faith which is easily described and yet difficult to achieve.

To look at it another way, the coordinator has to realize that he is not seeking power or control over the lives of other people. Rather, he must allow each person freely to choose the way in which he will live and die. This means the coordinator can testify to what he believes about life and death but cannot impose his beliefs on others. If the Spirit of Jesus is alive and at work among men, it speaks to the hearts of all men, but nothing will guarantee that any one person, including the coordinator, reechoes the voice of the Spirit.

The liberal-conservative battles over religious education are too simplistic. God is neither liberal nor conservative. For the coordinator to label some members of the parish one way or the other and then act towards them accordingly is truly "unprofessional" in terms of the Gospel. A firm and integrated faith will lead the coordinator to respect all with whom he works and to treat them accordingly. Much has already been written in other places about the development of life in faith, and space need not be taken here to repeat it. Suffice it to say here that faith will make a difference in the life of the coordinator and that difference should show.

Set Personal Parameters The coordinator who is striving to become a "professional" in the educational mission will find it helpful to set personal goals or parameters for personal decisions. The coordinator will also need to learn how to separate his personal goals from those of the community which he serves. On the one hand, he must be totally immersed in the community, sharing their hopes, aspirations, and problems; and yet, on the other hand, if he is to assume a leadership position, he must also have a vision which transcends the situation of the particular community he serves. A broad vision of what religious education is all about, the ability to see the daily successes and failures in perspective, is essential for survival and for leadership. This perspective can be gained partially through an articulation of personal goals or parameters.

A *parameter* is a constant used for measurement whose value varies with circumstances. Personal parameters for a coordinator would be the basic values and beliefs about self and religious education which would form the criteria for his decisions. This range of values helps the coordinator to see "good" effects even in "bad" decisions. For example, the Board of Education may vote down a great program which the coordinator has designed for the parish. The coordinator believes strongly in that program but more basically (personal parameters) he believes in the humanizing process by which the Board is free to choose or to reject. Thus he does not react to failure when the Board votes out a program; it is not taken personally.

Know Personal Strengths and Weaknesses Self-acceptance and self-discipline in the pursuit of valid goals are another characteristic of a professional coordinator. A person with great strengths is very apt to have great weaknesses. This is true for coordinators like anyone else. Learning how to utilize his strengths in the service of the community and how to compensate his weaknesses with the help of others is a process which a professional coordinator should strive to master.

This process, of course, begins with self-acceptance. If the coordinator can realize his own inherent worth despite his weaknesses, he can provide an atmosphere of acceptance and respect in which catechists and others are free to risk changing themselves.

PROFESSIONAL LIFE STYLE

It should again be noted that there is no real dichotomy between the coordinator's "professional" and his "personal" life styles. They are related aspects on a continuum which can be identified separately only for discussion purposes.

Learning Effectiveness The ability to use well one's time, talents, and available resources in the pursuit of goals is another of those characteristics which differentiates the professional coordinator from one who is attempting to fulfill the role.

There is an authority of office which is given by the faith community to the person who enters into the role of coordinator. Yet this authority of office must be augmented with an authority of leadership or an earned authority before the coordinator will become a true leader for that faith community. This earned authority is often referred to as prestige or influence. It is the quality which can be seen "when his subordinates permit their behavior to be guided by his decision without independently examining the merits of that decision" (1).

A coordinator who has achieved this earned authority will possess several qualities; namely, he will be well-informed, will consider alternatives to decisions, and will take a stand on issues after appropriate deliberation, and stick with it(2).

This prestige or earned authority (or authority of competence) comes not only from the personal qualities of the coordinator, but also from the professional skills which he has learned, that is, from his effectiveness in fulfilling the responsibilities assigned to him. Effectiveness is not a quality with which we are born; it has to be learned. And it involves the successful use of time, talents, and resources.

Time is a limitation which all people have in common; there are only twenty-four hours to each day. Hence, it is the way in which people use time that separates the effective persons from those who never seem to accomplish anything. The professional coordinator is a person who learns to use time well. Before a coordinator can begin to do this, however, he needs to know where he is presently spending his time and energies. A daily record over a month or two will give him a general picture of how much time he spends on which kinds of activities. Then the question becomes one of sorting out priorities that are related to his individual talents, responsibilities, and commitments. What kinds of activity consume what amount of time? What is being done by the coordinator that could be done equally as well by someone else? Which items take priority over which other items? Is there time planned for availability? for study and research? for involvement with the teachers and parents?

Planning each day, week, and month becomes the

next step. Once the regular activities are identified and the amount of time they consume is measured, then plans can be made. Time must also be alloted for the unexpected. The flow of daily events and people—especially in large parish situations—will consume much of the coordinator's time, and it will look as if he is very busy. Yet this may only be activity and not accomplishment. Planning for events and for ways to respond to events and to the daily flow of people separates the effective coordinator from the merely "busy" coordinator.

Religious educators have a neurotic twinge about being "available" and "being open." Much of this is excellent. In a technological world where people are viewed as replaceable parts, responding to another as a unique person and valuing him enough to be with him is a badly needed charism and one which Christian leaders should develop. But this availability is more properly the charism for the priest than for the coordinator. In the pastoral situation, however, the coordinator will also have to be available to the people, but at least he can plan his availability more carefully. Mornings might be used for planning and for study, and during this time the coordinator will "not be available." There are exceptions, of course, but during this time period the secretary would ordinarily not disturb the coordinator and would postpone phone calls and visits until later in the day. In the afternoon, the coordinator would follow up on these.

At first, this may look too "business-like" for religious educators, and it might be if it is followed too rigidly. More to the point, however, is the fact that the effective use of time is a professional skill and one which indicates that the coordinator takes himself, his work, and others seriously enough to want to make the best use of time for all these.

How each coordinator will learn this art of being

effective—that is, how he will earn the prestige or the authority of leadership—is an individual matter. The effective use of time is one of the key factors. Another is the establishing of goals and priorities.

Setting Priorities: All who are involved in the educational mission of the faith community have their own goals and priorities for what should be accomplished. The Annual Program and Budget approved by the Board of Education establishes the formal goals and priorities for the coordinator and the catechists for a given year. Yet the informal personal and program priorities remain. Bringing these into a working harmony is another characteristic of a professional coordinator.

Each person involved in the educational mission should be made aware of the priorities for the total program which have been set by the Board; the coordinator should not take this awareness for granted. Each person should also have the chance to express his own personal insights into what the educational mission is all about and why. Helping him to express this and to relate his personal priorities to the adopted priorities for that year is the coordinator's task. Unless all are working to achieve a common sense of direction, internal discord will develop and will eventually consume much time and energy.

The process of projecting the Annual Program and Budget allows for some of this harmonizing of personal and program priorities. Weekly "staff" meetings between the coordinator and those working regularly with the educational mission (catechists, secretaries, etc.) might be another vehicle for this. Other ways are also possible. The point is that the coordinator cannot afford to by-pass the setting of priorities which guide the actions of all involved with the educational mission, and all should know these priorities.

The chief question to ask in setting these priorities is: What can we contribute? What can we (all those involved) contribute toward the realization of the educational mission of this community? What can we contribute to the faith development of these young people? these adults? The outward emphasis of *educational service* should be primary and not the internal needs and priorities of the people involved. All the daily questions and problems should be resolved with this general concern foremost in mind: the educational mission, the reason why all are working together in that particular place to begin with.

Plan Improvements Even with priorities set and the chief focus on the contribution which all can make to the educational mission established, there will be innumerable daily problems and improvements to be made in the educational work. Approaching these in an organized manner is another characteristic of the professional coordinator.

There are several steps which have proven effective in many fields for improving a situation: (1) select a job to improve, (2) gather the facts, (3) challenge every detail, (4) develop a preferred solution, and (5) implement the improvements.

1) Select a Job to Improve: Defining the problem or selecting the job to improve is the key step; the better the definition of the problem or the identification of the task is, the more possible the solution becomes. For example, if the religious education program for adolescents is not working well, this might be selected as the primary job or area to improve. The adolescent program should be described in its component parts, i.e., the basic instructional style, the catechists involved, the curriculum materials used, the place, the time, and so

forth. Each sub-problem can be related to a more major problem until the basic problem to be solved is identified. This step is closely related to the second step, and the first draft of the problem may be revised several times after the first facts are known.

2) Gather the Facts: Why is the program working? Why isn't it working? How do we know? What evidence is there? What kinds of programs work well in general? What do we need here to meet the needs of our adolescents? And so forth . . .

Facts about all aspects of the task to be improved are gathered without applying them immediately to a program idea. In other words, after the brainstorming about the job or area to be improved, those involved then gather data about that area. The coordinator might form a committee of adolescents and help them gather opinions of others in a formal way; he might also meet with a group of parents of adolescents and discuss the strengths and weaknesses of the program.

After the facts are gathered they should be organized into some format by which they can be readily seen. Placing data on large charts which can be put up on the wall before the group working on the improvements is one way to do this. A mimeographed report might be another way. If mimeograph pages are used, it might be advisable not to staple them together or at least to staple only those pages of facts which go together and leave miscellaneous topics separate.

3) Challenge Every Detail: When the fact-gathering has been done, then the group can challenge all the reasons given for the success or failure of the job selected for improvement. Bringing in an outside person, e.g., a diocesan consultant, is also helpful at this time. An outsider is not "locked into" the local assumptions and

might be able to do a better job of challenging all the reasons and facts gathered.

4) Develop a Preferred Solution: When a probing session challenging all the facts is concluded, a new statement of the problem may emerge, or it may become evident that the problem is much larger than what can be solved or improved by that particular group. For example, the massive size of the parish may be the real problem affecting the religious education program for adolescents and not the actual program offered itself. This is a problem beyond the ability of the coordinator and the catechists. In this case, the group can decide to identify ways to involve others in working on that problem, or they can accept that larger problem as a necessary limitation and proceed to find ways to improve the selected job within that major handicap.

Whichever course of action is taken, the next step becomes one of projecting (brainstorming) the best way to improve the job or solve the problem. Again an outside person might help the group think up all kinds of solutions. The committees of adolescents and of parents mentioned above could also brainstorm preferred solutions. Eventually a number of improvement ideas will emerge and these can be worked out in depth by one or more persons so that detailed alternatives emerge.

Then the group has to weigh the cost of the alternatives, both in human and material resources, and the impact of the solution in terms of the total educational mission of the parish.

5) Implement the Improvement: When an alternative has been chosen, the group can work out a plan of action or begin to solve the problems inherent in implementing the preferred solution. How do we get sufficient funds? Where do we get interested people? How

do we convince the pastor? How do we convince the Board? What about the reaction of the Diocesan Office? These and many other implementation questions have to be raised and resolved.

This organized approach to improvement is a characteristic of a professional coordinator and a process which will help him to gain an authority of competence. Faith and Christianity are profoundly simple, but the organized procedures and institutions of finite men are not. It is not enough in an era of change for a coordinator to speak prophetically about what is wrong with the Church and with the times. He must be about the work of proclaiming the Word, of spreading the Gospel, and, in this era when the medium is the message, the way in which he works is also a large part of the message he wishes to teach. Effectiveness can be learned and the faith community has a right to expect a professional coordinator to learn to be effective in leading the educational mission.

GROWTH WITH OTHERS

In an opinion survey conducted as part of Project Coordinator, 81.1% of those who replied (64.1% were coordinators) indicated that they saw a purpose or a need for some kind of an association of professional religious educators. They saw this need in terms of sharing ideas (41.5%), developing professionalism among themselves (28.2%), mutual support (13.1%), and as a means to a national voice on issues (11.6%). This survey and personal contacts make it evident that coordinators as a newly developing profession feel a great need for mutual support and sharing. The question is, how is this best achieved?

The Professional Association The traditional way in which these needs are met is the professional association with its national and regional offices, annual convention, newsletters and/or publications, and individual memberships. Some 26.1% of the respondents indicated in one way or another that they favored this type of association to meet their needs. The significant fact is that some 75% did not describe the traditional professional association as the best means for meeting their felt needs. They attempted to describe some other vehicle.

Another sign of the need for a different mode for professional growth is the decline in the presently-existing professional organizations. There have been a number of professional associations within Protestant religious education which have voted themselves out of existence in recent years. Several affiliate associations of the National Education Association have been re-examining their effectiveness in recent years, especially the effectiveness of the annual conference and the newsletters and the publications.

The nature of a professional association—as historically constituted—would also seem to militate against the needs of coordinators for growth with others. Typically, professional associations have a national office with a small staff and some regional groupings with volunteer staff. In effect, the individual member forms a relationship with the national office—a one-to-one relationship—and develops some contacts with others throughout the country through the annual conferences. The development of local or regional groups generally lags, and so the ability of the professional association to assist the individual in facing local problems and to give the individual moral and professional support is limited.

Professional associations do seem to be successful

in bringing some new insights to bear upon common problems through their conferences and publications and in speaking as a national voice on issues of concern to the membership.

Given the present state of drift in religious education in the United States and Canada, with its lack of clarification of goals and processes, and the new nature of the role of the parish professional, this author would strongly recommend that coordinators think twice before forming a professional association. More effective avenues for growth with others should be created to meet the emerging needs of coordinators. The national voice can come through existing groups such as the Religious Education Association and the National Conference of Diocesan Directors. The introduction of new insights can come through existing religious and educational publications. The need for mutual support and for assistance with local problems will have to come from some other vehicle. Now is the time for parish professionals to read theology and education and to evolve their own catechetics.

A Conference of Growth Communities The Catechetical Forum might give a clue to one type of growth association which could be evolved by coordinators. Coordinators could form a small regional group which would meet and be self-determining relative to its organizational structure and program for development.

The group might be limited in membership through invitations. At first, this looks as if it is exclusive, but it need not be so. In order for a group of people to really get to know one another enough to become a support community, they have to maintain a relatively limited size and small turnover. In addition, the membership might include more people than coordinators themselves. Professional catechists (professional in the sense described here), Board members, college professors in related fields, and others could be invited to this regional group. It would seem that a regional, that is, New England or Mid-west or South-east rather than provincial or diocesan grouping would also be more beneficial for a sharing of viewpoints.

In such a support community, the ability of the members to know one another and to develop the potential of assisting one another is greater than is possible through the professional associations, even with local chapters. Typically associations need to form a constitution and to have by-laws and voting procedures and the like. Eventually these procedures get in the way. In the loose support community described here, the group itself annually or semi-annually determines their course of direction and program. A small executive committee might be needed, but since the group knows one another, the executive committee is more apt to be truly representative. The person picked to lead this support community for a year or more could also represent this community in a conference with similar leaders from other support communities if there were a reason for these leaders to meet or to speak on a national issue or movement other than through the existing channels.

Diocesan Coordinators Group Even with these groups in existence, there is probably sufficient reason, given the present state of development of the coordinator phenomenon, for coordinators to form an independent diocesan group—where there are a sufficient number of persons employed—to working collectively on local problems. Some diocesan offices have assisted such groups to form; others have held regular group meetings with the coordinators and, in effect, have such a group. In the case of the latter, however, the coordinator group is not usually independent of the Diocesan Office. This lack of independence is mutually detrimental. The diocesan office needs "independent" feedback on its work from persons in the field who are competent and interested. The coordinators need to struggle with local problems, taking the diocesan point of view into consideration as *only one* point of view if genuine creativity is to occur, and the need for such creativity in programming for the educational mission is acute.

Where there is an independent diocesan group of coordinators, the leader of the coordinator group should be present at meetings of the Diocesan Office to present the coordinators' point of view and vice versa. The independence of each in most areas should be carefully guarded, while at the same time fostering a mutual interdependence whereby the strengths of each are shared with the other.

PROFESSIONALLY UNPROFESSIONAL

As a final thought about keeping professional, I would like to stress that coordinators should become professionally unprofessional. This play on words is an attempt to articulate a feeling that faith and the educational mission are profoundly simple as well as complex and that the coordinator as a person called to the role of service for the Christian community should be greatly sensitive to both aspects of this paradox.

Perhaps growth as a professional means becoming more acutely aware of the need for others to assume the responsibility for their own destiny and growth in faith. The coordinator certainly has to be responsive to the people whom he serves, but he is not responsible for them. If he becomes too "professional" in handling the educational work, he removes the groping and the searching which are such intergral parts of the educational mission. The insecurity which accompanies the educational mission allows for the Spirit to speak in the midst of anguish and confusion. A certainty in faith borders on idolatry.

The North American culture of which we are a part stresses the need for technicians, or professionals, to handle all aspects of life. It is an easy temptation for the coordinator to want to become that type of a professional. And yet, if he does, he looses the ability to sense the pulse of life and of people (and of the Spirit) and becomes a "clanging gong or a tinkling symbol" albeit well-made and functioning well. To be human is to be imperfect and in the process of becoming with others. The pressure for accomplishment—another aspect of our culture—may push the coordinator to try to become so "good" at religious education that he becomes less than human, and the message which he wishes to communicate is lost in the jargon and in the techniques.

If the coordinator can see his role as a temporary one, temporary until that community can assume the leadership for their own educational mission, if he can strive to become professionally unprofessional, then he is more apt to assume his responsibilities with a "tentative" attitude (a human attitude) which will win him the authority of competence needed for leading the faith community in the realization of their educational mission. This attitude is perhaps the primary characteristic of the "professional" coordinator in this era of change.

NOTES FOR CHAPTER 9

1) Ronald F. Campbell, Luvern L. Cunningham, and Roderick F. McPhee, The Organization and Control of American Schools (Columbus, Ohio: Charles Merrill, 1965), p. 210.

2) *Ibid.*, p. 247ff.

Chapter Ten

FUTURE OF COORDINATORS?

"To look back across history and try to comprehend the great cyclic movements of the past is difficult enough; but to understand what is going on right now is infinitely harder. No one can be sure that he is reading the signs perceptively enough to predict what is coming"(1).

This statement is an apt warning for anyone who would seek to define the present status of religious education in America. Whether present and newly emerging movements, program designs, and organizations will continue to assist Christian people in fulfilling their educational mission in the 1970's, only history will finally tell. What is clear at the beginning of this new decade is that there is widespread confusion about the goals of religious education, about what kinds of educational strategies and teaching methods are effective for those goals, and about the personnel and organizations needed to achieve whatever it is that the Church attempts to accomplish in education.

This confusion exists particularly for professionals in religious education. Because this phenomenon is so new—it began roughly about 1967 in any significant way—it would be foolhardy to try to predict its future course. The variety of ways in which parish professional religious educators are being utilized and the many problems and frustrations which are presently plaguing this movement make it possible to raise only certain short range and long range questions. These questions are presented here with the hope that research and discussion will resolve them and raise others in time for the answers to be brought to bear upon the course of this movement.

IMMEDIATE QUESTIONS TO BE RESOLVED

Each parish Board and parish coordinator face innumerable questions in getting started into this new focus in parish religious education, questions which must be answered locally with diocesan leadership. There are some immediate questions, however, which should be discussed nationally by groups concerned about the movement toward parish professional religious educators. The following are among them and arise out of data from Project Coordinator, from interviews and consultations across the country, and from discussions with Diocesan Directors and parish coordinators.

Is there a valid need for a parish coordinator? This question has both immediate and long range implications. The immediate will be discussed here.

The question basically asks whether or not it is wise for a parish to select this alternative to its educational mission; it involves the other alternatives and their impact. Perhaps it would be better for the parish to expand the parochial school and develop adult religious education related to it. The role of the principal, therefore, would expand. The school religion teachers could become the resource persons for expanded parish work in religious education.

Another alternative might be to secure an administrator and several secretaries to implement the decisions of the Parish Council and to coordinate the implementation of the work of other parish groups such as the Board of Education. The "strength" of the total parish may be the most pressing priority over and above the importance of parish religious education. Freeing the pastor of the parish for total pastoral work and placing the running of the parish in the hands of an administrator who is responsible to the Parish Council may be the administrative move which will most effectively advance the total "strength" of the parish. This, in no way, is meant to say that religious education is not important; rather it is a questioning of the priorities for the total thrust of a parish.

This question becomes a national question in that the specific administrative alternatives and program guidelines which are sponsored by such groups as the National Catholic Education Association (NCEA) and the National Conference of Diocesan Directors (NCDD) do have an impact upon diocesan programs and policies and upon parish efforts. Hence, it is imperative that such national groups fulfill their responsibility toward this new phenomenon by presenting alternatives and their projected impact on the educational mission of the Church.

Should a coordinator be hired by the parish, by a group of parishes, or by the diocese? Because there simply are not a sufficient number of people prepared to work as parish coordinators at this time, a number of dioceses and parishes are securing coordinators to work in a regional capacity. Also, some dioceses are hiring the coordinators and sending them into parish areas as extensions of the Diocesan Office. This is most frequently an administrative decision, based upon what is possible. It does raise the question, however, of whether or not the ultimate goal is one coordinator in each parish. This, in turn, again points up the necessity for a clearer focus on the purpose of religious education (the nature of the educational mission) in this decade. If religious education is viewed rather technically as a highly specialized field, then the goal most likely would be to have one coordinator in each parish. If, however, religious education is viewed more in terms of a movement, then perhaps a coordinator in an area is what is needed to support the parish efforts.

The lines of jurisdiction between the diocesan office and the parish religious education programs will have to be clarified before the full impact of this administrative decision—parish or area—relative to hiring a coordinator can be seen. Perhaps provinces should get together and work out a common thrust for their area. Eventually, the strengths and weaknesses of these provincial plans could be compared and some national criteria formulated.

What is the "best" role for parish coordinators? Recognizing fully that there never can be an ideal role for parish coordinators, nevertheless, it is important that sufficient data be collected throughout the country, in order that several model roles can be formulated to serve as guides to parishes seeking to move into this area.

There is, at present, a wide variance on the roles designed for coordinators. Some parishes view them as *administrators*; others as *resource persons* or consultants. The difference should be more clearly shown in administrative models. This also applies to the difference between a parish coordinator and a regional coordinator. Instead of trying to find "the role" for a coordinator, several alternatives should be tried and the results compared.

What is the relationship of the parish coordinator to the parochial school and the principal? Until some clear indication can be given whether or not schools will become a diocesan system as compared with a system of parish schools, the relationship of the coordinator to the school principal and the religion teachers in the Catholic school will remain vague.

This is not a simple area to resolve. The school tradition within the educational mission of the Church is very strong. Coordinators are viewed as a threat to schools by some; as an alternative to schools by others. In the school tradition the principal is the chief educational leader of the parish under the Board of Education; and the Superintendent of Schools, as the diocesan leader under the Diocesan Board, is over religious education. In a parish, the coordinator, in the school tradition, would become a supervisor or consultant under the jurisdiction of the principal much like a language arts coordinator. The clash of these two traditions puts great strain and frustration upon all who are presently working in the educational mission of the Church.

As with questions mentioned above, some national leadership on this issue also is needed. A clearer articulation of the educational mission for the Church today (nationally), a statement which would include more than the school tradition, would definitely lessen the strain and frustrations felt locally. Meanwhile, local groups and dioceses will have to work out this relationship problem.

Should the coordinator be part of a pastoral team or work with the Board of Education (Parish Council)? In a number of places throughout the country, pastoral teams are being formed. Several persons — priest, religious and lay — work together as a team to serve the liturgical, educational and social action needs of the total parish community. In effect, they form a "corporate pastorate." What are the theoretical and the experiential advantages and disadvantages of this approach? What should be the relationship of the team to the parish groups: boards, committees, commissions, and councils? Does the team simply extend the parish's dependence upon the pastor in a more sophisticated form? Or is this a development in the concept of ministry?

This question, like the first one, is immediate in the sense that the decision should not be made with haste, that is, not until the implications are calculated as fully as possible.

What should be the salary schedule for parish coordinators? for religious working as parish coordinators? This question should receive some immediate attention, especially by national groups working with problems of religious life and service. Do sisters work a ten month year and depend upon the parishes for their further education? Are sisters to be hired individually by agreement (contract) with the parishes rather than by an agreement between the parish or diocese and the community? Should sisters receive salary based upon the assigned responsibilities, their education and their background? Or should sisters (religious in general) receive a uniform rate of salary?

What about the salary for lay coordinators? Can some national criteria be established to guide diocesan policy-making in this regard? Is this necessary? Is this necessary, perhaps, because of the lack of understanding locally (diocesan as well as parish) of the extent and nature of this job?

What should be the relationship of the coordinator to the Diocesan Office? This is another way of looking at the question: Who should hire the coordinator? Some dioceses would envision the coordinator as working for the parish (paid by them and responsible to their Board) but also administratively responsible to the Diocesan Director. This really raises the unresolved question of the jurisdiction of the Diocesan Office and Board of Education in relation to that of the parish and parish Board of Education.

LONG-RANGE QUESTIONS TO BE RESOLVED

The impact of this phenomenon of the parish professional cannot be understated. This movement qualitatively changes what is possible in religious education in the United States and Canada—although Canada is still insulated from this problem by a separate school system which is supported by the government. This latter fact should be kept in mind in discussions about parochiaid. The success of the separate school system of Canada cannot be discussed without also discussing the failure of the parishes to meet the needs of the youth attending the government schools.

For years, religious educators have dreamed of what religious education might be. School people dreamed also in a different way. Because there have been full-time teachers and principals in schools, the work of Catholic education has gone on often despite the efforts of the Diocesan School Offices. CCD parish programs have had to rely upon volunteers—the parish priests on a part-time basis—and diocesan leadership.

Hence, there was an inability to "show results" in the same way in which schools were able to see tangible evidence of their achievements. Now the situation is radically changed. Coordinators offer the potential of dreams as yet undreamed, new questions to be studied and resolved leading to new developments.

What if the parish coordinators were to become deacons? The term "deacon" is used here not to refer to becoming members of the clerical state; rather it is intended to refer to formally conferring the responsibility of Christian service. What if "non-professionals" were selected from each parish in the areas of liturgy, education, and social action and after a period of education, ordained deacons to serve that faith community?

What if parish coordinators were to become community change agents in education? Realizing the responsibility of the faith community to public education, would this responsibility be best fulfilled if a coordinator was hired by several parishes within a larger community (town, city, or suburb) to serve as an ombudsman or a change agent for all education? In such a role, this person would become an expert on education and religious education and would bring new information and insights to those already working with education in public schools and the Church and would become the focus for youth and adult dissatisfaction with education. If this would not be possible on the scale of the larger city, the coordinator might be asked to become an ombudsman for Christian education only or religious education in all the churches, or just for public education. It obviously would be difficult to get a public school board to hire such an ombudsman, but why couldn't the churches do so?

What if the Diocesan Office were to place coordinators in areas of the diocese as change agents? If all of the parishes are viewed as independent entities, responsible for their own educational programs, then the diocesan role can change rather drastically. The Diocesan Office could place coordinators in areas of the diocese leaving them free to effect change as they deemed possible rather than to implement one diocesan plan. In effect, the coordinator would be much like the 4-H or agricultural extension agents in farm states. He would have access to quality information about religious education from the Diocesan Office but would be free to influence parishes (and schools) in the manner in which he deemed best. He would be administratively linked in a loose fashion to the Diocesan Office but would have jurisdiction over no programs—simply asked to bring about change.

Research on innovation in farm ideas indicates that a certain percentage of farmers will innovate new ideas on their own with only moderate contact with the extension agents. The largest group to adopt new ideas after they have been tested by the innovators is also the one with the most contact with the extension agent. Those who are last to adopt a new idea also have the least amount of contact with the extension agents(2). Throughout this program, the farmers are totally free to adopt or not adopt new ideas as well as whether or not to sustain contact with the extension agent.

What if, therefore, coordinators were to become regional change agents for Christian education? or ombudsmen for Christian education? or ombudsmen for all education?

Is there a valid need for a professional parish religious educator? On the more theoretical side, the question must be raised again whether or not there is a valid role for a professional religious educator. It is part of the North American culture to specialize and to professionalize many aspects of life. Perhaps it is part of the faith community's educational mission to challenge this by showing that "ordinary people" using their native intelligence can grapple with educational problems. Perhaps faith is not "professional" and that far fewer "ministers" are needed to serve the faith community than are presently employed.

Should the coordinator work to improve the "system" which hires him or should he work to create a new "system"? Lastly, on the more personal side, parish coordinators wonder whether or not they should become proficient in achieving the aims of the parish which hired them or whether the question is not to work toward a new concept of parish itself? Perhaps improving the present parish structure is perpetuating the basic problem; namely, that the organizational approach to Christianity impedes the growth of Christianity. Is Christianity a free movement of the Spirit among people which does not need an institution or organization except at the very local level? Is the faith community moving out of its present organizational structure under the leadership of the Spirit? Will coordinators and people like them become the "ministers" of a new expression of Church?

RECOMMENDATIONS

Based upon the data from Project Coordinator (which will eventually be published in a *Project Report)* and upon contacts with coordinators and those working with coordinators throughout North America, I would like to make the following recommendations:

To Parish Coordinators
1) "Relax! Jesus Saves."
2) Don't fight the Diocesan Office. The solutions to problems in parish religious education cannot depend upon the Diocesan Office. You were hired to "solve" them. Use the strengths of the Diocesan Office but avoid a struggle for power over interparochial concerns. You will lose; even if you win, what have you gained?
3) Please get out of the box. As a Methodist Bishop used to say: "We should live our lives not pushed by our problems but led by our visions." There is a whole new vision of parish religious education to be discovered and tried. We are trapped by our past presuppositions and the Spirit demands that we leave these intellectual idols behind. If you hear the call from the wilderness, please heed it and let us know what you find. Become a professional and launch out into the unknown.

To Boards of Education
Make haste slowly. The hiring of a parish professional is a significant step. It has great potential, but parishes need to be quite clear about what it is that they expect of a coordinator before hiring him.

To Diocesan Offices
1) Assume leadership for this movement within the Diocese, but be careful of seeking to control it. If parish coordinators are to be freed to advance radically the movement of religious education in parishes, they will also have to be "freed" from the presuppositions and controls of the Diocesan Director. Diocesan Directors (I've been one) are limited by their own dreams and visions of religious education. These are similar in tone and direction with those of the parish coordinators, but the coordinators also see many things that are possible and desirable that directors cannot envision. The

coordinators will have to teach us as well as learn from us. And if they are really parish "professionals," they are peers in educational background—even though they hold a different responsibility and have different experiences.

2) Collect data about the work which parish coordinators are doing and will do—job descriptions, contracts, sample programs, and similar primary materials. We have been collecting sample texts and audio-visuals for years. Now we need to begin to collect a range of possible administrative ideas which coordinators and parishes interested in hiring coordinators can use. This data can also be shared with one another through the National Center and the National Conference of Diocesan Directors (NCDD).

3) Encourage coordinators, pastors working with coordinators, and possibly even Board members to meet regionally in an independent group to explore common problems. The Office can support and provide information for these meetings, but should be wary of trying to direct their course along a route which they see as valid. The direction of the movement of parish coordinators within a diocese should be a shared responsibility. The Director is ultimately responsible for the diocesan work, but he needs the imput from the coordinators for the diocesan decisions which affect them.

4) Plan for new vistas. With the development of the parish professional, the Diocesan Office can look forward to dropping many of its present services and developing new services. The coordinators can provide some insight into this also. A certain amount of diocesan staff time should be spent in action research—where should we be five years from now?

To the NCDD, NCEA, "CORED," and the REA
     Form a joint subcommittee to assess this national

phenomenon and formulate a national strategy regarding it.

The NCDD needs to be involved since the Diocesan Director will be the key resource person for leadership relative to parish coordinators in his diocese. The NCEA should be involved because the relationship of religious education to schools must be resolved if a common sense of direction or educational mission is to emerge. The REA and the Canadian National Religious Education Office should be involved also as the development of the parish professional has vast implications for ecumenical religious education and for parish religious education in Canada, as well as in the United States. And of course coordinators must be involved. The newly established organization for coordinators, CORED, is attempting to become a national voice for parish professionals. Whether or not it will become the representative body for coordinators, only history will decide. At this time, however, it is an organized voice articulating the concerns of parish professionals and hence it should be involved in the national discussions about the growth of this new focus in parish religious education. A subcommittee such as this could attack these short- and long-range questions as well as provide a better insight into what is possible and desirable with parish coordinators.

These recommendations are valuable not so much for their internal content but more for the concern which they highlight about the radical potential for change inherent in this new phenomenon. The issues to which they are addressed may have changed by the time of the publication of this book but the potential for change will not have been realized nor the extent of the growth of the parish professional realized. For these reasons, I would hope the recommendations could be taken seriously.

NOTES FOR CHAPTER 10

1) "Storm Signals," *A Climate for Individuality* (Washington, D.C.: American Association of School Administrators, ASCD, NEA, 1965), p. 9.

2) Subcommittee for the Study of Diffusion of Farm Practices, Adopters of New Farm Ideas (North Central Regional Extension Publication No. 13); (Lansing, Michigan: State University, Department of Agriculture). See also Herbert F. Lionberger, "Diffusion of Innovations in Agricultural Research and in Schools," Strategy for Curriculum Change (ASCD, NEA, 1965), pp. 29-54. Lionberger also gives an extensive bibliography on innovation diffusion, and acceptance of ideas.

POSTSCRIPT

Anyone who conducts research on a phenomenon or who writes a book tends to over-estimate the importance of his research or his subject, and I am no exception. The many contacts with coordinators and diocesan directors throughout the United States and Canada, however, have convinced me during these past two years since Project Coordinator began that the potential for radical change is building up fast. The high frustration level of most coordinators and diocesan directors seems to come from the tension they feel between what might be and what is, within the educational work of the Church. Like Pierre de Chardin these educators feel deeply that "today something is happening to the whole structure of human consciousness" and that the Gospel has much to say to that development. They want to be creative participants in fashioning a new heaven and a new earth and in building the brotherhood of man.

But the way is not yet clear and perhaps it will never be again. Nevertheless, these religious educators are prayerfully forging ahead. Whether they are heading from Egypt to Sinai or vice versa, only time will tell for sure. Meanwhile, those in a leadership position in religious education must continue to grapple with the question stated so well by Teilhard De Chardin: "Swept along by the tide of affairs, what can we do to see clearly and to act decisively?" This book was written to contribute to that dialogue.

Appendix A

NCEA MODEL
SUGGESTED CONSTITUTION
Diocesan Board of Education

("Voice of the Community" NCEA, used with permission)

ARTICLE I
Name, Purpose & Duties

Section 1: There is hereby established a Board, under the name of "Diocesan Board of Education," having the purpose and duties of governing all matters pertaining to education in the Diocese of _____. These shall be deemed to include Catholic schooling and all other formal educational activities, including all matters pertaining to the Diocesan Office of Education; the location, opening and closing of schools; the location, opening and closing of catechetical centers; the determination as to whether schools or catechetical centers shall be operated in given locations; classes; teachers; salaries; educational, athletic and related

301

programs; finances; standards of education; application of Christian principles to the educational programs; and all formal courses of religious education. All decisions of the Board of Education shall be binding upon the Superintendent of Education; the Office of Education: all subordinate Boards of Education; and the pastors, principals and staffs of the schools and catechetical programs within the Diocesan system.

ARTICLE II
Membership on the Board

Section 1. Number and Composition. The Board of Education shall be geographically and numerically representative of the Catholic community. It shall include clergy and laity. It shall have representation of the religious orders serving the Diocese.

Section 2. Election, Vacancies, Removal. The members of the Board shall be elected by a method to be established. Vacancies on the Board shall be filled in the same manner. Any member of the Board, other than an ex officio member, who is absent from two consecutive regular meetings of the Board shall, unless excused by action of the Board, cease to be a member.

Section 3. Tenure of Office. Each member shall hold office for the term of three years, provided, however, that in order that the terms may be staggered, and that one-third of the members of the Board may be elected in each year beginning three years from the date thereof, the initial terms shall be divided so that three members will have a term of five years, three members a term of four years, and three members a term of three years. The present and future members of the Board shall hold office until successors be elected or until prior resignation or death or until prior disqualification by absence from two consecutive Board meetings not excused as aforesaid. The priest and religious members shall be appointed on a three year basis with one term of renewal.

Section 4. Ex Officio Membership. The Bishop of the Diocese of _____ shall be an ex officio member of the Diocesan Board of Education.

ARTICLE III
Officers

Section 1. Creation of Officers. The officers of the Board shall consist of a President, Vice-President, a Recording Secretary and such assistants and additional officers as the Board may elect.

Section 2. The Superintendent of Education. The Board shall retain an executive officer who shall be the Superintendent of Education. Said officer shall be considered not a member of the Board.

Section 3. Officers shall be elected annually at the annual meeting of the Board designated for this purpose. They shall be from nominations submitted by a Nominating Committee appointed by the President and by any member from the floor; they shall hold office until the next annual election and thereafter until their successors are duly elected and qualified.

Section 4. The President shall act as Chairman of the Board and of any Executive Committee; shall be the executive head of the Board; shall appoint all committees unless otherwise specified by the Board; shall execute on behalf of the Board all written instruments except as otherwise directed by the Board; shall be responsible for the agenda to be used at meetings; shall be responsible for reporting the actions of the Board to the Bishop of _____; and in general shall perform all duties incident to the office of a President and such other duties as from time to time may be assigned to him by the Board.

Section 5. The Vice-President at the request of the President shall perform the duties and exercise the functions of the President and when so acting shall have the power of the President, and shall perform such other duties as delegated by the President.

Section 6. The Secretary shall keep the minutes of the meeting of the Board; shall see that all notices are fully given in accordance with the provisions of this constitution; shall be custodian of the records of the Board; shall see that the Board seal is affixed to all documents, the execution of which on behalf of the Board under a seal is duly authorized and when so affixed may attest the same; and in general, shall perform all duties incident to the office of the Secretary of the Board and such other duties as from time to time may be assigned by the President of the Board.

Section 7. The Assistant Officers shall have such duties as from time to time may be assigned to them by the Board or by the President.

ARTICLE IV
Meetings

Section 1. The Board shall meet monthly subject to change by the Board itself or to postponement by the President. Special or additional regular meetings shall be held whenever called by the President or by a majority of the Board. The regular meeting held in the month of May in each year, or if none is held in that month, then in the next month in which a regular meeting is held shall be designated the annual meeting for the purpose of election of officers and any annual report.

Section 2. All meetings may be held at such times and places within or without the State as may be fixed by the President or by a majority of the Board upon not less than ten days' notice. Notice of the place, day and hour of all meetings must be delivered in writing. All meetings of the Diocesan Board of Education are to be open meetings unless designated as being Executive. Decisions made in Executive sessions must be presented and voted on at open sessions before becoming effective.

Section 3. A majority of the entire Board is necessary for the transaction of business at meetings; and a majority vote of those present shall be sufficient for any decision or election.

Section 4. The Board may fix itself on rules of procedure but in the absence of such, Roberts "Rules of Order" shall apply.

ARTICLE V
Committees

Section 1. Executive Committee: The Board may provide for an Executive Committee of five (5) or more members, the President to be an ex officio member, and the other member or members to be elected by the

Board and serve at the pleasure of the Board; the President is to be the Chairman thereof. During intervals between meetings of the Board, the Executive Committee may possess and execute all of the powers of the Board conferred in this constitution, to the extent authorized by the resolution providing for the Executive Committee or by subsequent resolutions. The Executive Committee shall meet at the call of its Chairman and shall fix its own rules or procedures and notices to be given of its meeting. Meetings of the Executive Committee shall be open meetings. A majority shall constitute a quorum.

Section 2. Other Committees: The Board may by resolution provide for such other committees as it deems advisable and may discontinue the same at its pleasure. Each entity shall have such powers and shall perform such duties as may be assigned to it by the Board and shall be appointed and vacancies filled in the manner determined by the Board. In the absence of other direction, the President shall appoint all committees.

ARTICLE VI
Office of Education

Section 1. Constitution, Staff, Appointment. There shall be an Office of Education for the Diocese of ————; a Superintendent of Education who shall be the Executive Officer of the Board of Education and other staff positions as the Board may deem appropriate; the Superintendent shall have such compensation and term of employment as determined by the Board. Other staff members shall have such compensation and other terms of employment as the Superintendent determines subject to the approval of the Board.

Section 2. Duties and Powers. The Superintendent of Education shall be responsible directly to the Board for the implementation of its policies in the Diocese. The Office of Education shall be under the direction of the Superintendent and under his direction shall have immediate charge and control of the general administration and supervision of all formal education within the Diocese.

ARTICLE VII
Seal

Section 1. Seal. The Board's seal shall be the seal, an impression of which appears on the margin hereof.

ARTICLE VIII
Amendment of Constitution

Section 1. Amendment. This constitution may be amended, supplemented or repealed in whole or in part at any time by a two-thirds vote of all of the members of the Board.

APPENDIX

Some of the powers and functions of the Board of Education are worthy of special notice and therefore are listed below. This list, however, shall not be considered as exclusive or as restricting the powers of the Diocesan Board of Education in any way.

a. Establishment and Discontinuance of Schools. The Board of Education shall decide as to whether a parish or area shall be served by a formal school or by a catechetical center or by a combination thereof. No school of any grade, elementary, secondary, parish, interparochial, diocesan or catechetical center shall be established or expanded without the permission or initiative of the Board of Education. Existing schools or catechetical centers of whatever grade shall not be dissolved or discontinued, nor shall any part (for example an elementary school, kindergarten, primary grades, a catechetical program) be discontinued without the express and explicit permission of the Board. Any major changes in the operation or organization of a school or catechetical center of whatever level must be referred to the Diocesan Board of Education for approval. This shall be deemed to include patterns of dual enrollment, shared facilities, shared time and shared services.

b. Staffing of Schools. The permission of the Board of Education and of the Most Reverend Bishop is required before any religious order, congregation or society may be invited to staff a school or catechetical center in the diocese.

c. School Contract. The school contract or amendments thereto for the management and staffing of any parish or diocesan school or of any catechetical center or program must be approved by the Diocesan Board of Education. Normally, the contract will bear the signature of the Most Reverend Bishop, the President of the Board of Education, the appropriate superior of the religious congregation and, in the case of a parish school, the President of the parish Board of Education. (In the event that there is no parish Board of Education, the contract should be signed by the Reverend Pastor.)

d. Personnel. The Diocesan Board of Education reserves the right to certify administrative and teaching personnel and to withdraw certification for cause. All lay instructional personnel shall be contracted according to procedures and personnel policies determined by the Board of Education, Diocese of _____.

e. Buildings. All sites to be used for school buildings or catechetical centers, including faculty houses and convents, must be approved by the Diocesan Board of Education. The plans for such buildings and the type of equipment to be installed must be approved by the Board of Education. The interest of the Board of Education shall concentrate upon such matters as affect teaching and instruction, the safety of students, the well being of faculty and the conforming with State laws and regulations dealing with educational institutions. In each instance, the approval of the Board of Education must be obtained for all school and catechetical sites; plans and specifications; equipment, etc., for all schools, catechetical centers, faculty houses and convents. Before these are granted, final approval must be obtained from the Diocesan Building Committee.

f. Norms for Religious Instruction Outside the Catholic School. The Diocesan Board of Education has a special interest in establishing norms for those things that affect religious education outside the Catholic school. It shall have the right to prescribe standards for those teaching in such schools and centers; the type of equipment that shall be present; the quality of instructional materials to be used; the classroom environment and all other things affecting such education.

g. Activities. The Diocesan Board of Education reserves the right to approve all organized activities of schools and catechetical centers.

h. Community Relations. The Board of Education reserves the right of final approval over all relations of schools, catechetical centers or any part thereof to official or unofficial agencies of the community; city; county; state or nation.

i. Parent-Teacher Groups. The Diocesan Board of Education has the right of final approval over the charters and constitutions of all parent-teacher groups and other organizations of parents or other interested parties organized for working with educational programs.

Appendix B

RELIGIOUS EDUCATION MODEL
SUGGESTED CONSTITUTION
Diocesan Board of Education

PREAMBLE

Recognizing our responsibility to provide quality Christian education for youth and adults, We, the People of God of the Diocese of ——————, under the spiritual leadership of our Bishop, do hereby establish this Diocesan Board of Education.

ARTICLE I: PURPOSE

Section 1: The Diocesan Board of Education, representing the People of God of the Diocese (priest, religious and lay), has the primary responsibility for establishing the goals and policies regulating the programs of the Diocesan School Office and the Religious

Education Office (CCD) so that these truly serve the educational needs of the People of God, their parishes and schools in the Diocese.

Section 2: The Diocesan Board of Education, representing the Bishop, and the People of the Diocese, is also responsible for establishing directional goals and policies which will stimulate parishes especially through their Boards of Education to provide opportunities for quality Christian education for the youth and adults of the Diocese, education which is in keeping with the Gospel of Christ and the needs of the times.

Section 3: The Board of Education shall make recommendations to the (Catholic) College, to the Newman Campus Parishes and to other informal educational groups within the Diocese (CFM, Cursillo, TEC, etc.) regarding the relationship of their programs to the total education efforts of the Diocese.

Section 4: The goals and policies of the Diocesan Board of Education and the resulting programs of the Catholic School Office and the Religious Education Office (CCD) shall be limited only by the Bishop of the Diocese and/or the Diocesan Pastoral Council.

The Ordinary of the Diocese (and/or the Diocesan Pastoral Council) shall retain a veto power over the decisions of the Diocesan Board of Education. Decisions of the Board of Education shall be presented to the Ordinary and/or the Pastoral Council in writing. If they are returned by the Ordinary and/or the Pastoral Council with a veto in writing, they shall be reconsidered according to the suggestions of the veto. If they are not returned, the decisions shall become operative within sixty days.

ARTICLE II: FUNCTIONS

Section 1: In fulfilling its purpose in relationship to the Diocesan School Office and the Religious Education Office (CCD), the Diocesan Board shall do the following:

1. It shall review annually the goals, programs and budgets of the two offices to ensure that together they provide a comprehensive and coordinated approach to serving the educational needs of the People of God of the Diocese.
2. It shall (in conjunction with the Ordinary of the Diocese) secure adequate qualified personnel to head these offices, and upon recommendation of the Superintendent of Education secure adequate qualified personnel to staff them.
3. It shall provide adequate material resources for implementing the goals and policies of these Offices from (the Diocesan Development Fund), from the parishes and schools served and from governmental and private sources.
4. It shall provide for a process of evaluation of the effectiveness of these goals and programs in meeting the educational needs of the Diocese through these Offices (and other sources) and a process of reporting the educational needs and accomplishments to the People of God of the Diocese.

Section 2: In fulfilling its purpose in relationship to the Board of Education of parishes and schools, the Diocesan Board of Education upon the recommendation of the Superintendent of Education shall do the following:

1. It shall establish directional goals and policies re-

garding the movement and quality of all formal educational programs in the Diocese.

2. It shall adopt recommended policies regarding the qualifications and conditions of employment of all educational personnel (professional and non-professional) in the Diocese.

3. It shall adopt recommendations regarding the location, building and arrangement of educational facilities.

4. It shall adopt recommended standards and guidelines regarding the quality and level of achievement in the educational programs of the Diocese.

5. It shall regularly demand an evaluation of the effectiveness, relevance, authenticity, and quality of its own work, of the work of the Catholic School Office, the Religious Education Office (CCD), and of the total educational endeavor in the Diocese through its own processes of evaluation and through invitations to other groups concerned about the total development of the People of God of the Diocese, (Priests' Senate, Home and School, Parent groups, Parish Boards of Education, etc.).

6. It shall launch programs and procedures designed to advance the ability of parish and area Boards of Education to make responsible decisions effecting the quality of Christian education within the Diocese.

Section 3: In fulfilling its purpose in relationship to Colleges and the Newman Campus Parishes and other informal educational groups, the Diocesan Board of Education shall do the following:

1. It shall regularly invite representatives from these groups to present recommendations from their expertise regarding goals for the total development of Christian Education within the Diocese.

2. It shall upon advice of the Superintendent of Education make recommendations to these groups regarding the goals, policies and programs which they may enact to compliment the educational work of the Diocesan Board and of parish and area Boards of Education.

ARTICLE III: MEMBERSHIP

Section 1: The Diocesan Board of Education shall consist of eleven (11) members initially appointed and eventually elected by the Parish and area Boards of Education through a process to be determined. Nine (9) of the members shall be representatives of the People of God of the Diocese at large (laymen or women): one (1) shall be a priest and shall be appointed by the Ordinary; one (1) member shall be a religious representing the various religious communities serving within the Diocese and shall be appointed by the Major Superiors involved through a process of their own determination.

Section 2: Vacancies on the Board shall be filled in the manner described above. Any member of the Board, other than the ex-officio member, who is absent from two consecutive regular meetings of the Board shall, unless excused by the action of the Board, cease to be a member.

Section 3: Each member shall hold office for a term of three years, provided however, that in order that the terms may be staggered, and that one-third of the members of the Board may be elected in each year beginning three years from the date thereof, the initial terms shall be divided so that three (3) members will have a term of five years, three members shall have a term of four years and three (3) members for a term of three years. The present and future members of the Board shall hold office until successors be elected or until prior resignation or death or until prior disqualification by absence from two consecutive Board meetings not excused as aforesaid. The priest and religious members shall be appointed on a three year basis with one term of renewal.

Section 4: The Bishop of the Diocese and the President of the Pastoral Council shall be ex-officio members of the Diocesan Board of Education.

ARTICLE IV: OFFICERS

Section 1: The officers of the Board shall consist of a President, Vice-President, a Recording Secretary, and such assistants and additional officers as the Board may elect.

Section 2: The Board shall retain a Superintendent of Education as Executive Officer. The Executive Officer shall not be a member of the Board.

Section 3: Officers shall be elected at the annual meeting of the Board designated for this purpose. They shall be from nominations submitted by a Nominating Committee appointed by the President and by any member from the floor; they shall hold office until the next annual election and thereafter until their successors are duly elected and qualified.

Section 4: The President shall act as Chairman of the Board and of any Executive Committee; shall be the executive head of the Board; shall appoint all committees unless otherwise specified by the Board; shall execute on behalf of the Board all written instruments except as otherwise directed by the Board; shall be responsible (in consultation with the Superintendent of Education) for the agenda to be used at meetings; shall be responsible for reporting the actions of the Board to the Ordinary of the Diocese; and in general shall perform all duties incident to the Office of President and such other duties as from time to time may be assigned to him by the Board.

Section 5: The Vice-President at the request of the President shall perform the duties and exercise the functions of the President and when so acting shall have the power of the President, and shall perform such other duties as delegated by the President.

Section 6: The Secretary shall keep the minutes of the meeting of the Board; shall see that all notices are fully given in accordance with the provisions of this constitution; shall be custodian of the records of the Board; shall see that the Board seal is affixed to all documents, the execution of which on behalf of the Board under a seal is duly authorized and when so affixed may attest the same; and in general, shall perform all duties as from time to time may be assigned by the President of the Board.

Section 7: The Assistant Officers shall have duties as from time to time may be assigned to them by the Board or by the President.

ARTICLE V: MEETINGS

Section 1: The Board shall meet monthly subject to change by the Board itself or to postponement by the President. Special or additional regular meetings shall be held whenever called by the President or by a majority of the Board. The regular meeting held in the month of May in each year, or if none is held in that month, then in the next month in which a regular meeting is held shall be designated the annual meeting for the purpose of election of officers and any annual report.

Section 2: All meetings may be held at such times and places within or without the State as may be fixed by the President or by a majority of the Board upon not less than ten (10) days notice. Notice of the place, day and hour of all meetings must be delivered in writing. All meetings of the Diocesan Board of Education are to be open meetings unless designated as being executive. Decisions made in Executive sessions must be presented and voted on at open sessions before becoming effective.

Section 3: A majority of the entire Board is necessary for the transaction of business at meetings; and a majority vote of those present shall be sufficient for any decision or election.

Section 4: The Board may establish for itself rules of procedure but in the absence of such, Roberts "Rules of Order" shall apply.

ARTICLE VI: COMMITTEES

Section 1: The Board may provide for an Executive Committee of five (5) or more members, the President to be an ex-officio member and the other members to be elected by the Board and serve at the pleasure of the Board; the President is to be the Chairman thereof. During intervals between meetings of the Board, the Executive Committee may possess and execute all of the powers of the Board conferred in this constitution, to the extent authorized by the resolution providing for the Executive Committee or by subsequent resolutions. The Executive Committee shall meet at the call of its Chairman and shall fix its own rules or procedures and notices to be given of its meeting. Meetings of the Executive Committee shall be open meetings. A majority shall constitute a quorum.

Section 2: The board may by resolution provide for such other committees as it deems advisable and may discontinue the same at its pleasure. Each entity shall have such powers and shall perform such duties as may be assigned to it by the Board and shall be appointed and vacancies filled in the manner determined by the Board. In the absence of other direction, the President shall appoint all committees.

ARTICLE VII: OFFICE OF EDUCATION

Section 1: There shall be a Catholic School Office and a Religious Education Office (CCD) until such time as a unified Office of Education can be established. The Superintendent of Education shall coordinate the work of these two Offices working toward the establishment of one unified and comprehensive Office of Education. The Executive Officer shall have compensation and term of employment as determined by the Board in consultation with the Ordinary of the Diocese. Other staff members of these Offices shall have such compensation and terms of employment as the Executive Officer determines subject to the approval of the Board.

Section 2: The Superintendent of Schools and the CCD Director shall be responsible to the Board for implementation of its decisions in their areas of responsibility, through the Superintendent of Education.

Section 3: The Superintendent of Schools shall be responsible for the Catholic School Office and the services which this Office performs in relationship to the parish and area Boards of Education and schools of the Diocese. These services are presented annually in a Program and Budget Projection to the Board of Education for approval.

Section 4: The CCD Director is responsible for the Religious Education Office and the services which this Office performs in relationship to the parishes and the parish Boards of Education and their non-school religious education programs for youth and adults. These services are presented annually in a Program and Budget Projection to the Diocesan Board for approval.

ARTICLE IX: SEAL

Section 1: The Board's seal shall be the seal, an impression of which appears on the margin hereof.

BOARD MEMBERS: BISHOP:

President _____   _____

Vice President _____   SUPERINTEND. OF SCHOOLS:

Secretary_____   _____

(Priest Member) _____   CCD DIRECTOR:

(Religious Member)_____   _____

Date approved _____, 19 ____

APPENDIX
SECOND VATICAN COUNCIL'S DECREE ON CHRISTIAN EDUCATION

Importance of Education:
"The Sacred Ecumenical Council has considered with care how extremely important education is in the life of man and how its influence ever grows in the social progress of this age.

"Indeed the circumstances of our time have made it easier and at once more urgent to educate young people and, what is more, to continue the education of adults."

Universal Right of Education:
"All people of every race, condition and age, since they enjoy the dignity of a human being, have an inalienable right to an education that is in keeping with their ultimate goal, their ability, their sex, and the culture and tradition of their country, and also in fraternal association with other peoples in the fostering of true unity and peace on earth."

Right to Christian Education:
"Since all Christians have become by rebirth of water and the Holy Spirit a new creature so that they should be called and should be children of God, they have a right to a Christian education."

Parents: Primary Right:
"Since parents have given children their life, they are bound by the most serious obligation to educate their offspring and therefore must be recognized as the primary and principal educators. This role in education is so important that only with difficulty can it be supplied where it is lacking."

Society: Secondary Right:
"The family, which has the primary duty of imparting education, needs the help of the whole community. In addition, therefore, to the rights of parents . . . . , certain rights and duties belong indeed to civil society, whose role is to direct what is required for the common temporal good."

Church: Secondary Right:
"Finally in a special way the duty of educating belongs to the Church, not merely because she must be recognized as a human society capable of educating, but especially because she has the responsibility of announcing the way of salvation to all men, of communicating the life of Christ to those who believe, and, in her unfailing solicitude, of assisting men to be able to come to the fullness of this life."

Catechetical Instruction Essential:
"In fulfilling her educational role, the Church, eager to employ all suitable aids, is concerned especially about those who are her very own. Foremost among these is catechetical instruction, which enlightens and strengthens the faith, nourishes life according to the Spirit of Christ, leads to intelligent and active participation in the liturgical mystery and gives motivation to apostolic activity."

Importance of Schools:
"Among all educational instruments the school has a special importance . . . . No less than other schools does the Catholic school pursue cultural goals and the human formation of youth. But its proper function is to create for the school community a special atmosphere animated by the Gospel Spirit of freedom and charity, to help youth grow according to the new crea-

tures they were made through baptism as they develop their own personalities, and finally to order the whole of human culture to the news of salvation so that the knowledge the students gradually acquire of the world, life, and man is illuminated by faith."

Importance of CCD:
"Feeling very keenly the weighty responsibility of diligently caring for the moral and religious education of all her children, the Church must be present with her own special affection and help for the great number who are being trained in schools that are not Catholic. This is possible by the witness of the lives of those who teach and direct them, by the apostolic action of their fellow students, but especially by the ministry of priests and laymen who give them the doctrine of salvation in a way suited to their age and circumstances and provide spiritual aid in every way the times and conditions allow."

Catholic Colleges:
"The Church is concerned also with schools of a higher level, especially colleges and universities. In those schools dependent on her she intends that by their own principles, methods and liberty of scientific inquiry, in such a way that an ever deeper understanding in these fields will be obtained and that, as questions that are new and current are raised and investigations made according to the example of the doctors of the Church and especially St. Thomas Aquinas, there may be a deeper realization of the harmony of faith and science."

Newman Apostolate:
"Since the destiny of society and of the Church itself is intimately linked with the progress of young people pursuing higher studies, the pastors of the Church are to expend their energies not only on the spiritual life

of students who attend Catholic universities, but, solici-
tous for the spiritual formation of all their children,
that even at universities that are not Catholic there
should be associations and university centers under
Catholic auspices in which priests, religious and laity,
carefully selected and prepared, should give abiding
spiritual and intellectual assistance to the youth of
the university."

INDEX

Annual Program and Budget, 178,
185, 274
Authority
formal, 55
functional, 55
of competence, 55, 272
of office or of leadership, 271-272

Babcock, Bishop Allen, 3
Babin, Pierre, 205
Baltimore Catechism
theory of religious education, 200,
202-204
Bernardin, Bishop Joseph, 10
Blum, Rev. Virgil, 13
Board of Education, 24, 109-152
coordinator, 145-149
future of, 149-152
NCEA model constitution, 114-125
operation, 139-145
parish, 112-129
parish school, 107-112
President, 141-144
religious education model constitution, 123-125
responsibilities of, 128-136
responsibilities of members, 136-
139
special sessions and interim operations, 144-145
strengths, 125
weaknesses, 127-128
Bruner, Jerome, 198
Budget, 154 ff.
See also Program and Budget
Projection

Canadian National Religious Education Office, 297
Catechesis, 193-196
Catechetics, 6, 196-197
"old," 47-48
"new," 47-48
Catechist Preparation Programs,
206 ff.

assisting professional teachers,
219-221
consortium, 212-213
content, 209-210
evaluation of, 214-215
for adults, 215-219
goals, 207-209
instructional means, 211 ff.
Catechists, role of, 193-211
Catholic education, 113
economic factors, 13-17
sociological changes, 8-13, 15
Christian Community
ideal, 80-85
reality — 1970's, 85-98
Christian education, 196-197
Collins, Joseph B., 202
Combs, Arthur W., 188
Community of Religious Education
Directors. *See* CORED
Confraternity of Christian Doctrine
(CCD), 54-55
executive boards, 108-109, 228
Constitution for a Diocesan Board of
Education
NCEA model, 301-310
Religious Education model, 311-
324
Coordinator, 1, 6
as deacon, 292
contract-role description, 27-37
covenanted relationship and responsibilities, 49-51, 65-70
evaluation of, 63-65
finding a, 38-44
qualifications, 70-78
Religious Education, 5, 17, 53
rise of, 17
role, 47-49, 53-58
specialist and/or generalist, 56-57,
229
specific responsibilities, 58-63
See also Parish Coordinators
CORED (Community of Religious
Education Directors), 296-297